DATE DUE

DEMCO 38-296

Ethical concepts are, or purport to be, normative. They make claims on us: they command, oblige, recommend, or guide. Or at least when we invoke them, we make claims on one another. But where does their authority over us – or ours over one another – come from? Christine Korsgaard identifies four accounts of the source of normativity that have been advocated by modern moral philosophers: voluntarism, realism, reflective endorsement, and the appeal to autonomy. She traces their history, showing how each developed in response to the prior one and comparing their early versions with those on the contemporary philosophical scene. Kant's theory that normativity springs from our own autonomy emerges as a synthesis of the other three, and Korsgaard concludes with her own modified version of the Kantian account. Her discussion is followed by commentary from G. A. Cohen, Raymond Geuss, Thomas Nagel, and Bernard Williams, and a reply by Korsgaard. There is an introduction by Onora O'Neill.

THE SOURCES OF NORMATIVITY

Cambridge University Press gratefully acknowledges the co-operation of the President and Fellows of Clare Hall, Cambridge, under whose auspices the 1992 Tanner Lectures and Seminar (from which this book derives) were held.

THE SOURCES
OF NORMATIVITY

CHRISTINE M. KORSGAARD

with

G. A. COHEN

RAYMOND GEUSS

THOMAS NAGEL

BERNARD WILLIAMS

Edited by

ONORA O'NEILL

CAMBRIDGE
UNIVERSITY PRESS

Riverside Community College
Library
4800 Magnolia Avenue
Riverside, California 92506

BJ 1458.3 .K67 1996

Korsgaard, Christine M.

The sources of normativity

e University of Cambridge
eet, Cambridge CB2 IRP
NY 10011-4211, USA
ourne 3166, Australia

© Cambridge University Press 1996

First published 1996

Printed in Great Britain at the University Press, Cambridge

A catalogue record for this book is available from the British Library

Library of Congress cataloguing in publication data

Korsgaard, Christine M. (Christine Marion)
The sources of normativity / Christine M. Korsgaard with G. A.
Cohen . . . [et al.].
p. cm.
Includes bibliographical references and index.
ISBN 0 521 55059 9 (hardback). – ISBN 0 521 55960 x (paperback)
1. Normativity (Ethics) I. Title.
BJ1458.3.K67   1996
170′.44 – dc20   95–12848 CIP

ISBN 0 521 55059 9 hardback
ISBN 0 521 55960 x paperback

SE

Contents

vii

8 History, morality, and the test of reflection

9 Reply

Notes on the contributors

CHRISTINE M. KORSGAARD is Professor of Philosophy at Harvard University.

G.A. COHEN is Chichele Professor of Social and Political Theory and Fellow of All Souls, Oxford.

RAYMOND GEUSS is University Lecturer, Faculty of Social and Political Sciences at the University of Cambridge.

THOMAS NAGEL is Professor of Philosophy and Law at New York University.

BERNARD WILLIAMS is White's Professor of Moral Philosophy at the University of Oxford and Deutsch Professor of Philosophy at the University of California, Berkeley.

ONORA O'NEILL is Principal of Newnham College, Cambridge.

Acknowledgments

I want to thank Jerry Cohen, Raymond Geuss, Tom Nagel, and Bernard Williams for their helpful and challenging commentaries. I would also like to take this opportunity to thank the many others who have given me comments on these lectures as they have evolved. Charlotte Brown, Peter Hylton, and Jay Schleusener worked with me on the project from the beginning, reading and commenting on drafts and standing constantly ready to discuss the issues raised in them. I have benefited from extensive written and oral comments from Sissela Bok, Charles Crittenden, Richard Kraut, Arthur Kuflik, Richard Moran, Derek Parfit, Andrews Reath, Amélie Rorty, Thomas Scanlon, and Lawrence Thomas. I have discussed all or parts of the lectures with audiences at Bryn Mawr, the University of Connecticut, the University of Illinois at Urbana, the University of Maryland, Miami University, the University of Pennsylvania, and Temple University; at a conference on David Hume at Santa Clara University and at Robert Audi's NEH Summer Institute on Naturalism at the University of Nebraska; and of course at Cambridge University. I am also grateful to have been invited to discuss the material with the ethics discussion groups at Chapel Hill and in Chicago. It is a pleasure to thank all of these people for their criticisms and their help.

Introduction

Onora O'Neill

Normativity pervades our lives. We not merely have beliefs: we claim that we and others ought to hold certain beliefs. We not merely have desires: we claim that we and others ought to act on some of them, but not on others. We assume that what somebody believes or does may be judged reasonable or unreasonable, right or wrong, good or bad, that it is answerable to standards or norms. So far, so commonplace; but we have only to go a little further to find ourselves on the high seas of moral philosophy.

We will find ourselves at sea because there is huge disagreement about the source and the authority of norms on which we all constantly rely. The Tanner Lectures provide an outstanding opportunity to address and discuss such fundamental ethical questions. Thanks to the generous support of the Tanner Trustees, Tanner Lectures on Human Values are given at a total of eight different universities each year. The 1992 Tanner Lectures in Cambridge were given by Christine Korsgaard. Her lectures were followed by comments by G. A. Cohen, Raymond Geuss, Thomas Nagel, and Bernard Williams, and by extended and thoughtful discussion by a large audience. Thanks to the President and Fellows of Clare Hall, the occasion was congenial as well as invigorating. Since then texts have been exchanged, revised and refined and Christine Korsgaard has added a reply to her commentators. Needless to say, no unanimity has been achieved, but a vigorous approach to a set of topics that are central for ethics has been proposed, explored, and criticised.

The grasp of normativity which Christine Korsgaard seeks is practical, in two distinct senses. In the first place she is not looking for explanation, for a sociology of knowledge or a genealogy of morals, but for a grasp of ways in which normative claims may be vindicated. Secondly, she is principally interested in normative claims that are relevant to action rather than knowledge, and in particular in the normative claims of morality.

The normative claims of morality have acquired an unsavoury reputation. Obligations are accused of being constraining and forbidding, even repellent and corrupting. This image of morality was perfected by Nietzsche and is kept in good working order by many critics of 'modern moral philosophy', most of whom prefer the more attractive aspects of the ethical life – virtues and relationships, passions and affections. But normativity, as Korsgaard presents it, is not confined to principles and obligations. It is pervasive. Goodness and virtue too imply norms, to which we may or may not live up.

Korsgaard enters these contested waters briskly and boldly, and dispatches versions of some of the leading accounts of normativity in the first lecture. Voluntarisms will not do the job, unless there are authoritative legislators – which cannot be shown unless we already have an account of the source of some authoritative norms. Realisms, will not do the job, unless they can show that some actions, duties, or ends are intrinsically necessary. As Korsgaard sees it, the normative question slips through our fingers if we rely on these approaches.

The second lecture discusses attempts to locate normativity within rather than beyond human activity. Korsgaard discusses the positions of Hume, Mill, and Bernard Williams, then moves on to the strong claim that a Kantian position provides the best hope of locating the sources of normativity within human life. The crucial advance in all these writers depends on their recognition that human beings reflect, in the sense that they think about their own beliefs and desires, roles and traditions. Some of these they may accept upon reflection; others they may reject upon reflection. If reflection is the source of normativity, Korsgaard must show why reflective responses to some desires, intentions, or plans have normative force, so can be used to show that certain sorts of action are required. How can reflective responses, and in particular reflective endorsement, provide or constitute norms?

Korsgaard concludes that many sorts of reflective endorsement cannot. Some sorts of reflection may endorse actual beliefs or desires, but hardly vindicate them. For example, if a desire is endorsed only in the sense that its possession is the object of a second order desire, then it may become a stable aspect of character, but its normativity remains in doubt. So it is important to distinguish between different types of reflective scrutiny.

Some sorts of reflective scrutiny may be thought of as applying the norms of roles, as when somebody asks himself whether he may act in a certain way in his capacity as teacher, as nurse, as father. Such scrutiny tests action against received standards and norms. The actions that are endorsed as a result of this sort of reflective scrutiny presuppose rather than vindicate whatever norms are embedded in those roles. On Korsgaard's view there are analogous difficulties in some other sorts of reflective endorsement. For example, the Humean variety of reflective endorsement is inadequate 'the fact that we disapprove of injustice. . .can hardly be offered as a reason for endorsing our own disapproval of injustice', and she finds the versions of reflective endorsement that she reads into Mill and in Williams no more convincing.

However, Korsgaard has more time for reflective endorsement than her initial comments suggest. In particular she holds that there is a type of reflective scrutiny which can be used to discriminate morally acceptable from unacceptable ways of acting and living, and which constitutes a significant source of normativity. This more significant sort of reflective scrutiny is provided by using the Kantian test, as when somebody asks himself whether he can act on certain maxims (principles, intentions, projects) regardless of his particular roles, desires, etc., or, equivalently, whether those maxims could be universally adopted. In this case reflection does not invoke any 'external' or 'alien' considerations, such as the norms of roles or of traditions, state or other powers, or the current desires of those involved, which themselves demand further justification.

Kantian reflective scrutiny rejects any maxims which cannot be willed as universal laws. The rejection of those maxims identifies certain constraints from which it is possible to construct obligations or norms for all, rather than only for those who occupy certain roles or have certain desires. This sort of reflective endorsement is unlike others, in that it does not presuppose the prior justification of specific norms or desires. It will, Kant holds, be the appropriate sort of reflective scrutiny for identifying moral principles.

The only obligations to which this Kantian procedure can point are requirements not to act on maxims which cannot be universally adopted. Korsgaard's claim (which she does not develop in this work, but has discussed in earlier essays) is that if maxims which cannot survive this sort of reflective scrutiny – which cannot be willed as universal laws – are rejected, there will be constraints enough to elaborate a substantial account of obligations for all, regardless of particular roles or desires. Reflexivity of this sort provides a vindicable source of normativity not because some desire (say, the strongest) endorses another, or because some norm (say, that of a role) endorses some action, but because reflection reveals that some maxims can be principles for all, and others cannot.

An alternative way of looking at Kantian reflective scrutiny is to see it as asking whether adopting some maxim (intentions, principle, plan of action) can be seen as autonomous, that is as 'self-legislated'. 'Self-legislated' principles do not depend on appealing to the standards or norms of some arbitrary 'authority' (desire or tradition, Church or state); 'other legislated' principles invoke these spurious 'authorities'. The Kantian conception of autonomy or self-legislation is not that of some privileged expression of the self (the 'existentialist' misunderstanding of Kantianism); it is simply the obverse of the Kantian conception of heteronomy, which is a matter of relying on the law of another 'authority', which itself stands in need of, so cannot confer, vindication.

Korsgaard notes that the Kantian approach leaves it unclear what the scope of universal laws must be, and makes the partly unKantian suggestion that this must be settled by considering an agent's *practical identity*. Practical identities are those under which we act: as a member of a family, or of a community, as a citizen, or as a Member of the Kingdom of Ends. Human beings cannot live without some practical sense of identity; and (if Korsgaard is right) they cannot now get far without conceiving themselves as Members of the Kingdom of Ends. In acting with the practical identity of a Member of the Kingdom of Ends the forms of normativity that can be vindicated will correspond in scope as well as in form to the moral obligations which have traditionally been seen as endorsed by Kantian reflection.

There are plenty of strong claims and vigorous arguments here, and plenty of interesting suggestions about ways to read the history of ethics and about current controversies. Inevitably Korsgaard's commentators locate much to question and to disagree with. But over one matter there is no disagreement: few issues are more central to an adequate account of ethics as a whole than a convincing account of the sources of normativity.

Newnham College, Cambridge
1995

Excellence and obligation
a very concise history of western metaphysics
387 BC to 1887 AD

Christine Korsgaard

One should guard against thinking lightly of [the bad con-
science] merely on account of its initial painfulness and ugliness. For fundamentally it is the same active force that is at
work on a grander scale in those artists of violence and
organizers who build states . . . only here the material upon
which the form-giving and ravishing nature of this force
vents itself is man himself, his whole ancient animal self . . .
This secret self-ravishment, this artists' cruelty, this delight in
imposing a form upon oneself as a hard, recalcitrant, suffering material and of burning in a will . . . as the womb of all
ideal and imaginative phenomena, also brought to light an
abundance of strange new beauty and affirmation.

Nietzsche[1]

It is the most striking fact about human life that we have values. We
think of ways that things could be better, more perfect, and so of
course different, than they are; and of ways that we ourselves could
be better, more perfect, and so of course different, than we are.
Why should this be so? Where do we get these ideas that outstrip
the world we experience and seem to call it into question, to render
judgment on it, to say that it does not measure up, that it is not what
it ought to be? Clearly we do not get them from experience, at least
not by any simple route. And it is puzzling too that these ideas of a
world different from our own call out to us, telling us that things
should be like them rather than the way they are, and that we
should make them so.

Plato became Plato when Socrates made him see the problem.

---

[1] *The Genealogy of Morals*, II.17, p. 86.

In the *Phædo* he asks: why do we say that the two sticks are 'not exactly equal?'[2] Instead of seeing two sticks, lying side by side, that's that, we see them as if they were *attempting* something, endeavouring to be something that they are not. We see them as if they had in mind a pattern that they were trying to emulate, a pattern of equality that was calling out to them and saying 'be like me!' And if we see them this way then the pattern must be in our own minds too. You cannot look at two sticks and say: 'Oh look at the two sticks, trying and failing to be equal!' unless your own mind contains an idea of the equal, which is to say, the perfectly equal. Plato called such a thing a form, because it serves as a kind of pattern, and said we must have known them in another world.

The fact of value is a mystery, and philosophers have been trying to solve it ever since. But it is essential to see that during the transition from the ancient to the modern world a *revolution* has taken place – in the full sense of that resonant word. The world has been turned upside down and inside out, and the problem of value has become the reverse of what it was before. And here is why:

Plato and Aristotle came to believe that value was more real than experienced fact, indeed that the real world is, in a way, value itself. They came to see the world we experience as being, in its very essence, a world of things that are trying to be much better than they are, and that really are much better than they seem. It would be hard to convey this in a few lines to someone unfamiliar with their metaphysical systems. Plato believed that the essence of a thing is the form in which it participates. A thing's true nature and its perfect nature are one and the same. Form, which is value, is more real than the things which appear to us to participate in but fall short of it. Aristotle believed that the *actuality* of a thing is its form, which makes it possible for the thing to do what it does and therefore to be what it is. The reality of a thing is its activity. Form is more real than the matter, since matter is just the potential for form, the possibility of acting in a certain way.[3] And yet form is also perfection. For Plato and Aristotle, being guided by value is a matter of being guided by the way things ultimately *are*.

---

[2] *Phædo* 74–76, pp. 56–58.
[3] Here I have in mind *Metaphysics* VIII (H)–IX (⊖) especially.

In ethics, this way of viewing the world leads to what we might call the idea of excellence. Being guided by the way things really are is, in this case, being guided by the way *you* really are. The form of a thing is its perfection, but it is also what enables the thing to be what it is. So the endeavour to realize perfection is just the endeavour to be what you are – to be *good at being what you are*. And so the ancients thought of human virtue as a kind of excelling, of excellence.

Now the revolution I'm talking about happened gradually, but the seeds of it were already present in what Plato and Aristotle thought. For after all, even in this world of value, this world in which the real was the good, something has to have been amiss. For things at least look *to us* as if they are pretty imperfect. If all things are striving for perfection, why do they fail? What holds them back? What could? Plato, I believe, thought that the problem was in *us*, that sense experience itself was a kind of illusion, or perhaps that the badness of the world was an illusion produced by the perspective of sense. And because the problem was in us, he put forth, in the *Phædrus*, a doctrine of the Fall.[4] But like his Christian followers, he had to leave it as a mystery; he could give no real explanation of why we fell. Aristotle didn't give an explanation either, but he gave the problem a name: *hyle*, matter. The form of thing is its perfection, but if a thing doesn't reach its perfect form then ultimately it is because there is some reluctance, some recalcitrance, some resistance in its matter: the matter refuses, so to speak, to take the form.

I'm not sure about Plato. But at least in ethics, Aristotle doesn't seem to have made much of the problem. A well-brought up person would not need to have excellence forced upon him – he would move naturally towards the achievement of his perfect form. Indeed what I've just said is a tautology, a sort of definition of 'well-brought up'. In Greek thought, becoming excellent is as natural as growing up. We need to learn virtue; but it is as we learn language, because we are human and that is our nature. But what about those who are not well-brought up, or perhaps have the sort of native material defects that at their worst make a person a natural slave?

---

[4] *Phædrus* 246–249, pp. 493–496.

Aristotle isn't much interested in them in the *Nicomachean Ethics*, but they do come up, in the very last section of the book. And Aristotle suggests that in this case there is a remedy: it is law.

As its detractors love to point out, the idea of obligation is naturally associated with the idea of law. And obligation differs from excellence in an important way. When we seek excellence, the force that value exerts upon us is attractive; when we are obligated, it is compulsive. For obligation is the imposition of value on a reluctant, recalcitrant, resistant matter. Obligation is the compulsive power of form. Excellence is natural; but obligation – as Nietzsche says in the passage I have quoted – is the work of art.

This is why in the Christian era, obligation began to play a greater role in moral thought than it had done before. For then we turned our attention to the problem of fallen humanity, and we saw that the fallen human being is a reluctant, recalcitrant, resistant matter. For the Christian thinkers, we, humanity, are what is wrong with the world. We are the reason why the world, being good, is yet not good; we are the resistant matter; in a sense we are matter itself. (Think of Christian horror of the body, of our material nature.) In Augustine's hands the Form of the Good is transformed into a person, a lawgiver, God, whose business is to impose excellence on a reluctant, recalcitrant, resistant humanity. Why we were this way of course remained a mystery, the mystery of the Fall. But the upshot was that we became obligated.

The enemies of obligation think that now that God is dead, or anyway not the source of ethics, we can dispense with obligation, or put it back into its proper place, the sphere of justice and contract, where ethics naturally shares a border with the law. For the rest, we can go back to an ethics of excellence alone. But the death of God did not put us back into Plato and Aristotle's world. For in the meantime the revolution has completed itself. We no longer think that we are what's wrong with the world. We are no longer at all puzzled about why the world, being good, is yet not good. Because for us, the world is no longer first and foremost form. It is *matter*. This is what I mean when I say that there has been a revolution, and that the world has been turned inside out. The real is no longer the good. For us, reality is something *hard*, something which resists reason and value, something which is recalcitrant to form.

If the real and the good are no longer one, value must find its way into the world somehow. Form must be imposed on the world of matter. This is the work of art, the work of obligation, and it brings us back to Kant. And this is what we should expect. For it was Kant who completed the revolution, when he said that reason – which is form – isn't in the world, but is something that we impose upon it. The ethics of autonomy is the only one consistent with the metaphysics of the modern world, and the ethics of autonomy is an ethics of obligation.

And Nietzsche was right when he warned the enemies of obligation not to think of it lightly because it was born in pain and ugliness. Obligation is what makes us human. Or anyway, so I will argue.

The normative question

Christine Korsgaard

> Do not merely show us by argument that justice is superior to
> injustice, but make clear to us what each in and of itself does
> to its possessor, whereby the one is evil and the other good.
>
> Plato[1]

INTRODUCTION

I.I.I.

In 1625, in his book *On the Law of War and Peace*, Hugo Grotius
asserted that human beings would have obligations 'even if we
should concede that which cannot be conceded without the utmost
wickedness, that there is no God, or that the affairs of men are of
no concern to Him'.[2] But two of his followers, Thomas Hobbes
and Samuel Pufendorf, thought that Grotius was wrong.[3] However
socially useful moral conduct might be, they argued, it is not really
obligatory unless some sovereign authority, backed by the power of
sanctions, lays it down as the law. Others in turn disagreed with
them, and so the argument began.

Ever since then, modern moral philosophers have been engaged
in a debate about the 'foundations' of morality. We need to be
shown, it is often urged, that morality is 'real' or 'objective'. The

---

[1] Plato, *Republic* II, 367b, p. 613.

[2] Grotius, *On the Law of War and Peace*. Schneewind I, p. 92. I owe a great debt to Jerome
Schneewind for drawing my attention to this stretch of the historical debate, and especially for encouraging me to read Pufendorf.

[3] See Hobbes, especially *Leviathan* (1651), and Pufendorf, *On the Law of Nature and Of Nations*
(1672) and *On the Duty of Man and Citizen According to Natural Law* (1673). More detailed references will be given in the discussion that follows.

early rationalists, Samuel Clarke and Richard Price, thought that they knew exactly what they meant by this.[4] Hobbes had said that there is no right or wrong in the state of nature, and to them, this meant that rightness is mere invention or convention, not something real.[5] Hobbes meant that individuals are not obligated to obey the laws of social cooperation in the absence of a sovereign who can impose them on everyone.[6] But the rationalists took him to mean what Bernard Mandeville had later ironically asserted: that virtue is just an invention of politicians, used to keep their human cattle in line.[7]

But what exactly is the problem with that? Showing that something is an invention is not a way of showing that it is not real. Moral standards exist, one might reply, in the only way standards of conduct *can* exist: people believe in such standards and therefore regulate their conduct in accordance with them. Nor are these facts difficult to explain. We all know in a general way how and why we were taught to follow moral rules, and that it would be impossible for us to get on together if we didn't do something along these lines. We are social animals, so probably the whole thing has a biological basis. So what's missing here, that makes us seek a philosophical 'foundation'?

The answer lies in the fact that ethical standards are *normative*. They do not merely *describe* a way in which we in fact regulate our conduct. They make *claims* on us; they command, oblige, recommend, or guide. Or at least, when we invoke them, we make claims on one another.[8] When I say that an action is right I am saying that you ought to *do* it; when I say that something is good I am recom-

[4] See Clarke, *A Discourse Concerning the Unchangeable Obligations of Natural Religion, and the Truth and Certainty of the Christian Revelation. The Boyle Lectures 1705*; and Price, *A Review of the Principal Questions in Morals* (1758). More detailed references will be given in the discussion that follows.

[5] Hobbes, *Leviathan*, 1.13, p. 90 .   [6] Hobbes, *Levaithan*, 1.15, p. 110 .

[7] See Mandeville, *The Fable of the Bees: or, Private Vices, Public Benefits*, especially the section 'An Enquiry into the Origin of Moral Virtue', pp. 41–57. Mandeville himself denied that he meant either that virtue is unreal or that it is not worth having. See for instance 'A Vindication of the Book', pp. 384ff.; and also *An Enquiry into the Origin of Honor*, in Schneewind II, pp. 396–398.

[8] For this thought see Kant, *Critique of Judgment*, especially part I, division I, book I, 'The Analytic of the Beautiful'. Kant argues that when we judge something beautiful we not only take pleasure in it, but demand that everyone do so.

mending it as worthy of your choice. The same is true of the other concepts for which we seek philosophical foundations. Concepts like knowledge, beauty, and meaning, as well as virtue and justice, all have a normative dimension, for they tell us what to think, what to like, what to say, what to do, and what to be. And it is the force of these normative claims – the right of these concepts to give laws to us – that we want to understand.

And in ethics, the question can become urgent, for the day will come, for most of us, when what morality commands, obliges, or recommends is *hard*: that we share decisions with people whose intelligence or integrity don't inspire our confidence; that we assume grave responsibilities to which we feel inadequate; that we sacrifice our lives, or voluntarily relinquish what makes them sweet. And then the question – *why?* – will press, and rightly so. Why should I be moral? This is not, as H. A. Prichard supposed, a misguided request for a demonstration that morality is in our interest (although that may be one answer to the question).[9] It is a call for philosophy, the examination of life. Even those who are convinced that 'it is right' must be in itself a sufficient reason for action may request an account of rightness which this conviction will survive. The trouble with a view like Mandeville's is not that it is not a reasonable explanation of how moral practices came about, but rather that our commitment to these practices would not survive our belief that it was true.[10] Why give up your heart's desire, just because some politician wants to keep you in line? When we seek a philosophical foundation for morality we are not looking merely for an explanation of moral practices. We are asking what *justifies*

---

[9] Prichard, 'Does Moral Philosophy Rest on a Mistake?' and 'Duty and Interest'. Prichard's argument is discussed in detail below.

[10] Actually, as Hume and Hutcheson both argued, there are also problems about the explanatory adequacy of Mandeville's view. Neither Hume nor Hutcheson names Mandeville, but that he is their target is clear. Mandeville had suggested that politicians create the desire to be virtuous by praising virtue, and so by appealing to our pride. Hume and Hutcheson's answer is that if there were not a basis in human nature for the pleasure we take in being praised for our character and actions, the ideal of virtue could neither be made intelligible to nor motivate us. Politicians might turn the ideal of virtue to their own use but could not conceivably have invented it from whole cloth and foisted it upon animals whose only conception of the good is getting what they want. For Hume's discussion see the *Enquiry Concerning the Principles of Morals*, p. 214. For Hutcheson's see the *Inquiry Concerning the Original of our Ideas of Beauty and Virtue*, in Raphael I, p. 291.

the claims that morality makes on us. This is what I am calling 'the
normative question'.

THE PROBLEM

1.2.1

Most moral philosophers have aspired to give an account of morality which will answer the normative question. But the issue of *how*
normativity can be established has seldom been directly or separ-
ately addressed, as a topic in its own right. My purpose in these lectures will be to do just that; to explore the various ways in which
modern moral philosophers have tried to establish the normativity
of ethics.

Before I begin discussing particular theories, however, I want to
define the normative question a little more clearly, and to show
how it differs from certain other questions with which it is readily
confused. I will therefore begin with a schematic account of the
tasks of moral philosophy, in order to show where in its enterprise
the normative question arises. Since many moral philosophers
have not addressed the question directly, it is not always clear what
their answers are. When we want to know what, according to some
philosopher, makes morality normative, this will show us where to
look.

It is obvious that human beings apply ethical concepts – the
concepts of goodness, duty, obligation, virtue, and justice – to
certain states of affairs, actions, properties of actions, and personal
characteristics. The philosopher is, in the first instance, concerned
with three important features of these concepts. First, what exactly
do they mean, or what do they contain: that is, how are they to be
analyzed or defined? What is meant by saying something is good,
or right, or a duty? Second, of course, to what do they apply?
Which things are good, and which actions are right or obligatory?
And third, the philosopher wants to know where ethical concepts
come from. How did we come into possession of them, and how
does it come about that we use them? Did we get them from
reason, experience, God, or a prior existence in Plato's world of
Forms? What features of our minds, or actions, or the world insti-

gated us to develop these concepts and apply them to actions and characters? Let me call those three questions – what moral concepts mean or contain, what they apply to, and where they come from – a theory of moral concepts. In the first instance, then, the philosopher wants to produce a theory of moral concepts.

Now moral concepts play a practical role in human life, and they have a quite particular kind of importance. And this shows up in the fact that on the occasions when we use them we are influenced in certain practical and psychological ways, both actively and reactively. Let me review some familiar facts: when you think an action is right, you think you ought to do it – and this consideration at least frequently provides you with a motive for doing it.[11] Sometimes this can be a very strong motive. Many people throughout the course of history have been prepared to die for the sake of doing what they thought was right, or of avoiding what they thought would be terribly wrong. Similarly, when you think that a characteristic is a virtue you might aspire to have it, or be ashamed if you don't. Again this can be very strong: people's lives and happiness can be blighted by the suspicion that they are worthless or unlovely specimens of humanity. If you think that a characteristic is a vice, you might seriously dislike someone for having it: if it is bad enough, you may exclude that person from your society. Indeed your whole sense that another is for you a *person*, someone with whom you can interact in characteristically human ways, seems to depend on her having a certain complement of the moral virtues – at least enough honesty and integrity so that you are neither a tool in her hands nor she in yours. And finally, there are the phenomena of reward and punishment. Many people believe that good people or people who do good things deserve to have good things happen to them and that bad people or people who do bad things deserve to have bad things happen to them. Some people have even thought that this is so important that God must have organized the world so that people will get what they deserve. When we use moral concepts, then, we

---

[11] By saying this I do not mean to imply that 'internalism' – the view that moral judgments necessarily motivate – is necessarily true. Even 'externalists' usually think that rightness is a motivating consideration sometimes, although it might only be through the mediation of other motives. The relation between the views advanced in these lectures and the internalism/externalism dispute is discussed in lecture 2, 2.4.2.

use them to talk about matters which for us are important in very deep, strong, and profoundly practical ways.

Let me call this whole set of facts 'the practical and psychological effects of moral ideas'. I remind you of them, obvious as they are, because I think it is important to remember that a theory of moral concepts is answerable to them, and even more important to see that it is answerable to them in *two distinct ways*. First of all, the practical and psychological effects of moral ideas set a criterion of *explanatory adequacy* for a theory of moral concepts. Our theory of moral concepts must contain resources for explaining why and how these ideas can influence us in such deep ways. Perhaps the best way to illustrate this point is to think about a moral theory that is inadequate in this regard. Hume accused the rationalists of exactly this sort of failure when he famously said:

Since morals, therefore, have an influence on the actions and affections, it follows, that they cannot be deriv'd from reason; and that because reason alone, as we have already prov'd, can never have any such influence.[12]

It turns out that Hume's argument for this point is inadequate, for he does not really *prove*, as he puts it here, that reason cannot motivate.[13] Yet his criticism is still well-taken. The rationalists certainly did not explain *how* reason provides moral motivation. They simply asserted that it does. For Samuel Clarke, for instance, it is a fact about certain actions that they are 'fit to be done'. It is a self-evident truth built into the nature of things, in the same way that mathematical truths are built into the nature of things (whatever that way is). But people do not regulate their actions, love, hate, live, kill, and die for mathematical truths. So Clarke's account can leave us completely mystified as to why people are prepared to do these things for moral truths. And this is the element of truth in Hume's criticism. The rationalists did not explain why morality seems so important to us and moves us in the ways that it does.

That is the first way in which a theory of moral concepts is answerable to the practical and psychological effects of moral

---

[12] Hume, *A Treatise of Human Nature*, III.1.i, p. 457.
[13] I argue for this in more detail in 'Skepticism about Practical Reason'.

ideas. They provide a criterion of *explanatory adequacy*. But the practical importance we accord to moral concepts is not merely a curious fact about those concepts which an adequate theory needs to explain. When we do moral philosophy, we also want to know whether we are *justified* in according this kind of importance to morality. People who take up the study of moral philosophy do not merely want to know why those peculiar animals, human beings, think that they ought to do certain things. We want to know what, if anything, *we* really ought to do. This is the second way in which the theory of moral concepts is answerable to these effects. They provide a criterion of *normative* or *justificatory adequacy*.

Perhaps this is clearest when the claim morality makes on you is dramatic. If I claim that you ought to face death rather than do a certain wrong action, I had better be prepared to back that claim up with an account of what makes the action wrong which is powerful enough to show that something worth dying for is at stake. But really this demand on moral theory is always there. Even when the claims of morality are not so dramatic, they are pervasive in our expectations of ourselves and each other. So these claims must be justified. That is the normative question.

The real threat of moral scepticism lies here. A moral sceptic is not someone who thinks that there are no such things as moral concepts, or that our use of moral concepts cannot be explained, or even that their practical and psychological effects cannot be explained. Of course these things can be explained somehow. Morality is a real force in human life, and everything real can be explained.[14] The moral sceptic is someone who thinks that the explanation of moral concepts will be one that does not support the claims that morality makes on us. He thinks that once we

---

[14] Derek Parfit reminds me that this may not be true of certain very general facts, such as, say, that the universe exists. I suppose someone might regard the existence of values or reasons as a highly general fact of that kind, absent some other explanation. But suppose someone undertook to be *sceptical* about morality because he thought that (1) morality could only be grounded in this sort of general inexplicable fact – values, like the universe, would have to just be there if they existed at all – and (2) there is no reason to believe that they are. Such a sceptic would still have to think that the human delusion that morality is real can be explained and that the true explanation of this delusion would undercut people's commitment to morality.

see what is really behind morality, we won't care about it any more.

It is easy to confuse the criteria of explanatory and normative adequacy. Both, after all, concern questions about how people are motivated to do the right thing and why people care about moral issues so deeply. And certainly a theory of moral concepts which left the practical and psychological effects of moral ideas *inexplicable* could not even hope to *justify* those effects. Nevertheless the issue is not the same. The difference is one of perspective. A theory that could explain why someone does the right thing – in a way that is adequate from a third-person perspective – could nevertheless fail to justify the action from the agent's own, first-person perspective, and so fail to support its normative claims.

To see this, consider a nice stark example. Suppose someone proposes a moral theory which gives morality a genetic basis. Let's call this 'the evolutionary theory'. According to the evolutionary theory, right actions are those which promote the preservation of the species, and wrong actions are those which are detrimental to that goal.[15] Furthermore, the evolutionary theorist can prove, with empirical evidence, that because this is so, human beings have evolved deep and powerful instincts in favour of doing what is right and avoiding what is wrong. Now this theory, if it could be proved, would give an account of our moral motives which was adequate from the point of view of explanation. Our moral instincts would have the same basis and so the same kind of power as the sexual drive and the urge to care for and defend our children. And we know from experience that those instincts can induce people to do pretty much *anything*, even things which are profoundly detrimental to their own private interests or happiness.

But now ask yourself whether, if *you* believed this theory, it would be adequate from *your own* point of view. Suppose morality demands that you yourself make a serious sacrifice like giving up your life, or hurting someone that you love. Is it really enough for you to think that this action promotes the preservation of the

---

[15] This is the same example G. E. Moore used for what is really, at bottom, the same purpose. See his 'The Conception of Intrinsic Value', pp. 255–257. As I argue later, there is a problem about reducing normative ideas to natural ones, and it is in part this problem that motivates Moore's belief in the non-natural character of value.

species? You might find yourself thinking thoughts like these: why after all should the preservation of the species count so much more than the happiness of the individuals in it? Why should it matter so much more than my happiness and the happiness of those I care most about? Maybe it's not worth it. Or suppose the case is like this: there are Jews in your house and Nazis at the door. You know you will get into serious trouble, even risk death yourself, if you conceal the Jews. Yet you feel morally obligated to risk death rather than disclose the presence of the Jews. But now you know that this motive has its basis in an instinct designed to preserve the species. Then you might think: why should I risk death in order to help preserve the species that produced *the Nazis*?

I want you to notice something about this example. Suppose that last thought – 'Preserving the species that produced the Nazis is not worth the risk of dying' – could move you to ignore the claims of morality. We might now question whether the evolutionary theory does provide an adequate explanation of moral motivation after all. If it were true, people would not act morally or at least would only do so as long as they were kept in the dark about the source of their moral motivation. You might be tempted to think that this shows that the problem is at bottom one of explanation after all, but that would be a mistake. Although the case is fanciful, we can imagine it this way: given the strength of the moral instinct, you would find yourself overwhelmed with the urge to do what morality demands even though you think that the *reason* for doing it is inadequate. Perhaps the pain of ignoring this instinct breaks you down, like the pains of torture or extreme starvation. Then you might be moved by the instinct even though you *don't* upon reflection endorse its claims. In that case the evolutionary theory would still explain your action. But it would not *justify* it from your own point of view. This is clear from the fact that you would wish that you didn't have this instinct, that you wish you could make it go away, even though given that you have it, it remains adequate to move you.

That case, as I said, is fanciful, but it does bring something important out. While it is true that a theory which cannot justify moral conduct normally also cannot explain why anyone who believes that theory acts morally, the basic philosophical problem here is not one of explanation. The case of the evolutionary theory shows that a theory could be adequate for the purposes of explanation and still not answer the normative question. And there is an important reason for this. The question how we explain moral behaviour is a third-person, theoretical question, a question about why a certain species of intelligent animals behaves in a certain way. The normative question is a first-person question that arises for the moral agent who must actually do what morality says. When you want to know what a philosopher's theory of normativity is, you must place yourself in the position of an *agent* on whom morality is making a difficult claim. You then ask the philosopher: must I really do this? Why must I do it? And his answer is his answer to the normative question.

I.2.2

To be successful, there are three conditions which the answer must meet. All of these conditions spring from the position from which the normative question arises, the first-person position of the agent who demands a justification of the claims which morality makes upon him.

First, the answer must actually succeed in *addressing* someone in that position. It must not merely specify what we might say, in the third person, *about* an agent who challenges or ignores the existence of moral claims. Every moral theory defines its concepts in a way that allows us to say something negative about people who do that – say, that they are amoral or bad. But an agent who doubts whether he must really do what morality says also doubts whether it's so bad to be morally bad, so the bare possibility of this sort of criticism settles nothing. And I think it can be misleading to try to imagine what we might helpfully say, in the second person, to some *other* agent who challenges morality's claims. After all, some other agent might refuse to listen to reason, or to listen at all. He might be insincere and contentious; he might just be looking for a way to evade his duty, rather than asking the question because he really wants to know. For this exercise to work, we have to eliminate these possibilities, and imagine that this other agent is sincere and reasonable, and does really want to know. But that just shows that the answer we need is really the first-person answer, the one that satis-fies *us* when we *ourselves* ask the normative question.[16]

The second condition follows from the first. Because we our-selves are both to ask and to answer the normative question, a successful normative theory must meet a condition which is some-times called 'transparency'.[17] Usually this is thought of as a prop-erty of explanations. If a theory's explanation of how morality motivates us essentially depends on the fact that the source or nature of our motives is concealed from us, or that we often act blindly or from habit, then it lacks transparency. The true nature of moral motives must be concealed from the agent's point of view if those motives are to be efficacious. Suppose that people came to believe Mandeville's theory or the evolutionary theory, and as a result they gave up their moral practices. Then those accounts would lack transparency. Now because of the possibility I men-tioned a moment ago – the possibility that we might still be influ-enced by a motive we do not endorse – what we need here is transparency in a broader sense. It is not merely that the explana-tion must still go through when the agent understands himself completely. The justification must still go through as well. A nor-mative moral theory must be one that allows us to act in the full light of knowledge of what morality is and why we are susceptible to its influences, and at the same time to believe that our actions are justified and make sense.

Finally, I believe that the answer must appeal, in a deep way, to our sense of who we are, to our sense of our identity. As I have been emphasizing, morality can ask hard things of us, sometimes even that we should be prepared to sacrifice our lives in its name. This places a demanding condition on a successful answer to the nor-mative question: it must show that sometimes doing the wrong thing is as bad or worse than death. And for most human beings on

---

[16] These points have been brought out, although not exactly in these terms, by Philippa Foot, particularly in 'Moral Arguments'. Foot says that if someone listens to what we take to be a good moral argument and then says 'so what?' then we should want 'to know how he met the case put to him' (p. 97). What we want to know, of course, is whether he met it in a way that would change our *own* minds about it if we understood it. See also Bernard Williams's discussions in chapter 1 of *Morality: An Introduction To Ethics* and in *Ethics and the Limits of Philosophy*, pp. 22–26.

[17] See Williams, *Ethics and the Limits of Philosophy*, pp. 101–102.

most occasions, the only thing that could be as bad or worse than death is something that for us amounts to death – not being ourselves any more. This is not an unfamiliar thought. Most people, contemplating extreme old age, hope that they will die rather than exist for years in a condition of severely diminished intelligence, altered character, or with an inability to recognize and interact with those whom they have loved for years. The thought is 'that would not be me any more' and one would rather be dead. If moral claims are ever worth dying for, then violating them must be, in a similar way, worse than death. And this means that they must issue in a deep way from our sense of who we are.

1.2.3

It is often thought, though obscurely, that the normativity of ethics poses a special problem for *modern* moral philosophers. The Modern Scientific World View is supposed to be somehow inimical to ethics, while in different ways, the teleological metaphysics of the ancient Greek world and the religious systems of Medieval Europe seemed friendlier to the subject. It is a little hard to put the point clearly and in a way that does not give rise to obvious objections, but both of these earlier outlooks seem to support the idea that human life has a purpose which only is or can be fulfilled by those who live up to ethical standards and meet moral demands. And this is supposed to be sufficient to establish that ethics is really normative, that its demands on us are justified. They are justified in the name of life's purpose. While the Modern Scientific World View, in depriving us of the idea that the world has a purpose, has taken this justification away.

Whether this is true or not, the moral philosophy of the modern period can be read as a search for the source of normativity. Philosophers in the modern period have come up with four successive answers to the question of what makes morality normative. In brief, they are these:

1 Voluntarism. According to this view, obligation derives from the command of someone who has legitimate authority over the moral agent and so can make laws for her. You must do the right thing because God commands it, say, or because a political sove-

reign whom you have agreed to obey makes it law. Normativity springs from a legislative will. This is the view of Pufendorf and of Hobbes.

2 Realism. According to this view, moral claims are normative if they are true, and true if there are intrinsically normative entities or facts which they correctly describe. Realists try to establish the normativity of ethics by arguing that values or obligations or reasons really exist, or, more commonly, by arguing against the various forms of scepticism about them. This kind of argument has been found in the work of rational intuitionists ever since the eighteenth century. It was advanced vigorously by Clarke and Price in the eighteenth century and by Prichard, Moore, and Ross in the early twentieth century.[18] It is also found in the work of some contemporary moral realists, including Thomas Nagel.[19]

3 I call the third view 'Reflective Endorsement'. This view is favoured by philosophers who believe that morality is grounded in human nature. The philosopher's first job is to explain what the source of morality in human nature is, why we use moral concepts and feel ourselves bound by them. When an explanation of our moral nature is in hand, we can then raise the normative question: all things considered, do we have reason to accept the claims of our moral nature, or should we reject them? The question is not 'are these claims true?' as it is for the realist. The reasons sought here are practical reasons; the idea is to show that morality is good for us. Arguments with this structure can be found in the tradition, in the work of Hutcheson, Hume, and John Stuart Mill, and, in contemporary philosophy, in the work of Bernard Williams.

4 The Appeal to Autonomy. This kind of argument is found in Kant and contemporary Kantian constructivists, especially John Rawls. Kantians believe that the source of the normativity of moral claims must be found in the agent's own will, in particular in the fact that the laws of morality are the laws of the agent's own will and that its claims are ones she is prepared to make on herself. The capacity for self-conscious reflection about our own actions

---

[18] Clarke, *A Discourse Concerning the Unchangeable Obligations of Natural Religion*; Price, *A Review of the Principal Questions in Morals*; Prichard, *Moral Obligation and Duty and Interest: Essays and Lectures by H. A. Prichard*; Moore, *Principia Ethica*; and Ross, *The Right and the Good*.

[19] In *The Possibility of Altruism* and *The View from Nowhere*. But see n. 68 below.

confers on us a kind of authority over ourselves, and it is this authority which gives normativity to moral claims.

During the modern period, each of these accounts of normativity developed in response to the prior one, sometimes as a result of criticism, more often when the implications of the earlier view were pressed a little harder. In this lecture and the next one I am going to describe this historical process, comparing earlier versions of these accounts with those on the contemporary scene. The Kantian account of obligation is the culmination of this historical development, and in lecture 3 I will present an updated version of that account which I take to be true. Finally, in lecture 4, I will address the question of the scope of our obligations – that is, of who can obligate us, and why – and then return to the question of normative scepticism.

In the rest of this lecture I will discuss the first two accounts of normativity: voluntarism and realism.

1.2.4

One warning about the way I will proceed seems in order. My focus in these lectures is on the normativity of *obligation*. But in certain moral theories, the question about what makes obligation normative cannot be separated from questions about what makes goodness or virtue normative, and so those questions will come up too. And I will also have things to say, by way of comparison, about the normativity of knowledge and meaning.

The very use of such comparisons may strike some as controversial. As I said before, many of the concepts that interest philosophers are normative ones: obligation, rightness, goodness, meaning, knowledge, beauty, and virtue are all concepts that, in various ways, claim to direct us, to guide our thoughts, desires, and actions. In that broad sense, they are all normative concepts. Yet you might think that no unified account of their normativity is possible, and that for two reasons. First, of course, they are used in the context of different subjects, and to address different problems. Second, and just as importantly, our sense of their normativity, of *how* they direct us, is different. Do they push or do they pull, are they carrots or sticks? Obligation, the most obtrusively normative of these concepts, seems sternly to command; while beauty only to attract and meaning perhaps to suggest. So it might look as if these various concepts have different kinds of normativity.[20] Nevertheless, recognizable versions of the four views I have just described do show up when philosophers try to deal with the problem of normativity in areas other than ethics, and I take that fact to be significant. I believe that a unified account of normativity is possible, and while I will not try to argue for that here, it will show up in the way I proceed.

VOLUNTARISM

1.3.1

As I mentioned at the beginning of this lecture, Grotius asserted that human beings would have obligations even if God did not exist to give us laws. Because of that remark, he is often identified as the first *modern* moral philosopher.[21] But the credit for that should really go to Hobbes and Pufendorf. For they were the first to identify clearly the special challenge which the Modern Scientific World View presents to ethics, and to construct ethical theories in the face of that challenge.

According to Pufendorf, the actions of human beings, like every other form of physical motion, are in themselves morally indifferent. Values are not found in the world of nature at all. Instead, Pufendorf says, intelligent beings must impose moral values on nature. He says:

Now as the original way of producing physical entities is creation, so the way in which moral entities are produced can scarcely be better expressed than by the word *imposition*. For they do not arise out of the intrinsic nature of the physical properties of things, but they are superadded, at the will of intelligent entities, to things already existent and physically complete, and to their natural effects.[22]

And Hobbes opens his most famous ethical treatise with this apparently unpromising reflection:

---

[20] I thank Nicholas White for reminding me of some of these points.
[21] I owe this point to Schneewind. See Schneewind 1, pp. 88–89.
[22] Pufendorf, *The Law of Nature and of Nations*, in Schneewind 1, p. 171.

For seeing life is but a motion of Limbs, the beginning whereof is some
principal part within; why may we not say, that all *Automata* (Engines that
move themselves by springs and wheeles as doth a watch) have an artificial
life? For what is the *Heart*, but a *Spring*; and the *Nerves*, but so many *Strings*;
and the *Joynts*, but so many *Wheeles*, giving motion to the whole Body, such
as was intended by the Artificer?[23]

And he proceeds to construct a completely mechanistic explanation of how human beings work and an ethics that is based upon it.

Pufendorf and Hobbes ask how nature, an indifferent and
mechanical world of matter in motion, can come to be imbued
with moral properties. Interestingly, both traced obligation ultimately to divine command, not so much because they hung on to a
medieval or religious conception of the world, but rather because
they had *adopted* the Modern Scientific World View.[24] They
believed that it *takes* God or a Godlike sovereign to impose moral
properties on the indifferent world of nature. Grotius, although not
deeply concerned about the metaphysics of value, had been a
realist by default, for he believed that normative claims are simply
there, part of the framework of the universe. He tells us that what
makes the laws of nature, as moral laws were called, different from
positive laws, is that the acts which they enjoin or forbid 'are, in
themselves, either obligatory or not permissible . . . by their own
nature'.[25] But Pufendorf and Hobbes disagreed. Pufendorf criticized Grotius explicitly for maintaining that 'some things are
noble or base of themselves . . . and that these form the object of
natural and perpetual law'. Instead he held that:

since . . . moral necessity . . . and turpitude . . . are affections of human
actions arising from their conformity or non-conformity to some norm or
law, and law is the bidding of a superior, it does not appear that [they] . . .
can be conceived to exist before law, and without the imposition of a
superior.[26]

---

[23] Hobbes, *Leviathan*, introduction, p. 9.
[24] Of course voluntarism is not a product of the modern period. Many medieval Christian
thinkers were voluntarists who thought morality depends on the will of God. I don't take this
to be a problem for the point I am making here, since the medieval view that human beings
need to have values imposed on them by law anticipates the modern view that the world is
material and so morally indifferent. I say a little more about these points in the prologue.
[25] Grotius, *On the Law of War and Peace*, in Schneewind, 1, p. 98; I have put together clauses
from two sentences.
[26] Pufendorf, *On The Law of Nature and of Nations*, in Schneewind, 1, p. 175.

And Hobbes of course maintained that there is no obligation until a sovereign capable of enforcing the 'laws of nature' is in power. Obligation must come from law, and law from the will of a legislating sovereign; morality only comes into the world when laws are made.

1.3.2

Pufendorf and Hobbes shared two other views of which their critics sometimes failed to see the importance. First, voluntarism is often criticized on the grounds that the sovereign can apparently make anything right or wrong. And many theological voluntarists have held that to be true. But Pufendorf and Hobbes thought that the *content* of morality is given by reason independently of the legislative will. They agreed that good and evil, prudence and imprudence, and in a way even justice and injustice, are objectively identifiable attributes of states of affairs and of the actions which produce them. As Pufendorf puts it:

> this indifference of physical motion in the actions of men is maintained by us only in respect to morality. For otherwise actions prescribed by the law of nature have . . . the native power to produce an effect good and useful to mankind, while actions similarly forbidden produce a contrary effect. But this natural goodness and evil does by no means constitute an action in the field of morals.[27]

No legislator is needed to give content, at least in a general way, to the ideas of the good and the right. What is good is what is naturally beneficial to people; what is right and just is what makes harmonious social life possible. So most human beings in most circumstances have reason to want what is good and, at least as a group, to do what is right, independently of law or obligation. But in the absence of God, Pufendorf wrote, the precepts of morality 'though they might be observed for their utility, like the prescriptions doctors give to regulate health, they would not be *laws*' for 'they get *the force of law* only upon the presupposition[s] that God exists'.[28] And Hobbes, after laying out the laws of nature, says:

---

[27] Pufendorf, *On the Law of Nature and of Nations*; in Schneewind I, p. 176.
[28] Pufendorf, *On the Duty of Man and Citizen*, p. 36.

These dictates of Reason, men use to call by the name of Lawes; but improperly: for they are but Conclusions, or Theoremes concerning what conduceth to the conservation and defence of themselves; whereas Law, properly is the word of him that by right hath command over others.[29]

So the role of the legislator is to make what is *in any case* a good idea into *law*.

Second, both Pufendorf and Hobbes believed that no one could be a legislator without the power to impose sanctions to enforce his law. And it is frequently inferred that the point of these sanctions is to provide the subjects of the law with motives to obey it.[30] Actually, however, both of these philosophers thought that morally good action is action which proceeds from what we would now call the motive of duty.[31] One does the right thing because it is the right thing, because it is the law, and for no other reason. Pufendorf says that civil and natural obligations:

agree in this respect, that a man should do, of his own accord and by an intrinsic motive, the things which they demand of him. This forms the main difference between obligation and compulsion . . .[32]

Hobbes says that 'a man is obliged to do what he is commanded' and 'COMMAND, is where a man saith, *Doe this*, or *Doe not this*, without expecting any other reason than the Will of him that says it'.[33] This, Hobbes tells us, distinguishes command from mere counsel, where the reason for action is given by the good of the one who is counselled.

And from this ariseth another difference, that a man may be obliged to do what he is Commanded; as when he has covenanted to obey: But he cannot be obliged to do as he is Counselled, because the hurt of not following it, is his own; or if he should covenant to follow it, then is the Counsel turned into the nature of a Command.[34]

---

[29] Hobbes, *Leviathan* I.15, p.111.

[30] See for instance Schneewind in the introduction to *Moral Philosophy from Montaigne to Kant*, in Schneewind I, p. 22.

[31] While Pufendorf is almost ignored by contemporary moral philosophers, there is a great deal of controversy about Hobbes's views on moral motivation and obligation and a substantial recent literature on the topic. For references see Richard Tuck's introduction to *Leviathan*, p. xliii. A complete defence of the view I set forward here would require taking on the issues raised by that controversy, but this is not the place for that.

[32] Pufendorf, *On the Law of Nature and of Nations*, in Schneewind I, p. 180 .

[33] Hobbes, *Leviathan* II.25, p. 176.   [34] Hobbes, *Leviathan* II.25, p. 177.

Hobbes illustrates this distinction in a discussion of Holy Scripture:

> *Have no other Gods but me; Make to they selfe no graven Image* . . . &c are Commands; because the reason for which we are obliged to obey them, is drawn from the will of God our King, whom we are obliged to obey. But these words, *Sell all thou hast; give it to the poore; and follow me*, are Counsell; because the reason for which we are to do so, is drawn from our own benefit; which is this, that we shall have *Treasure in heaven* . . . these words, *Repent, and be Baptized in the Name of Jesus*, are Counsell; because the reason why we should so do, tendeth not to any benefit of God Almighty . . . but of our selves, who have no other means of avoiding the punishment hanging over us for our sins past.[35]

This makes it clear that if sanctions were supposed to provide the motives for obeying moral laws, then moral laws would be mere counsels, not commands. Or in Pufendorf's language if the sanctions were motives, then the laws would compel rather than obligate. So sanctions are not the right sort of motives to support obligation. And this is why Hobbes says:

> A Just man, therefore, is he that taketh all the care he can, that his Actions may be all Just; and an unjust man is he that neglecteth it . . . nor does an Unrighteous man, lose his character, for such Actions, as he does, or forbearers to do, for feare: because his Will is not framed by the Justice, but by the apparent benefit of what he is to do.[36]

A good person does the right thing for what Pufendorf calls an intrinsic motive: because it is the law, and his will as Hobbes says is 'framed' by that fact.

1.3.3

Why then are sanctions needed? The answer is that they are necessary to establish the authority of the legislator. Pufendorf says:

> An obligation is introduced into a man's mind by a superior, by one who has not only the strength to inflict some injury on the recalcitrant, but also just cause to require us to curtail the liberty of our will at his discretion.[37]

---

[35] Hobbes, *Leviathan* II.25, pp. 178–179. [36] Hobbes, *Leviathan* I.15, p. 104.
[37] Pufendorf, *On the Duty of Man and Citizen*, p. 28.

And Hobbes says:

The Right of Nature, whereby God reigneth over men, and punisheth those that break his Lawes, is to be derived, not from his Creating them . . . but from his *Irresistible Power*.[38]

And, more generally, Hobbes adds, 'To those therefore whose Power is irresistible, the dominion of all men adhereth naturally. . .'[39]

Pufendorf and Hobbes thought that the legislator's power to enforce the law was necessary to give moral commands the special force of *requirement*. A homely example will illustrate their point. Suppose you are a student in my department. Then my colleagues and I are in a position to require you to take a course in logic. We are in this position because we have authority over you, and we have authority over you in part because we can impose a sanction on you. If you refuse to take the logic course, you will not get a degree from us. Now I want you to notice several things about this. First of all, the scenario does not in the least imply that our decision to make you study logic must be arbitrary. It may be a very good idea for philosophy students to study logic, and that may be why we require it. If we are good at our jobs and worthy of our authority, we will have some such reason. In a similar way the laws which God or the Hobbesian sovereign requires us to obey are precepts of reason, determined independently of any arbitrary legislative will. Yet it is not merely their reasonableness that obligates us to obey them, just as it is not merely the benefits of studying logic that obligates students in my department to take the logic course. For if you are a philosophy student but are not in my department, I can give you all sorts of excellent reasons why you should take a course in logic, and you will not thereby be *required* to take one. In Hobbes's language, that will still be only counsel, not command. And that is why authority requires a sanction.

And there is a further implication. Suppose again that you are a student in my department, and consider your *motive* for taking the logic course. There are three possibilities. First, you might take it because you grasp the reasons for which we require it. You see that

---

[38]   Hobbes, *Leviathan* II.31, p. 246.   [39]   Hobbes, *Leviathan* II.31, p. 247.

it is a good idea, and you are moved by that fact. Second, even if you think the requirement arbitrary and unnecessary, you may take the course out of fear of being denied your degree – because of the sanction. Or, third, you may take it simply because it is a required course. The important point is that the third motive is appropriate here. While you may very well grasp the reasons why we require the course, and it may even be true that for those reasons you would have taken it anyway, there is something a little odd about saying that is your motive. Since it is required you would have to take it in any case. But there is no reason to suppose that therefore you only take it out of fear of being denied your degree, as it were cringingly. The fact that it's a required course is, under the circumstances, itself a reason.[40] This is the picture of obligation, and of what it is to act from the moral motive, which Hobbes and Pufendorf have in mind. And according to this picture neither moral obligation nor its proper and characteristic motive, the motive of duty, is possible unless there is a legislator backed by the power of sanctions who can lay down the law.

1.3.4

Let me sum up. Hobbes and Pufendorf believed that the content of morality is given by natural reason. What morality demands of us is what it is reasonable for us, at least as a group, to do. The rules of morality are the rules that make social life possible, and social life is necessary for human beings. And Hobbes and Pufendorf clearly supposed that in many cases this consideration could be motivationally sufficient as well. Pufendorf, especially, says that in the absence of obligation we would still do what is right because it is useful. The legislator is not invoked to supply the content of morality or even to explain why people are often motivated to do what is right.[41] The legislator is necessary to make *obligation* possible, that is, to make morality normative.

---

[40] There is further discussion of this example in lecture 3, 3.3.4.
[41] Of course, because of free-rider problems, this sort of consideration could not explain why everybody does what is right. But since there is no such fact to explain, that is not a problem.

REALISM

1.4.1

Samuel Clarke, the first defender of realism, was quick to spot
what he took to be a fatal flaw in the view I have just described.
Hobbes, Clarke complains, tries to derive obligation from the
social contract, from our agreement to obey the laws of a sovereign
who will make social cooperation possible. But why are we obligated to conform to the social contract? Clarke says:

> To make these *compacts* obligatory [Hobbes] is forced . . . to recur to an
> antecedent *law of nature*: and this destroys all that he had before said. For
> the same law of nature which obliges men to *fidelity*, *after* having made a
> compact; will unavoidably, upon all the same accounts, be found to oblige
> them, *before* all compacts, to *contentment* and mutual *benevolence* . . .[42]

If the need to establish a cooperative system can obligate us to
conform to a social contract, why doesn't that same need obligate
us to behave ourselves in cooperative ways in the first place? Or, if
we say that obligation comes from the fact that the laws have been
made by the sovereign, what then are we to say about why we are
obligated to obey the sovereign? Again Clarke complains:

> that compacts ought to be faithfully performed, and obedience to be duly
> paid to civil powers: the obligation of *these things* [Hobbes] is forced to
> deduce entirely from the internal reason and fitness of the things them-
> selves . . .[43]

Pufendorf had tried to explain why we are obligated to obey the
sovereign by defining a notion of legitimate authority. He stipu-
lated that the superior who is able to obligate us must have these
two attributes: 'not only the strength to inflict some injury upon the
recalcitrant but also just cause to require us to curtail the liberty of
our will at his discretion'.[44] He goes on to explain:

> The reasons which justify a person's claim to another's obedience are: if
> he has conferred exceptional benefits on him; if it is evident that he wishes

[42] Clarke, *A Discourse Concerning the Unchangeable Obligations of Natural Religion*, in Raphael I,
p. 219.
[43] Clarke, *A Discourse Concerning the Unchangeable Obligations of Natural Religion*, in Raphael I,
p. 221.   [44] Pufendorf, *On the Duty of Man and Citizen*, p. 28.

the other well and can look out for him better than he can for himself; if at the same time he actually claims direction of him; and finally, if the other party has voluntarily submitted to him and accepted his direction.[45]

So the authority of the legislator springs not only from his power to impose sanctions, but also from our gratitude for his benefits, or from his benevolent wisdom, or from our own contractual acts. But the difficulty with this solution is obvious. If we have no antecedent obligation to be grateful to benefactors, or to submit to the guidance of benevolent wisdom, or to honour our agreements, how can these things confer legitimate authority on the legislator? And if we do have a natural obligation to these things, then why may we not have other natural obligations as well? The very notion of a legitimate authority is already a normative one and cannot be used to answer the normative question.

Hobbes has a way of avoiding this last problem, but it is at a serious cost. He says flatly that God's authority does not depend on our gratitude or on His graciousness, but simply on His irresistible power.[46] And he concludes that this is true of the authority of the political sovereign as well. But this gives rise to a problem. The sovereign's authority now consists entirely in his ability to punish us. Although sanctions are not our motive for obedience, they are the source of the sovereign's authority and so of our obligations. I am obligated to do what is right only because the sovereign can punish me if I do not. Well, suppose I commit a crime and I get away with it. Then the sovereign was not able to punish me. And if my obligation sprang from his ability to punish me, then I had no obligation. So a crime I get away with is no crime at all. If irresistible power is just power unsuccessfully resisted, then authority is nothing more than the successful exercise of power, and things always turn out right. For no one can ever do what he lacks the power to do.[47]

The problem here is a general one, which applies to any attempt to derive normativity from a natural source of power. Suppose the

---

[45] Pufendorf, *On the Duty of Man and Citizen*, p. 28.
[46] Hobbes, *Leviathan* II.31, p. 246; quoted above.
[47] Strictly speaking, crime is still possible. If the sovereign catches me and punishes me, then I did something wrong. But wrongdoing is always punished, for if it is not, then it was not wrongdoing after all. So although not everything that happens is right, there is still a sense in which everything turns out right.

authority of obligation derives from the power of our sympathetic motives. Then if you lack sympathetic motives, you lack obligations. Your obligations vary along with your motives, and so you can do no wrong. Suppose, as Hume sometimes seemed to think, that the authority of our reasons for action must be derived from the strength of our desires. Then you will always do what you have reason to do, and you can do no wrong. As Joseph Butler would later point out, this sort of argument shows that authority cannot be reduced to any kind of power. And the relation in which moral claims stand to us is a relation of authority, not one of power.[48]

1.4.2

So we are faced with a dilemma. If we try to derive the authority of morality from some natural source of power, it will evaporate in our hands. If we try to derive it from some supposedly normative consideration, such as gratitude or contract, we must in turn explain why that consideration is normative, or where its authority comes from. Either its authority comes from morality, in which case we have argued in a circle, or it comes from something else, in which case the question arises again, and we are faced with an infinite regress.

The realist's response is to dig in his heels. The notion of normativity or authority is an irreducible one. It is a mistake to try to explain it. Obligation is simply there, part of the nature of things. We must suppose certain actions to be obligatory in themselves if anything is. According to Clarke, it is a fact about certain actions that they are fit to be done. Or as Richard Price puts it:

all actions, undoubtedly, have a *nature*. That is, *some character* certainly belongs to them, and somewhat there is to be *truly* affirmed to them. This may be, that some of them are right, others wrong. But if this is not allowed; if no actions are, *in themselves*, either right or wrong, or anything of a moral and obligatory nature, which can be an object to the understanding; it follows, that, in themselves, they *are* all indifferent.[49]

---

[48] See Butler, 'Upon Human Nature', sermon II of the *Fifteen Sermons Preached at the Rolls Chapel* and of the *Five Sermons*, pp. 39–40 .

[49] Price, *A Review of the Principal Questions in Morals*, pp. 47–48. See also Raphael II, pp. 146–147. Schneewind II, p. 591.

Some actions are simply intrinsically right. And if that is so, it is senseless to ask why we are obligated to do them. Because of these views, Clarke and Price were primarily polemical writers. They could not prove that obligation was real, and instead they devoted their efforts to rebutting what they took to be sceptical attacks on morality.

Let me digress a moment. In fairness to Clarke, it must be noticed that his view is ambiguous. Clarke sometimes says that it is their reasonableness that makes certain actions obligatory, and this admits of two possible interpretations. One may understand him to mean that the reasonableness of actions makes them obligatory in themselves, and there is some evidence that this is what he meant. For at times he seems – or perhaps pretends – not to realize that Hobbes (and Pufendorf) distinguished between an action's being reasonable and its being morally obligatory or required. Clarke argues as if Hobbes's view, that there is no right or wrong in the state of nature, commits him to the belief that in the state of nature all actions are equally reasonable or unreasonable. At one point, after a stretch of polemic generated by this assumption, Clarke concludes:

And in like manner all others, who upon any pretence whatsoever, teach that good and evil depend originally on the constitution of positive laws, whether divine or human; must unavoidably run into the same absurdity. For if there be no such thing as good or evil in the nature of things, antecedent to all laws; then neither can any one law be better than another . . . but all laws equally, will be either arbitrary and tyrannical, or frivolous and needless; because the contrary might with equal reason have been established, if, before the making of the laws, all things had been alike indifferent in their own nature.[50]

But on other occasions it sounds as if Clarke is anticipating Kant's view – which I will explain in lecture 3 – that obligation derives from the dictate of the agent's own mind. For example, Clarke says:

For the judgment and conscience of a man's own mind, concerning the reasonableness and fitness of the thing, that his actions should be conformed to such or such a rule or law, is the truest and formalist *obligation* . . .
. . . For no man willingly and deliberately transgresses this rule in any

[50] Clarke, *A Discourse Concerning the Unchangeable Obligations of Natural Religion*, in Raphael I, pp. 195–196.

great and considerable instance, but he acts contrary to the judgement and reason of his own mind, and secretly reproaches himself for doing so. And no man observes and obeys it steadily . . . but his own mind commends and applauds him for his resolution, in executing what his conscience could not forbear giving its assent to, as just and right.[51]

Here the normative force derives not from the intrinsic reasonableness of the action alone, but from the fact that the agent determines herself to do what is reasonable. Clarke himself does not seem to have noticed the difference between these two views, nor do any of his followers, before Kant, seem to have picked it up. Price, who says that obligation itself is a property of actions, is more straightforward a realist: his view of rightness anticipates G. E. Moore's view of goodness as an indefinable non-natural property.

And in general, early twentieth-century rational intuitionism, represented by the work of Prichard, Ross, and Moore, follows the pattern I described earlier: it digs in its heels, and insists on the irreducible character of normativity. This is clearest in Prichard's classic essays: 'Does Moral Philosophy Rest on a Mistake?' and 'Duty and Interest'. Prichard argues that it makes no sense to ask why you should be moral. If I give you a moral reason – such as, 'it is your duty' – then my answer is circular, since it assumes you should be moral. If I give you a self-interested reason – such as, 'it will make you happy' – then my answer is irrelevant. That is not the reason why you should be moral; you should be moral because it is your duty. If a question admits only answers that are either circular or irrelevant then it must be a mistake to ask it. And if that is the question of moral philosophy, Prichard thinks, then moral philosophy rests on a mistake. Obligations just exist, and nobody needs to prove it.[52]

---

[51] Clarke, *A Discourse Concerning the Unchangeable Obligations of Natural Religion*, in Raphael I, pp. 202–203; Schneewind I, p. 301.

[52] Actually Prichard's argument takes a detour through the idea that the moral reason for doing an action is that the action is good or realizes some sort of good. Prichard argues that if this means that the action *ought to be brought about*, for its own sake or its consequences, then it presumes the notion – and the reality – of obligation. If it means what Kant thought – that the action is intrinsically good because it issues from or embodies a good will – it again presupposes the notion and the reality of obligation, since a good will is one that acts from the sense of obligation. Prichard concludes that 'The sense of obligation to do, or of the rightness, of an action of a particular kind is absolutely underivative and immediate'. ('Does Moral Philosophy Rest on a Mistake?', p. 7)

1.4.3

As these arguments show, realism is a metaphysical position in the exact sense criticized by Kant. We can keep asking why: 'Why must I do what is right?' – 'Because it is commanded by God' – 'But why must I do what is commanded by God?' – and so on, in a way that apparently can go on forever. This is what Kant called a search for the unconditioned – in this case, for something which will bring the reiteration of 'but why must I do that?' to an end. The unconditional answer must be one that makes it impossible, unnecessary, or incoherent to ask why again. The realist move is to bring this regress to an end by fiat: he declares that some things are *intrinsically* normative. Prichard joins Clarke and Price in asserting this about obligatory actions, while Moore thought there were intrinsically good states of affairs.[53] The very nature of these intrinsically normative entities is supposed to forbid further questioning. Having discovered that he needs an unconditional answer, the realist straightaway concludes that he has found one.

A comparison will help to show why this is metaphysical. Consider the cosmological argument for the existence of God, which purports to prove God's existence by proving that there must be a necessarily existent being. It runs this way: somewhere there must be an Entity whose existence is necessary in itself. For if an entity is contingent, it can either exist or not exist. How then can we explain its existence? Well, some other entity must have brought it into being, have made it exist. What then about this other entity? Is it necessary or contingent? If it is contingent then what in turn made it exist? In this way we generate a regress, which can only be brought to an end if some Entity exists necessarily, that is, if there is some Entity about which it is impossible, unnecessary or incoherent to ask why It exists. So there must be such an Entity, and that is God.

As Hume pointed out in his *Dialogues Concerning Natural Religion*, there are two problems here.[54] First of all, so far as the argument goes, *anything* could be the necessary being. It could be matter, or

[53] See Moore, *Principia Ethica* and also 'The Conception of Intrinsic Value'.
[54] Hume, *The Dialogues Concerning Natural Religion*', part IX.

the universe, or the sun. In placing the necessity in God, the cosmologist has simply placed it where he wanted to find it. And second, unless you assume that even contingent beings must in some sense be necessary – that is, that there must be an explanation which shows that they *must* have existed – the argument cannot even get started.[55]

Moral realism is like that. Having discovered that obligation cannot exist unless there are actions which it is necessary to do, the realist concludes that there are such actions, and that they are the very ones we have always thought were necessary, the traditional moral duties. And the same two problems exist. The realist like the cosmologist places the necessity where he wanted to find it. And the argument cannot even get started, unless you assume that there are some actions which it is necessary to do.

But when the normative question is raised, these are the exact points that are in contention – whether there is really *anything* I must do, and if so whether it is *this*. So it is a little hard to see how realism can help.

1.4.4

Yet realism is seen by many as the only hope for ethics, the only option to scepticism, relativism, subjectivism, and all the various ways of thinking that the subject is hopeless. There are, I think, two reasons for this. One is clear from the arguments which I have just reviewed. It can look as if granting the existence of intrinsically normative entities is the only way to bring the endless reiteration of the question 'why must I do that?' to an end, and still save obligation. The other is based on a confusion. Realism may be defined in a way that makes it look like the *logical* opposite of scepticism, say for instance as the existence of moral truth. But considered as a substantive position, realism actually involves more than that.

---

[55] It may not be obvious that Hume makes this second argument but it is implied by one he does make. Hume has Cleanthes say 'In such a chain too, or succession of objects, each part is caused by that which preceded it, and causes that which succeeds it. Where then is the difficulty?' (p. 190). That of course amounts to a denial that the items in the 'chain' need be in any sense necessary. Each link may simply be contingent upon the one before it. It is worth noting that the cosmologist Cleanthes explicitly quotes in the course of his criticism is Samuel Clarke.

Let me explain. There is a trivial sense in which everyone who thinks that ethics isn't hopeless is a realist. I will call this *procedural* moral realism, and I will contrast it to what I will call *substantive* moral realism. Procedural moral realism is the view that there are answers to moral questions; that is, that there are right and wrong ways to answer them. Substantive moral realism is the view that there are answers to moral questions *because* there are moral facts or truths, which those questions ask *about*.

To see the difference, it helps to consider normative realism more generally. The procedural normative realist thinks that when we ask practical questions like 'what must I do?' or 'what is best in this case?' or 'how should I live?' there are correct and incorrect things to say. This is not just a view about morality. Suppose the correct answer to the question 'how should I live?' is 'just as you like'. Then people deluded by duty who don't live as they like would be making a *mistake*. The view that there is *no* normative truth about action is the view that it is impossible to fail to do what you have reason to do, or should do, or ought to do: it is the view, more or less, that it doesn't matter what you do. Procedural normative realism isn't completely trivial, for it does have an opposite, but that opposite is a kind of nihilism. The denial of procedural normative realism says that there is no ought, should, must, or reason at all.

But procedural realism does not require the existence of intrinsically normative entities, either for morality or for any other kind of normative claim. It is consistent with the view that moral conclusions are the dictates of practical reason, or the projections of human sentiments, or the results of some constructive procedure like the argument from John Rawls's original position.[56] As long as there is some correct or best procedure for answering moral questions, there is some way of applying the concepts of the right and the good. And as long as there is some way of applying the concepts of the right and the good, we will have moral and more generally normative truth. Statements implying moral concepts will be true when those concepts are applied correctly.

---

[56] See *A Theory of Justice*, part I. Rawls characterizes his conception of justice as a 'Kantian constructivist' one in 'Kantian Constructivism in Moral Theory: The Dewey Lectures 1980'.

Perhaps an example will help here. Most people suppose that the means/end relation is normative, in the sense that the fact that a certain action is a means to your end provides you with a reason to do it. Very few people have ever supposed that this requires an adjustment in the metaphysics of the Modern Scientific World View, say, by the introduction of intrinsically normative entities into our ontology. But how then do we establish that this relation is normative? One plausible answer comes from Kant. Kant tells us that the means/end relation is normative because of a principle of practical reason which he calls the hypothetical imperative. The hypothetical imperative tells us that if we will an end, we have a reason to will the means to that end. This imperative, in turn, is not based on the recognition of a normative fact or truth, but simply on the nature of the will. To will an end, rather than just wishing for it or wanting it, is to set yourself to be its cause. And to set yourself to be its cause is to set yourself to take the available means to get it.[57] So the argument goes from the nature of the rational will to a principle which describes a procedure according to which such a will must operate and from there to an application of that principle which yields a conclusion about what one has reason to do. And Kant of course thought that in a similar way, moral principles could be shown to be principles of practical reasoning which are based on the nature of the will and yield conclusions about what we ought to do. There are then facts, moral truths, about what we ought to do, but that is not because the actions are intrinsically normative. They inherit their normativity from principles which spring from the nature of the will – the principles of practical reasoning.

What distinguishes substantive from procedural realism is a view about the relationship between the answers to moral questions and our procedures for arriving at those answers. The procedural moral realist thinks that there are answers to moral questions *because* there are correct procedures for arriving at them. But the substantive moral realist thinks that there are correct procedures for answering moral questions *because* there are moral truths or facts which exist independently of those procedures, and

---

[57] Kant, *Foundations of the Metaphysics of Morals*, pp. 414–417; in Beck's translation, pp. 31–35.

which those procedures track.[58] Substantive realism conceives the procedures for answering normative questions as ways of *finding out* about a certain part of the world, the normative part. To that extent, substantive moral realism is distinguished not by its view about what kind of truths there are, but by its view about what kind of subject ethics is. It conceives ethics as a branch of knowledge, knowledge of the normative part of the world.

1.4.5

Substantive moral realism has been criticized in many ways. It has been argued that we have no reason to believe in intrinsically normative entities or objective values. They are not harmonious with the Modern Scientific World View, nor are they needed for giving scientific explanations. Since the time of Hume and Hutcheson, it has been argued that there is no reason why such entities should motivate us, disconnected as they are from our natural sources of motivation. Many of these criticisms have been summed up in John Mackie's famous 'Argument from Queerness'. Here it is in Mackie's own words:

If there were objective values, then they would be entities or qualities or relations of a very strange sort, utterly different from anything else in the universe. Correspondingly, if we were aware of them, it would have to be by some special faculty of moral perception or intuition, utterly different from our ordinary ways of knowing everything else . . .
Plato's Forms give a dramatic picture of what objective values would have to be. The Form of the Good is such that knowledge of it provides the knower with both a direction and an overriding motive; something's being good both tells the person who knows this to pursue it and makes him pursue it. An objective good would be sought by anyone who was acquainted with it, not because of any contingent fact that this person, or every person, is so constituted that he desires this end, but just because the end has to-be-pursuedness somehow built into it. Similarly, if there were objective principles of right and wrong, any wrong (possible) course of action would have not-to-be-doneness somehow built into it.[59]

And nothing, Mackie suggests, could be like that.

---

[58] Substantive realism is a version of procedural realism, of course; what distinguishes it is its account of *why* there is a correct procedure for answering moral questions.
[59] J. L. Mackie, *Ethics: Inventing Right and Wrong*, pp. 38, 40 .

Mackie doesn't really prove that such entities couldn't exist, any more than Hume really proves that reason cannot motivate. But like Hume, he has a point, although I think it is not the point he meant to make. If someone finds that the bare fact that something is his duty does not move him to action, and asks what possible motive he has for doing it, it does not help to tell him that the fact that it is his duty just is the motive. That fact isn't motivating him just now, and therein lies his problem. In a similar way, if someone falls into doubt about whether obligations really exist, it doesn't help to say 'ah, but indeed they do. They are *real* things'. Just now he doesn't see it, and herein lies his problem.

To see this, go back to the case where you are being asked to face death rather than do a certain action. You ask the normative question: you want to know whether this terrible claim on you is justified. Is it really true that this is what you *must* do? The realist's answer to this question is simply 'Yes'. That is, *all* he can say is that it is *true* that this is what you ought to do. This is of course especially troublesome when the rightness of the action is supposed to be self-evident and known through intuition, so that there is nothing more to say about it. If the realist is not an intuitionist, of course, he can go back and review the reasons why the action is right. Prichard says explicitly that it is only because people sometimes need to do this before they can see the necessity of an action that the question 'why should I be moral?' appears to make sense when actually it does not.[60] We need to remind ourselves that the action promotes pleasure, or meets a universalizability criterion, or fosters social life. But this answer appears to be off the mark. It addresses someone who has fallen into doubt about whether the action is really required by morality, not someone who has fallen into doubt about whether moral requirements are really normative.

Now to be fair to Prichard, it is clear from his essays that he takes words like 'right' and 'obligatory' to imply normativity by definition. These terms, as he sees it, are normatively loaded, so that it is incorrect to *say* that an action is right or obligatory unless we are already sure that we really have to do it. In one

---

[60] See Prichard, 'Does Moral Philosophy Rest on a Mistake?', p. 8.

sense, that's fine: it is six of one, half dozen of the other, whether we ask 'is this action really obligatory?' or 'is this obligation really normative?' If we take obligation to imply normativity, then the first question is the same as the second. The trouble with Prichard's way of talking about these matters is more a heuristic one. The question 'Is this action really obligatory?' can be understood as a question about whether moral concepts have been applied correctly in this case – whether, for instance, the requirement can really be derived from the categorical imperative or the principle of utility or some other moral principle. And that is a different question from the question how this obligation or any obligation can be normative. Prichard's way of approaching the matter therefore leads us to confuse the question of correct application with the question of normativity. And this actually happened to Prichard himself. For it led him to think that once we have settled the question of correct application, there can be nothing more to say about the normative question.[61]

And that is the problem with realism: it refuses to answer the normative question. It is a way of saying that it cannot be done. Or rather, more commonly, it is a way of saying that it need not be done. For of course if I *do* feel confident that certain actions really are required of me, I might *therefore* be prepared to believe that those actions are intrinsically obligatory or objectively valuable, that rightness is just a property they have. Just listen to what Samuel Clarke says:

These things are so notoriously plain and self-evident, that nothing but the extremist stupidity of mind, corruption of manners, or perverseness of spirit, can possibly make any man entertain the least doubt concerning them.[62]

Well, obviously *he* isn't worried. But suppose you are? Perhaps his confidence will make you take heart, but it is hard to see how else this could help.

---

[61] See lecture 2, 2.3.2, for discussion of a parallel problem in Prichard's attitude towards scepticism about belief. The point is perhaps even clearer in that case.

[62] Clarke, *A Discourse Concerning the Unchangeable Obligations of Natural Religion*, in Raphael 1, p. 194; Schneewind, 1, p. 296.

The difficulty here is plain. The metaphysical view that intrinsically normative entities or properties exist must be *supported by* our confidence that we really do have obligations. It is because we are confident that obligation is real that we are prepared to believe in the existence of some sort of objective values. But for that very reason the appeal to the existence of objective values cannot be used to support our confidence. And the normative question arises when our confidence has been shaken, whether by philosophy or by the exigencies of life. So realism cannot answer the normative question.

1.4.6

Some contemporary realists, such as Thomas Nagel, have argued that realism need not commit us to the existence of curious metaphysical objects like Plato's Forms or Moore's non-natural intrinsic values. According to Nagel, we need only determine whether certain natural human interests, like our interest in having pleasure and avoiding pain, have the normative character which they appear to us to have. The point is not to look for some sort of specially normative *object*, but to look *more objectively* at the apparently normative considerations that present themselves in experience. That you are, say, in pain, *seems* like a reason to change your condition; the question is whether it is one.[63] Utilitarianism itself can be seen as a naturalistic form of realism, and versions of it have been defended as such by contemporary realists like Brink and Railton.[64] Contemporary realists argue that there is no need to make the right and the good into mysterious metaphysical entities. Nothing seems more obviously normative than pleasures and pains, or desires and aversion, or our natural interests. So the realist need not assume, as Mackie supposes, that believing in objective values is believing in some sort of peculiar entities. We need only believe that reasons themselves exist, or that there are truths about what we have reason to do.[65]

---

[63] Thomas Nagel, *The View From Nowhere*, p. 157.
[64] See for instance Brink, *Moral Realism and the Foundations of Ethics*, especially chapter 8; and Railton, 'Moral Realism', 189ff.   [65] Nagel, *The View from Nowhere*, p. 144.

But if we take Mackie's point in the way that I have suggested, this leaves the problem in place. For how do we determine that these reasons or truths exist?[66] Like his rationalist predecessors, Nagel asserts that all we can do is rebut the sceptical arguments against the reality of reasons and values. Once we have done that, there is no special reason to doubt that they exist.[67] And then when you see something that appears to be a reason, such as, say, your desire to avoid pain, the best explanation of this appearance is that that's what it is – it's a reason.[68]

And there's nothing wrong with that. But it is an expression of confidence and nothing more. Just listen to what Thomas Nagel says:

In arguing for this claim, I am somewhat handicapped by the fact that I find it self-evident.[69]

---

[66] In the passage quoted, Mackie asserts that a moral realist must be an intuitionist – that is, must believe there is some special faculty of moral knowledge, 'different from our ordinary ways of knowing everything else'. Nagel would deny that his view has this implication, but he does not say what, on his view, something's 'appearing to be a reason' consists in.

[67] Nagel, *The View From Nowhere*, pp. 143–144. Nagel says: 'it is very difficult to argue for such a possibility [the reality of values], except by refuting arguments against it' (p. 143). Compare this little snatch of dialogue: 'Is there nothing truly wrong in the . . . misery of an innocent being? – "It appears wrong *to us*." – And what reason can you have for doubting, whether it appears what *it is*?' Except for the old-fashioned syntax, that could be Nagel arguing against Mackie. But it is Richard Price arguing against Hutcheson. *A Review of the Principal Questions in Morals*, p. 45.

[68] Nagel, *The View From Nowhere*, p. 141. What he actually says is 'The method is to begin with the reasons that appear to obtain from my own point of view and those of other individuals; and ask what the best perspectiveless account of those reasons is'. Because Nagel believes in the existence of reasons, rather than Platonic Forms or Moorean non-natural properties, it would be easy to suppose that he is only what I have here called a 'procedural realist'. Actually the issue is a bit complicated. I categorize him here as a substantive realist because he seems to believe, as the passage quoted shows, that our relation to reasons is one of *seeing* that they are there or *knowing* truths about them. As I have just argued, there is a way in which this view of ethics as an epistemological subject is the essential characteristic of substantive realism. But in part II of my paper 'The Reasons We Can Share: an Attack on the Distinction between Agent-Relative and Agent-Neutral Values' I argue that it is *possible* to understand the projects Nagel prosecutes in both *The Possibility of Altruism* and *The View From Nowhere* as constructivist projects, and that Nagel himself wavers between that way and a realist way of construing his own work. If we read Nagel as a constructivist then he is only a procedural realist.

[69] Nagel, *The View from Nowhere*, pp. 159–160 . Actually he says this about the idea that pain and pleasure provide 'agent-neutral' rather than 'agent-relative' reasons. But he says things pretty much like this about whether reasons exist at all. For instance on p. 157 he says that if there is no special reason to doubt the existence of reasons then denying that pain provides a reason to change your situation 'seems meaningless'.

Nagel's *manners* are better than Samuel Clarke's, but his predicament is the same. He isn't worried.

1.4.7

Now I'd like to pause for a moment and say something I hope will be helpful about why the normative question slips so easily through our fingers. Earlier I said that in a sense Prichard *is* asking the normative question. For him 'obligation' is a normatively loaded word. If 'obligation' is a normatively loaded word, then the normative question is whether certain actions are really obligatory. If 'reason' is the normatively loaded word, as Nagel thinks, then the normative question is whether obligations give us reasons. If 'objective' is a normatively loaded word, as Mackie seems to think, then the normative question is whether obligations are really objective, and so on.

Discussion of normativity often founder because of unexamined assumptions about the normatively loaded word. There are two problems here. First, philosophers making different assumptions about which is the normatively loaded word may fail to understand each other.[70] The second and perhaps more serious problem is that all of the ways of formulating the normative question that I have just mentioned suffer from the fact that they are readily confused with different questions. As I pointed out in my discussion of Prichard, the question whether the action is 'really obligatory' can be confused with the question whether the moral concept really applies to the action. In a similar way, the question whether an obligation really provides a reason can be confused with the question whether it provides an adequate motive.[71] Again, the question whether the obligation is *objective* can be confused with the question whether the moral concept is one

---

[70] Arguably, this is why Clarke supposed that Hobbes was committed to the view that everything is equally reasonable or unreasonable in the state of nature. (See 1.4.2 above.) Clarke takes 'reason' to be the normatively loaded word, while I hope it is clear from the discussion of voluntarism that Hobbes and Pufendorf did not do that. As a result, Clarke is unable to understand what Hobbes is saying.

[71] This is one of the main things that leads people to confuse explanatory and normative adequacy.

whose application is determinate, or sufficiently 'world-guided'.[72] In all of these cases, the philosopher is led to think that settling the other question, whatever it is, is a way of settling the normative question. And in all of these cases it is not.

This tendency to conflate the normative question with other questions often results in the normative question being blocked or ignored. And it is worth noticing that that is not the only resulting problem. The conflation can also prevent the *other* question, whatever it might be, from being answered in a reasonable way, because of what we might think of as interference from the normative question. The best example of this is G. E. Moore's famous 'open question' argument.[73] Moore argued that no matter what analysis we give of 'good', it is an open question whether the objects picked out by that analysis are good. And he concluded that 'good' must therefore be unanalyzable, and further that therefore we can only know which things are good through intuition. But the force of the open question argument clearly comes from the pressure of the normative question. That is, when the concept of the good is applied to a natural object, such as pleasure, we can still always ask whether we should really choose or pursue it. This should not lead us to conclude that the concept of the good, or any other normative concept, cannot be defined in a way that guides its application. Conflation of the normative question with other questions is what drives Moore and others to the view that moral concepts must be simple and indefinable, and as a result to intuitionism.

Part of what I have tried to do in this lecture is to raise the normative question in a way that is independent of our more ordinary normative concepts and words. No doubt this has sometimes been confusing as I have tried to describe and compare the views of philosophers who use different terms to imply normativity. The point is not that I think that there is no normatively loaded word. Of course we will have to use some words to imply normativity, but

<hr />

[72] This may have been what misled Sidgwick into thinking that only the principles of utility and of egoism can be obligatory, for his attack on common sense morality focuses largely on the fact that common sense moral concepts are indeterminate. At least if pleasure and pain can be measured, Sidgwick thinks that egoism and utilitarianism are 'world-guided'. See Sidgwick, *The Methods of Ethics*, especially chapter XIII. I discuss Sidgwick's concern with determinacy, although from a somewhat different point of view, in my paper 'Two Arguments Against Lying'. [73] Moore, *Principia Ethica*, pp. 15–17.

we can choose any of the above ways of talking or others. All that matters there is that we agree, so that we will understand each other. But the interesting question is not how we decide to talk about the issue. The interesting question is why there should be such an issue: that is, why human beings need normative concepts and words. And substantive realism is not merely the view that 'obligation' (as Prichard thinks) or 'good' (as Moore thinks) or 'reason' (as Nagel thinks) are normative words which we know how to apply. It is a view – and a false one – about why human beings have normative words.

1.4.8

What is really wrong with substantive realism is its view about the source of normativity. Why do we use normative concepts like good, right, reason, obligation? According to the substantive realist it is because we grasp that there are things that have normative properties. Some things *appear* normative, and there is no reason to doubt that they are what they seem. We have normative concepts because we've spotted some normative entities, as it were wafting by.

According to substantive realism, then, ethics is really a theoretical or epistemological subject. When we ask ethical questions, or practical normative questions more generally, there is something about the world that we are trying to find out. The world contains a realm of inherently normative entities or truths, whose existence we have noticed, and the business of ethics, or of practical philosophy more generally, is to investigate them further, to learn about them in a more systematic way. But isn't ethics supposed to be a practical subject, a guide to action? Well, the realist will grant that the eventual point is to apply all this knowledge in practice. According to the substantive realist, then, the moral life is the most sublime feat of technical engineering, the application of theoretical knowledge to the solution of human problems. And in general human life and action consist in the application of theories, theories about what is right or good.[74]

---

[74] In fact that is what realism takes action itself to be: a form of technology. Aristotle firmly distinguishes *praxis* or action from *technē* or production (see *Nicomachean Ethics* VI.4), but a substantive realist has no way to make this distinction.

1.4.9

I've just been criticizing moral realism for asserting that we have moral concepts because we have noticed some moral entities in the universe. There's another argument on the contemporary scene that makes what looks like a similar criticism, but takes this criticism as a reason for moral scepticism. Since I am not arguing for scepticism, I want to say something about that. This other argument is that we have no reason to believe in the existence of moral entities or facts, because we do not need to assume the existence of such entities or facts in order to explain the moral phenomena. We need to assume that physical entities and facts exist in order to explain our observations of and beliefs about the 'external world', but we do not need to assume that moral facts or entities exist in order to explain our moral beliefs and motives. Explanations of those can proceed in entirely psychological terms. So, the argument suggests, the best explanation of why I see a rock is that there is one. But the best explanation of why I disapprove of killing is that I was brought up in a certain way.[75]

A more carefully formulated version of this argument has some force against substantive moral realism, and this is a point I will come back to. But I want to start by saying what I think is wrong with this argument. As it is stated, this argument looks as if it should work against *any* form of normative realism. It should have just as much force against the existence of *theoretical* normative truth (that X is a reason to *believe* Y) as it does against *practical* normative truth (that X is a reason to *do* Y). We can after all explain the occurrence of people's beliefs merely in terms of the causes of those beliefs, and leave their reasons out of it. Even if people's beliefs are caused by their thoughts about what reasons they have, we can explain the beliefs simply as caused by those thoughts. This does not commit us to saying that the reasons which appear in the contents of those thoughts are real. I may tell the truth because I think lying wrong, but in order to explain my honesty you need not suppose that my reason is real. It is enough that I think so. In the

---

[75] The *locus classicus* is perhaps Gilbert Harman, *The Nature of Morality: an Introduction to Ethics*, chapter 1.

same way, I may believe that I am mortal because I am human, but in order to explain why I believe I am mortal you need not suppose that my reason is real. Again it is enough that I think so. So we don't need to assume that theoretical reasons exist in order to explain the occurrence of beliefs.[76] But we cannot coherently take that fact as a *reason* to doubt that there is any such thing as a reason for belief. For if there is no such thing as a reason for belief, there is *ipso facto* no reason for believing this argument.[77] And – to echo Clarke himself – if instead we admit there are reasons for belief, then why not admit that there are reasons for action as well?

The trouble with drawing sceptical conclusions from the fact that a belief in normative truth is not needed to explain what people think or do is that it assumes that explanation and description of the phenomena is the sole or primary function of human concepts. That amounts to supposing that the business of human life is the construction and application of theories. And the reason the argument has some force against substantive realism is that substantive realism implicitly shares that assumption. The substantive realist assumes we have normative concepts because we are aware that the world contains normative phenomena, or is characterized by normative facts, and we are inspired by that awareness to construct theories about them.

But that is not why we have normative concepts. The very enterprise we are engaged in right now shows why we have those: it is because we have to figure out what to believe and what to do. Normative concepts exist because human beings have normative problems. And we have normative problems because we are self-conscious rational animals, capable of reflection about what we ought to believe and to do. That is why the normative question can be raised in the first place: because even when we are inclined to believe that something is right and to some extent feel ourselves

---

[76] Actually, however, there is a problem explaining how human beings could come to have the illusion that there are such things as theoretical and practical reasons if no such things exist at all. But the reason why we have the concept of a 'reason' does not therefore have to be that we *notice* that such things exist.

[77] Harman and others who have used this argument could still be Pyrrhonian sceptics, and use the consideration that we have no reason to believe in reasons to produce a suspension of all rational judgment. But this does not seem to have been what most of them had in mind.

moved to do it we can still *always* ask: but is this really true? and must I really do this?

Normative concepts like right, good, obligation, reason, are our names for the solutions to normative problems, for what it is we are looking for when we face them. And if we sometimes succeed in solving those problems, then there will be normative truths: that is, statements which employ normative concepts correctly. So it is true that the assumption of a realm of inherently normative entities or objective values is not needed to explain the existence of normative concepts, or the resulting existence of a category of normative truths. It is not because we notice normative entities in the course of our experience, but because we are normative animals who can question our experience, that normative concepts exist.

CONCLUSION

1.5.1

Contemporary defences of substantive moral realism almost always arise in the same way. They are always initiated by *somebody else*, a self-proclaimed spokesperson for the Modern Scientific World View. Whether this person really exists, or only haunts the anxious dreams of the moral philosopher, does not really matter. Armed with the distinction between facts and values, or brandishing Ockham's razor like a club, the spokesperson for the Modern Scientific World View declares that there cannot be ethical knowledge, that we can explain the moral phenomena without positing the existence of moral entities or facts, or that intrinsically normative entities are just too queer to exist. And the moral philosopher, frantic with the sense of impending loss, rushes to the defence of ethical knowledge. And almost nobody pauses to ask whether knowledge of ethical objects, or indeed any sort of knowledge at all, is really what we want here in the first place.

Is the normative question a request for knowledge? To raise the normative question is to ask whether our more unreflective moral beliefs and motives can withstand the test of reflection. The Platonic realist thinks that we can answer that question by taking a closer look at the *objects* of our beliefs and motives, to discover whether they are really the True and the Good. Nagel thinks we should take a closer look at the beliefs and motives themselves, to discover whether they are really reasons. But no such *discovery* is ever made. The realist's belief in the existence of normative entities is not based on any discovery. It is based on his *confidence* that his beliefs and desires are normative.

So even if it is true, realism cannot answer the normative question. But why should this matter? If confidence can support a metaphysics which in turn is supposed to support the claims of morality, why can't confidence support the claims of morality more directly?

In the next lecture I will examine the views of some philosophers who have rejected the idea that knowledge is what we need for normativity, and put something more like confidence in its place. According to these philosophers, morality is not grounded in our apprehension of truths about objective values. It is grounded in human nature and certain natural human sentiments. Once we understand what it is in our nature that gives rise to morality and what its consequences are, we can then raise the normative question: whether it is good to have such a nature, and to yield to its claims. According to these thinkers, the capacity of our moral motives to survive the test of reflection is not a test for something else, the existence of a normative entity. It is normativity itself.

Reflective endorsement

Christine Korsgaard

under what conditions did man devise these value judgments good and evil? *and what value do they themselves possess?* Have they hitherto hindered or furthered human prosperity? Are they a sign of distress, of impoverishment, of the degeneration of life? Or is there revealed in them, on the contrary, the plenitude, force, and will of life, its courage, certainty, future?

Nietzsche[1]

INTRODUCTION

2.1.1

At the end of the last lecture I argued that normativity is a problem for human beings because of our reflective nature. Even if we are inclined to believe that an action is right and even if we are inclined to be motivated by that fact, it is always possible for us to call our beliefs and motives into question. This is why, after all, we seek a philosophical foundation for ethics in the first place: because we are afraid that the true explanation of why we have moral beliefs and motives might not be one that sustains them. Morality might not survive reflection.

The view I am going to describe in this lecture takes its starting point from that thought. It applies one of the best rules of philosophical methodology: that a clear statement of the problem is also a statement of the solution. If the problem is that morality might not survive reflection, then the solution is that it might. If we find upon reflecting on the true moral theory that we still are

[1] Nietzsche, *The Genealogy of Morals*, preface, 3, p. 17.

49

inclined to endorse the claims that morality makes on us, then morality will be normative. I call this way of establishing normativity the 'reflective endorsement' method.

2.1.2

The reflective endorsement method has its natural home in theories that reject realism and ground morality in human nature.[2] In the modern period it makes its first appearance in the work of the sentimentalists of the eighteenth century. They explicitly rejected the realism of the rationalists, and argued that the moral value of actions and objects is a projection of human sentiments. As Hume famously says:

Take any action allow'd to be vicious: Wilful murder, for instance. Examine it in all lights, and see if you can find that matter of fact, or real existence, which you call vice. In which-ever way you take it, you find only certain passions, motives, volitions and thoughts. There is no other matter of fact in the case. The vice entirely escapes you, as long as you consider the object. You can never find it, till you turn your reflexion into your own breast, and find a sentiment of disapprobation, which arises in you, towards this action. Here is a matter of fact; but 'tis the object of feeling, not of reason. It lies in yourself, not in the object.[3]

Strictly speaking, we do not disapprove the action because it is vicious; instead, it is vicious because we disapprove it. Since morality is grounded in human sentiments, the normative question cannot be whether its dictates are true. Instead, it is whether we have reason to be glad that we have such sentiments, and to allow ourselves to be governed by them. The question is whether morality is a good thing for us.

Of course the sentimentalists were not the first to ground morality in human nature. Some of the classical Greek philosophers, in particular Aristotle, did so as well. So it is not surprising that the reflective endorsement method has re-emerged in some recent moral thought of Aristotelian inspiration, namely that of Bernard

---

[2] But see the discussion of Mill below.
[3] Hume, *A Treatise of Human Nature*, III.1.i, pp. 468–469.

Williams.[4] Like Hume, Williams rejects realism and defends in its place a theory which grounds morality in human dispositions. And like Hume, he finds that the answer to the normative question rests in whether those dispositions are ones we have reason to endorse. Hume and Williams find in reflective endorsement a way of grounding ethics which is an alternative to realism. John Stuart Mill, unlike them, is a kind of realist, for he believes that the desirable or the pleasant has objective value. But Mill does not think that sort of realism settles the question of the normativity of obligation. So he, too, turns to the method of reflective endorsement.

My purpose in this lecture is to explain this method of establishing normativity in more detail and to defend it against certain natural objections which arise from the realist camp. My aim is not to criticize this view. Instead, I will end by saying why I think the logical consequence of the theory of normativity shared by Hume, Mill, and Williams is the moral philosophy of Kant.

DAVID HUME

2.2.1

The choice of Hume as the major traditional representative of a theory of normativity might seem perverse. The pose Hume strikes in his moral philosophy is that of the scientist, whose task is to explain the origin of moral ideas. In his essay 'Of the Different Species of Philosophy', Hume firmly separates two different ways of treating moral philosophy, which we may call 'theoretical' and 'practical'. Theoretical or 'abstruse' philosophers:

regard human nature as a subject of speculation; and with a narrow scrutiny examine it, in order to find those principles, which regulate our

---

[4] These remarks will naturally raise the question whether Aristotle himself used the reflective endorsement method. Williams, in some passages I will be quoting later, makes a good case for the claim that reflective endorsement is at least involved in Aristotle's method of justifying morality. But Aristotle's teleological conception of the world adds another element to his conception of normativity. In these lectures I am addressing modern methods of establishing normativity, so I have not discussed Aristotle's views directly. What I think about them will, however, become apparent in the course of the next two lectures.

understanding, excite our sentiments, and make us approve or blame any particular object, action, or behaviour.[5]

Practical philosophers, by contrast, are interested in inciting us to good conduct. Hume says:

As virtue, of all objects, is allowed to be the most valuable, this species of philosophers paint her in the most amiable colours; borrowing all helps from poetry and eloquence, and treating their subject in an easy and obvious manner, and such as is best fitted to please the imagination, and engage the affections.[6]

Hume compares the theoretical philosopher to an anatomist and the practical philosopher to a painter.[7] The business of the anatomist is to explain what causes us to approve of virtue; the business of the painter is to make virtue appealing. And Hume styles himself a theoretical philosopher: his aim is to reveal the elements of the mind's 'anatomy' which make us approve and disapprove as we do.

The odd thing about this way of dividing up the philosophical enterprise is that the normative question seems to fall between the cracks. Neither the anatomist nor the painter seems to be interested in the *justification* of morality's claims. The theoretical philosopher is concerned only with providing a true explanation of the origin of moral concepts. The practical philosopher is a preacher or a Mandevillian politician. His task is to get people to behave themselves in socially useful ways, and he is prepared to use 'all helps from poetry and eloquence'. So we have explanation on the one hand and persuasion on the other, but no branch of moral philosophy which is concerned with justification.

It is not that Hume takes it for granted that morality's claims can be justified to the individual. He thinks it is conceivable that knowledge of the true moral theory would undermine the commitment of individuals to moral conduct. Yet as he also says:

And though the philosophical truth of any proposition by no means depends its tendency to promote the interests of society; yet a man has

---

[5] Hume, *Enquiry Concerning Human Understanding*, p. 6.
[6] Hume, *Enquiry Concerning Human Understanding*, p. 5.
[7] Hume, *Enquiry Concerning Human Understanding*, pp. 9–10; *A Treatise of Human Nature*, iii. iii.6, pp. 620–621. I owe a debt to Charlotte Brown for many useful discussions of this issue.

but a bad grace, who delivers a theory, however true, which . . . leads to a practice dangerous and pernicious. Why rake into those corners of nature which spread a nuisance all around? Why dig up the pestilence from the pit in which it is buried? The ingenuity of your researches may be admired, but your systems will be detested; and mankind will agree, if they cannot refute them, to sink them, at least, in eternal silence and oblivion. Truths which are *pernicious* to society, if any such there be, will yield to errors which are salutary and *advantageous*.

But although he admits that this could happen, he thinks that it doesn't. Even though he is not supposed to be a practical philosopher, Hume cannot resist pointing out that his account of the origin of moral ideas *does* make virtue attractive.

But what philosophical truths can be more advantageous to society, than those here delivered, which represent virtue in all her genuine and most engaging charms, and make us approach her with ease, familiarity, and affection? The dismal dress falls off, with which many divines, and some philosophers, have covered her; and nothing appears but gentleness, humanity, beneficence, affability; nay, even at proper intervals, play, frolic, and gaiety. She talks not of useless austerities and rigours, suffering and self-denial. She declares that her sole purpose is to make her votaries and all mankind, during every instant of their existence, if possible, cheerful and happy . . .[8]

So Hume thinks that his account of morality, though itself theoretical and abstruse, can be used by the practical philosopher to good effect.[9]

---

[8] Hume, *Enquiry Concerning the Principles of Morals*, p. 279.

[9] Hume sent Francis Hutcheson the manuscript of book III of *A Treatise of Human Nature*, and among Hutcheson's criticisms was that it 'wants a certain Warmth in the Cause of Virtue'. In his reply Hume developed and appealed to his distinction between the anatomist and the painter, emphasizing the difficulty of combining these roles:

Where you pull off the Skin, & display all the minute Parts, there appears something trivial, even in the noblest Attitudes and most vigorous Actions: Nor can you ever render the Object graceful or engaging but by clothing the Parts again with Skin and Flesh, and presenting only their bare Outside. An Anatomist, however, can give very good advice to a Painter . . . And in like manner, I am perswaded, that a Metaphysician may be very helpful to a Moralist; though I cannot easily conceive these two Characters united in the same Work.

A few lines later, however, he adds 'I intend to make a new Tryal, if it be possible to make the Moralist & Metaphysician agree a little better.' I speculate that the conclusions of the *Treatise* and the *Enquiry*, whose arguments I cite here, are that new trial. All of the passages in this note are from letter 13 of *The Letters of David Hume*, pp. 32–33. This letter can also be found in Raphael II, pp. 108–109.

One can, of course, take Hume to be saying merely that his theory is a gold mine for practical philosophers. But I think he has something more in mind. Normativity is not the provenance of either the theoretical or the practical philosopher because it will emerge, if it does emerge, in the way the two sides of philosophy interact. If the true account of our moral nature were one that made us want to reject its claims, then practical philosophers, as the guardians of social order, would have to make sure that the truth was not known. But if practical philosophers can get people to accept the claims of morality simply by telling them the truth about the nature of morality, then the claims of morality are *justified*. Hume is claiming that his theory is normative. Or so I will now argue.

2.2.2

Obviously if we are going to raise the question whether we can endorse our moral nature, we must appeal to some standard, in terms of which we may judge morality to be good or bad. Morality must be endorsed or rejected from a point of view which itself makes claims on us and so which is itself at least potentially normative. An example will help.

In the last lecture I described an evolutionary moral theory which, I claimed, was an example of normative failure. As a moral agent, you might decide that moral claims, if they are made on you in the name of the preservation of the species, are not justified. We may now understand that case as a failure of reflective endorsement. In giving the example, I appealed to several different kinds of considerations which might lead you to challenge morality's authority, considerations which arise from different points of view. One is that doing your duty might make you unhappy, a problem which arises from the point of view of self-interest. Another is that doing your duty might be harmful to others, a problem which arises from the point of view of benevolence or sympathy, of our natural concern about others, leaving morality aside.[10] A third, which arose in the case of the person who is required to risk his life

[10] Hutcheson called this natural concern for others the public sense. (See Raphael I, p. 301.) He called every point of view from which we approve or disapprove a 'sense', and for him the question of normativity, as we will see later, is a question about the harmony of the various approving 'senses'.

to conceal some Jews from the Nazis, was that it might seem paradoxical that you should be asked to endure evil merely to promote the existence of the species that generated that evil. This is a problem of what we might call direct reflexivity: morality may be found unsatisfactory from the moral point of view itself. Thus the reflective dissonance that might lead you to reject the authority of moral claims can arise from any of a number of points of view we use in assessing motives and actions. In Hume's case, the points of view from which morality is assessed are, first, the point of view of self-interest, and second, the point of view of the moral sense itself. I begin with the first.

2.2.3

According to Hume, moral judgments are based on sentiments of approval and disapproval which we feel when we contemplate a person's character from what he calls 'a general point of view'.[11] Taking up the general point of view regulates our sentiments about a person in two ways. First, we view the person not through the eyes of our own interests, but instead through the eyes of our sympathy with the person herself and her friends, family, neighbours, and colleagues.[12] We are sympathetically pleased or pained by the good or bad effects of her character on those with whom she usually associates, the people Hume calls her 'narrow circle'.[13] Second, we judge her characteristics according to the usual effects of such characteristics, rather than according to their actual effects in this or that case. As Hume puts it, we judge according to 'general rules'.[14]

These two regulative devices bring a kind of objectivity to our moral judgments. Judging in sympathy with the narrow circle and according to general rules, we are able to reach agreement, in the sense of a convergence of sentiments, about a person's character. We all approve and disapprove of the same characteristics, and as a result we come to share an ideal of good character.[15] A person of

---

[11] Hume, *A Treatise of Human Nature*, III.3.i, pp. 581–582.
[12] Hume, *A Treatise of Human Nature*, III.3.i, p. 582.
[13] Hume, *A Treatise of Human Nature*, III.3.iii, p. 602.
[14] Hume, *A Treatise of Human Nature*, III.3.i, p. 585.
[15] Universality of this sort might fail across cultures or epochs, because different qualities might be useful in different times and places. Patriotism is a virtue in a world of warring nation states, but might become a vice in a world that aspires to greater unity. These differences, however, being explicable, do not really damage the universality of the account.

good character, one whom we judge to have the virtues, is one who is useful and agreeable to herself and her friends. Since people love those who have useful and agreeable qualities, and since the perception of a lovable quality in ourselves causes pride, virtue is a natural cause of pride, and vice in the same way of humility. And since pride is a pleasing sentiment and humility a painful one, we have a natural desire to be proud of ourselves and to avoid the causes of humility. This gives us a natural desire to acquire the virtues and avoid the vices. The normative question then is whether we really have reason to yield to these desires, and to try to be virtuous people.

I think this is the question Hume is raising in the last section of the *Enquiry Concerning the Principles of Morals* when he says this:

Having explained the moral *approbation* attending merit or virtue, there remains nothing but briefly to consider our interested *obligation* to it, and to inquire whether every man, who has any regard to his own happiness and welfare, will not find his account in the practice of every moral virtue.[16]

Hume proceeds to detail the ways in which the practice of virtue contributes to the moral agent's happiness. His fourfold division of the virtues into qualities useful and agreeable to self and others enables him to do this in very short order. No argument is needed to defend the qualities that make you useful and agreeable to yourself, for those contribute to your happiness by definition. Almost as little is required to defend the qualities that make you *agreeable* to others. As Hume says:

Would you have your company coveted, admired, followed; rather than hated, despised, avoided? Can anyone seriously deliberate in the case?[17]

To defend the qualities that are *useful* to others, Hume borrows a famous argument from Joseph Butler.[18] In order to be happy, we must have some desires and interests whose fulfilment will bring us satisfaction. And other-directed desires and interests are just as good for this purpose as self-absorbed ones. Indeed in many ways

[16] Hume, *Enquiry Concerning the Principles of Morals*, p. 278.
[17] Hume, *Enquiry Concerning the Principles of Morals*, pp. 280–281.
[18] Butler, 'Upon the Love of Our Neighbor', sermon 11 of the *Fifteen Sermons Preached at the Rolls Chapel*; sermon 4 of the *Five Sermons*.

they are better. Hume reminds us that any desire 'when gratified by success, gives a satisfaction proportioned to its force and violence'. But benevolent desires have the additional advantages that their 'immediate feeling . . . is sweet, smooth, tender, and agreeable' and that they make others like us and make us pleased with ourselves.[19] To be a morally good person, then, is conducive to your happiness or at least not inconsistent with it.

Now one might think that this argument is not intended to show anything about the goodness of being subject to motives of moral *obligation*, and that therefore it cannot show anything about the normativity of obligation. For according to Hume's account a *naturally* virtuous person is one who acts, not from the motive of duty or obligation, but simply from some natural motive, such as benevolence, which a spectator would approve. No reason why you are *obligated* to perform virtuous actions has been given by the argument or is required by it; you perform virtuous actions because you have natural motives to do so; and the argument has simply shown that this is a good way for you to be.

But this would not be correct. For first, Hume admits that in a case where a person is aware of lacking a virtuous moral motive, he may hate himself upon that account, and may perform the action without the motive, from a certain sense of duty, in order to acquire by practice, that virtuous principle, or at least, to disguise to himself, as much as possible, his want of it.[20]

And second, it turns out that in the case of what Hume calls the *artificial* virtues such as justice, this sense of duty is the motive that is normally operative.[21] According to Hume the first or natural motive for participating in a system of justice is self-interest. But this is not the usual motive for performing just *actions*, for just actions, taken singly, do not necessarily or even usually promote self-interest. What promotes self-interest is the existence of the *system* of justice. But the connection between individual just actions and the system is too 'remote' to sustain interested motivation.[22] Instead, Hume argues, sympathy with the public interest causes us

[19] Hume, *Enquiry Concerning the Principles of Morals*, p. 282.
[20] Hume, *A Treatise of Human Nature*, III,2.i, p. 479.
[21] Hume, *A Treatise of Human Nature*, III.2.i, p. 479.
[22] Hume, *A Treatise of Human Nature*, III.2.ii, p. 499.

to disapprove of all unjust actions on account of their general tendency to bring down the system.[23] And this sympathy grounds a sense of duty which motivates us to avoid injustice. We avoid injustice because we would disapprove of ourselves – that is, we would feel humility – if we did not.

Furthermore, there are cases in which this sense of duty is the *only* available motive, for it can happen that an action, while it is of the type that tends to bring down the system of justice, will not in fact do that system any harm at all, and that the agent knows that. This is the plight of the famous 'sensible knave' who poses the most difficult challenge to Hume's account of 'interested obligation'. As Hume says:

> Treating vice with the greatest candour, and making it all possible concessions, we must acknowledge that there is not the smallest pretext for giving it the preference above virtue, with a view to self-interest; except, perhaps in the case of justice, where a man, taking things in a certain light, may often seem to be a loser by his integrity. And though it is allowed that, without a regard to property, no society could subsist; yet according to the imperfect way in which human affairs are conducted, a sensible knave, in particular incidents, may think that an act of iniquity or infidelity will make a considerable addition to his fortune, without causing any considerable breach in the social union and confederacy . . .

This is, of course, a version of the familiar free-rider problem. The sensible knave wants to know why he should not profit from injustice when it will not damage his interests by endangering the system of justice. And here is Hume's surprising answer:

> I must confess that, if a man think that this reasoning much requires an answer, it will be a little difficult to find any which will appear to him satisfactory and convincing. If his heart rebel not against such pernicious maxims, if he feel no reluctance to the thoughts of villainy or baseness, he has indeed lost a considerable motive to virtue; and we may expect that his practice will be answerable to his speculation . . . Inward peace of mind, consciousness of integrity, a satisfactory review of our own conduct; these are circumstances, very requisite to happiness, and will be cherished and cultivated by every honest man, who feels the importance of them.[24]

---

[23] Hume, *A Treatise of Human Nature*, III.2.ii, pp. 499–500.
[24] Hume, *Enquiry Concerning the Principles of Morals*, pp. 282–283.

There's an old joke about a child who's glad he doesn't like spinach, since then he'd eat it, and he hates the disgusting stuff. Hume appears at first sight to be giving us that sort of reason for being glad we don't like injustice. *Of course* integrity will be cherished by honest people who feel the importance of it. But the sensible knave is questioning exactly that importance. The fact that we disapprove of injustice and therefore of ourselves when we engage in it can hardly be offered as a reason for endorsing our own disapproval of injustice.

Actually, however, in Hume's theory it can. Hume's theory of sympathy allows him to argue that an individual is likely to experience humility when he acts unjustly regardless of whether or not he believes that there is good reason to disapprove of the unjust action in the case at hand. For it follows from Hume's account of sympathy that the sentiments of others are contagious to us. And their sentiments about ourselves, in particular, have a tendency to get under our skins. So the fact that *other people* will disapprove and dislike the sensible knave will be sufficient to provide him with feelings of disapproval and dislike of himself. Of course a knave will try to keep his knavish actions secret. But unless he is very hardened indeed, even the knowledge that others *would* hate him if they knew what he is up to will be enough to produce humility and self-hatred when he acts unjustly. As Hume says:

By continual and earnest pursuit of a character, a name, a reputation in the world, we bring our own deportment and conduct frequently in review, and consider how they appear in the eyes of those who approach and regard us. This constant habit of surveying ourselves as it were, in reflection, keeps alive all the sentiments of right and wrong, and begets, in noble natures, a certain reverence for themselves as well as others, which is the surest guardian of every virtue.[25]

So Hume's reply to the sensible knave is not circular. Morality provides a set of pleasures of its own, a set of pleasures which the knave loses out on. Because of sympathy, the sense that you are lovable and worthy in the eyes of others makes you lovable and worthy in your own. For the same reason, the sense that you are

---

[25] Hume, *Enquiry Concerning the Principles of Morals*, p. 276.

detestable in the eyes of others makes you detestable in your own. And morality provides these feelings regardless of whether you think that morality is justified or not. This fact enables Hume to add the familiar claim that virtue is its own reward to his list of the ways in which virtue promotes self-interest without any circularity at all. Together, all of these arguments establish what Hume calls our 'interested obligation' to be moral.

2.2.4

The arguments I've just detailed give rise to two closely related criticisms, which issue from the realist camp. First, you might think that Hume is not giving an account of the normativity of morality, but simply an account of our motives to be moral, and one that falls afoul of Prichard's famous argument at that.[26] We should not practise virtue because it is in our interest, but rather for its own sake, so Hume's argument is irrelevant. But it is clear that Hume is not saying that we should perform *particular* virtuous or obligatory actions because it serves our own interest to do so. He is saying that it is in our interest to be *people who practise virtue for its own sake*. This is especially clear in the Butlerian argument used to defend the virtues that are useful to others. Neither the immediately agreeable sensations of benevolence nor its gratifications are available to anyone who is not genuinely and wholeheartedly concerned about others. The Butlerian argument is not meant to show that morality promotes some set of interests you already have, but rather that moral interests are good ones to have. What the argument establishes is the harmony of two potentially normative points of view, morality and self-interest.[27]

This shows something interesting, I think, about how the reflective endorsement theorist conceives the problem of normativity. Human beings are subject to practical claims from various

---

[26] For a discussion of Prichard's argument see lecture 1, 1.4.2.

[27] The argument can therefore be seen as establishing what Rawls calls 'congruence'. See *A Theory of Justice*, p. 399. Rawls's own argument that justice is a good for the just person, in section 86 of that work, is a congruence argument. On the use of congruence arguments among the eighteenth-century British Moralists, see Charlotte Brown, 'Hume Against the Selfish Schools and the Monkish Virtues'.

sources – our own interests, the interests of others, morality itself. The normative question is answered by showing that the points of view from which these different interests arise are congruent, that meeting the claims made from one point of view will not necessarily mean violating those that arise from another. And that in turn shows how the threat is conceived. The threat is that the various claims which our nature makes on us will tear us apart. The reflective endorsement strategy can be seen as a kind of answer – in Hume's case, an anticipatory answer – to the sorts of worries about morality voiced by Nietzsche and Freud. The concern is that morality might be bad or unhealthy for us. Indeed I think it is instructive that so many readers of Nietzsche and Freud take it to be obvious that they are some sort of moral sceptics, although neither ever says that he is. One possible explanation is that these readers implicitly accept the reflective endorsement view. The claim that morality is hurting us is automatically seen as a challenge to its normativity. We reply to the challenge by showing that morality's claims are not going to hurt us or tear us apart.

The second realist objection carries Prichard's worry to a higher level. This time the objector grants that Hume's argument is not offered to us as a wrongheaded theory of moral motivation, but rather as an attempt to establish normativity by showing that morality is good. But it says that even as such it fails. An argument that shows that virtue is good from the point of view of self-interest only shows that morality is extrinsically good, or extrinsically normative. But what we need for normativity is to show that morality is intrinsically good or intrinsically normative. And now we come back to a thought familiar from our encounter with realism: that only something intrinsically normative can satisfy the demand for unconditional justification.

At this point it will help to turn to an earlier view Hume held about normativity. The arguments I have been detailing up until now are for the most part from the *Enquiry Concerning the Principles of Morals.* In *A Treatise of Human Nature,* Hume appealed to a more specific version of the reflective endorsement account, which I call 'normativity as reflexivity'. This view can help to answer the realist's worry.

2.2.5

Since Hume does not set this view out explicitly, I will start by explaining the grounds on which I attribute it to him. Book I of *A Treatise of Human Nature* ends in a mood of melancholy despair and scepticism; while book III concludes in a mood of triumphant affirmation. And this is because at the end of book I, Hume finds that '[T]he understanding, when it acts alone, and according to its most general principles, entirely subverts itself, and leaves not the lowest degree of evidence in any proposition, either in philosophy or common life.'[28] Whereas at the end of book III, Hume concludes that the moral sense 'must certainly acquire new force, when reflecting on itself, it approves of those principles, from whence it is deriv'd, and finds nothing but what is great and good in its rise and origin'.[29] The understanding, when it reflects on its own operations, falls into doubt about and so subverts itself. But the moral sense approves of and so reinforces itself. Therefore scepticism about the understanding is in order, but scepticism about morality is not.

These facts suggest that Hume is relying on an account of normativity which is completely general, applying to any kind of purportedly normative claim. Let me define two terms that will help express this view. Call a purportedly normative judgment a 'verdict', and the mental operation that gives rise to it a 'faculty'. The faculty of understanding gives rise to beliefs, which are verdicts of conviction. The moral sense gives rise to moral sentiments or verdicts of approval and disapproval. The faculty of taste gives rise to verdicts of beauty. According to this theory a faculty's verdicts are normative if the faculty meets the following test: *when the faculty takes itself and its own operations for its object, it gives a positive verdict.*

Hume clearly thinks that the understanding fails this test. A belief, according to Hume, is a sentiment of conviction, a lively idea of the thing believed. He argues that the harder we press the question whether we ought to believe our beliefs or whether they are likely to be true, the more the degree of our conviction – that is, the liveliness or vivacity of the ideas – will tend to diminish. So the more we reason about whether reasoning is likely to lead us to the

---

[28] Hume, *A Treatise of Human Nature*, I.4.vii, pp. 267–268.
[29] Hume, *A Treatise of Human Nature*, III.3.vi, p. 619.

truth, the less confidence in the results of reasoning we will end up having.[30] The understanding in this way 'subverts itself' when it reflects on its own operations.[31]

But the moral sense passes the reflexivity test. In the conclusion of the *Treatise*, Hume says:

> Were it proper in such a subject to bribe the readers assent, or employ any thing but solid argument, we are here abundantly supplied with topics to engage the affections. All lovers of virtue . . . must certainly be pleas'd to see moral distinctions deriv'd from so noble a source, which gives us a just notion both of the *generosity* and *capacity* of our nature. It requires but very little knowledge of human affairs to perceive, that a sense of morals is a principle inherent in the soul, and one of the most powerful that enters into the composition. *But this sense must certainly acquire new force, when reflecting on itself, it approves of those principles, from whence it is deriv'd, and finds nothing but what is great and good in its rise and origin* . . . not only virtue must be approv'd of, but also the sense of virtue: And not only that sense, but also the principles from whence it is deriv'd. So that nothing is presented on any side, but what is laudable and good.[32]

Reflection on the origin of our moral sentiments only serves to strengthen those sentiments. The moral sense approves of its own origins and workings and so it approves of *itself*.

2.2.6

I believe that Hume got the idea for this theory of normativity from the moral sense theorist Francis Hutcheson. In his *Illustrations*

---

[30] See Hume, *A Treatise of Human Nature*, 1.4.i, pp. 180–185.

[31] I ignore a complication here. Hume is less sceptical about beliefs concerning matters in 'common life' than about metaphysical beliefs, but for a somewhat odd reason. Hume means quite literally that philosophical enquiry into the grounds of belief tends to diminish the force and vivacity of belief. When we reason about reasoning itself, Hume thinks that we will lose confidence in it, and this loss of confidence subverts our confidence in any other piece of abstract reasoning. But beliefs about common life are, so to speak, hardier, because of their connection to perception and to ideas which for us are forceful and vivacious. The reasoning that leads us to scepticism is itself an abstract piece of reasoning and cannot successfully oppose these more vivacious thoughts. We can only remain sceptical about beliefs in common life so long as we keep the sceptical arguments before our minds, which we cannot do while we are thinking about common life. Scepticism about metaphysical beliefs is more enduring. I set these rather strange views forward in more detail in an unpublished paper, 'Normativity as Reflexivity: Hume's Practical Justification of Morality'.

[32] Hume, *A Treatise of Human Nature*, III.3.vi, p. 619, my emphasis.

on the Moral Sense, Hutcheson imagines a rationalist who objects that judgments of good and evil cannot come from a moral sense, because we judge our senses themselves to be good or evil.[33] For instance, we approve of a benevolence-approving moral sense, while we would deplore a malice-approving moral sense. These judgments would be trivial if they came from the benevolence-approving moral sense itself. The argument is a variant on one familiar argument against theological voluntarism – that if God determines what is good and evil then we cannot significantly judge God himself to be good – and like that argument it is intended to drive us to realism. Hutcheson replies this way:

A sense approving benevolence would disapprove that temper which a sense approving malice would delight in. The former would judge of the latter by his own sense, so would the latter of the former. Each one would at first view think the sense of the other perverted. But, then, is there no difference? Are both senses equally good? No, certainly, any man who observed them would think the sense of the former more desirable than of the latter; but this is because the moral sense of every man is constituted in the former manner. But were there any nature with no moral sense at all observing these two persons, would he not think the state of the former preferable to that of the latter? Yes, he might, but not from any perception of moral goodness in the one sense more than in the other. Any rational nature observing two men thus constituted with opposite senses might by reasoning see, not moral goodness in one sense more than in the contrary, but a tendency to the happiness of the person himself, who had the former sense in the one constitution, and a contrary tendency in the opposite constitution.[34]

His point is that goodness of a sense must be assessed from some point of view from which we judge things to be good or bad, and that we have a limited number of such points of view to which we can appeal. We can judge the moral sense from the point of view of the moral sense itself; we can judge it from the point of view of benevolence towards others; or we can judge it from the point of view of our own self-interest.[35] What we cannot do is get outside of all of the points of view from which we judge things to be good or bad and still coherently ask whether some-

[33] Hutcheson, *Illustrations on the Moral Sense*, p. 133.
[34] Hutcheson, *Illustrations on the Moral Sense*, pp. 133–134.
[35] Hutcheson, *Illustrations on the Moral Sense*, pp. 133–134.

thing is good or bad. There is no place outside of our normative points of view from which normative questions can be asked.

The same argument can of course be made about the normativity of the verdicts of the understanding. If we fall into doubt about whether we really ought to believe what we find ourselves inclined to believe – that is, if we fall into doubt about whether our beliefs are true – we cannot dispel the doubt by comparing our beliefs to the world to see whether they are true. We have no access to the world except through the verdicts of the understanding itself, just as we have no access to the good except through the verdicts of the various points of view from which we make judgments of goodness.[36] The only point of view from which we can assess the normativity of the understanding is therefore that of the understanding itself.

It is this line of thought, I believe, that gave Hume the idea for the reflexivity test. It is, of course, complicated in the moral case by the fact that there is more than one point of view from which we can assess things as good or bad. This is what, in the later work, leads Hume to use the more general reflective endorsement test instead. But we can see reflexivity and reflective endorsement as working together. For one of the reasons that the moral sense approves of itself *is* that morality contributes to our happiness, and the moral sense approves of anything that contributes to people's happiness.

2.2.7

Now let's go back to the more general form of the realist's objection. This was that the reflective endorsement test only shows that morality is extrinsically normative, whereas what we want to show is that it is intrinsically normative. The addition of the reflexivity test does show that, or rather, it shows something that is very close. It shows that *human nature*, moral government included, is

---

[36] In the case of the good or the obligatory, realists often think that an appeal to intuition will help at this point: that is, they think that the fact what seems good *really is* good is confirmed by intuition. In the case of belief, no one will be tempted to think an appeal to intuition is going to help. If each of our original beliefs has to be seconded by an intuitive belief that beliefs are true, what in turn is to support that intuitive belief? The asymmetry exists because, as I argued in lecture 1, moral realists think that ethics is a theoretical subject and that our relation to value is itself one of knowledge or belief. They see scepticism about knowledge as a further stretch of scepticism rather than as something parallel to scepticism about the good or the right.

intrinsically normative, in a negative version of the sense required by the realist argument: there is *no intelligible challenge* that can be made to its claims. Within human nature, morality can coherently be challenged from the point of view of self-interest, and self-interest from the point of view of morality. Outside of human nature, there is no normative point of view from which morality can be challenged. But morality can meet the internal challenge that is made from the point of view of self-interest, and it also approves of itself. It is human nature to be governed by morality, and from every point of view, including its own, morality earns its right to govern us. We have therefore no reason to reject our nature, and can allow it to be a law to us. Human nature, moral government included, is therefore normative, and has authority for us.

Perhaps a comparison will make this thought seem more familiar. According to the teleological ethics of the ancient world, to be virtuous is to realize our true nature, to be the best version of what we are. So it is to let our own nature be a law to us. And the Greeks thought that since our own good would be realized in being the best version of what we are, we have every reason to be virtuous. Sentimentalism can be seen as a kind of negative surrogate of the teleological ethics of the ancient world. According to the sentimentalists, we have *no reason not to be* the best version of what we are.[37]

---

[37] This is actually even clearer in Butler, who like Hume argues for the congruence of interest and morality, but who also employs classical teleological notions freely. (See Butler, sermons 1–3 of the *Fifteen Sermons* and of the *Five Sermons*, 'Upon Human Nature' and the preface, especially pp. 14–15.) There is another way to put this argument which brings it a little closer to that of the voluntarists. If it is in our interest to be moral, then we suffer for being immoral. And if we suffer for being immoral, then our nature is in a position to punish us for being immoral. And by the voluntarist criterion of authority, that means that our nature has authority over us, and is in a position to give us laws. I do not know whether Hume had exactly this in mind, but I have sometimes thought it is the best way to understand Shaftesbury, on whom Hume certainly drew. Hutcheson understood Shaftesbury to be saying that interest is our *motive* for being moral, and many commentators have followed him in this. (See Hutcheson, *Inquiry Concerning the Original of Our Ideas of Beauty and Virtue*, in Raphael I, p. 263. Shaftesbury is not referred to by name, but is the 'some other moralist[s]' referred to in the first full paragraph of the page.) But if I am right, Shaftesbury is saying that morality has authority over us because it can punish us, and our motive, for Shaftesbury just as for Hobbes and for Pufendorf, is the motive of duty. One piece of evidence for this is the fact that Shaftesbury places so much emphasis on the fact that we will be made miserable by guilt, shame, and remorse if we are bad. (See Shaftesbury, *Characteristics of Men, Manners, Opinions, Times*, pp. 305–317.) If Shaftesbury were merely trying to say that morality is normative because it promotes our interests, this appeal would be circular in the same way that Hume's appeal to the sensible knave's loss of the pleasures of self-approval appears at first to be.

BERNARD WILLIAMS

2.3.1

This brings us to a recent attempt to revive the virtue-oriented ethics of the ancient world. In chapters 8 and 9 of *Ethics and the Limits of Philosophy*, Bernard Williams argues that there is a contrast between the kind of objectivity we can hope to find in science and that which we can hope to achieve in ethics. Williams accepts a form of realism in the case of science, but rejects it in the case of ethics.

Williams frames this contrast in terms of convergence, that is, in terms of what might lead us to the best kind of agreement. In science, the ideal form of convergence would be this: we come to agree with one another in our beliefs because we are all converging on the way the world really is. In ethics, this sort of convergence is unavailable, and so another must be found.[38] This, as we will see, is where reflective endorsement comes in.

2.3.2

Williams begins by solving a problem in the formulation of his contrast. The problem is essentially the same as the one that drove Hume to suppose that only a reflexivity test could establish the normativity of belief: that we can't go outside of our beliefs in order to determine whether they match the world, or whether they correctly capture 'the way the world really is'. Williams puts the problem this way. We have a certain way of conceptualizing the world, a conceptual scheme. One thing we might mean in talking about 'the way the world really is' is whether we have applied our concepts correctly. If we say that grass is green we have and if we say that it is pink we have not. This notion is unproblematic, but it seems to leave us no room to query our way of conceptualizing the world itself.

It is interesting to note that Prichard argues that this is correct: that is, he argues that there *is* no room to query our way of

---

[38] Williams, *Ethics and the Limits of Philosophy*, p. 136.

conceptualizing the world.[39] Just as he thinks the only way to resolve a doubt about whether we are 'really obligated' – whether obligation is normative – is to review the reasons why the action is right, so he thinks the only way to resolve a doubt about whether our beliefs are true is to review the reasons for those beliefs – in the language I am using here, to make sure that the concepts we use have been applied correctly. Here as before, the normative question slips through our fingers because it is asked in the wrong way. By asking the normative question in the form 'is my belief really true?' Prichard is led to confuse it with the question whether my concepts have been applied correctly.

But the normative question is a question about the status of the concepts, not about whether they have been correctly applied. Is our conceptual scheme adequate? Is it the correct one, or the best one, or the one that captures the most, or the one that captures what is 'really true' about the world? Philosophers will of course disagree on whether any of these questions are coherent and, if so, which one of them is the right one to ask. But since science leads us to modify our conceptual scheme, and we think of these modifications as improvements, it does appear that some such question is in order.

Williams proposes that we can capture the distinction between the way the world really is and the way it seems to us by the formation of a kind of limiting conception which he calls 'the "absolute conception" of the world'.[40] The idea involves a contrast between concepts which are more and less dependent on the particular perspective from which we view the world. For instance, we use colour categories because we are visual, so colour concepts like 'green' and 'pink' are dependent on something about our own particular perspective. The concept of a certain wavelength of light might be less dependent.

Williams associates two other properties with a concept's greater independence from our particular perspectives. First, our use of concepts which are more dependent on our own perspectives will be explained in terms of a theory that employs concepts which are

---

[39] Prichard, 'Does Moral Philosophy Rest on a Mistake?', pp. 14–15.
[40] Williams, *Ethics and the Limits of Philosophy*, p. 139.

less dependent. So for instance our use of colour concepts might be explained by a theory of vision which employs wavelength concepts. Relatedly, and importantly, this theory (or some yet more absolute theory in which it is embedded) will also *justify* our belief that colour vision is a form of *perception*, that is, a way of learning about the world, by the way that it explains it.[41] Colour vision is a way of learning about the world because it gives us information about wavelengths, or something yet more ultimate, which we take to be part of reality. Second, the more independent of our own perspective a concept is, the more likely it is that it could be shared by investigators who were unlike us in their ways of learning about the world. Suppose that there are rational creatures on Mars who cannot see colours but do something more like hear them, or perhaps feel them in the form of vibrations. They could not use colour concepts but they might be able to use wavelength concepts. The more independent concepts are more shareable.

Williams thinks that the nearest thing we have to a conception of 'the way the world really is' is the conception of the world that is maximally independent of our own perspective. And if we and the alien investigators actually began to converge on such a conception (and of course to agree on what judgments are correct within it) then we would have reason to believe we were converging on what the world is really like. This would be the best case of convergence for science: our theories would come to converge with the theories of other investigators because all of us were converging on the way the world is.

2.3.3

I think there is a problem with this view, which I will just mention and then lay aside. It concerns the question why we should think that human ways of *cognizing* things are less speciosyncratic and therefore more shareable with alien investigators than human ways of *perceiving* things. Cognition does seem less perspective-dependent than perception, but the air of obviousness about that may come from the way we hammer out perceptual conflicts

---

[41] Williams, *Ethics and the Limits of Philosophy*, p. 149.

among ourselves, and it may have no wider application. We do, of course, encounter other species who perceive the world differently than we do (although so far none of them are scientific investigators). So we can easily imagine rational scientific investigators who perceive the world differently, say like highly intelligent bats. But why should we be confident that our ways of cognizing the world are less dependent on our particular perspective than our ways of perceiving it and so would be more shareable with them? And, relatedly, how can we tell that one way of cognizing things is more perspective-dependent than another? Presumably, Williams's answer to these worries will appeal to the first of the two properties he associates with greater independence of perspective, the order of scientific explanation.[42] That is, he will argue that perceptual concepts should be judged to be more dependent on the peculiarities of our perspective than cognitive ones *because* we can explain the way we use the perceptual ones in terms of the purely cognitive ones. When we are ranking purely cognitive concepts for their dependence on perspective, the order of explanation is the only thing that could be our guide. So the order of explanation will turn out to be criterial of independence.[43] But this is where there is a problem. The view that the order of scientific explanation determines which of our concepts are less dependent on our perspective and so more shareable with alien investigators seems to *presuppose* that what science gives us is a perspective-independent way of conceptualizing the world. That is, it seems to presuppose that what science gives us is knowledge of what the world is really like.

I am inclined to conclude from this that Williams's realism about

[42] As Peter Hylton pointed out to me, if Williams does appeal to the order of explanation in the way I am suggesting then it has to be *scientific* explanations – that is, explanations whose *purposes* are scientific ones – which are in question. The everyday explanations of our own conduct which we offer to one another do not privilege the conceptual over the perceptual in this way. If I am trying to explain to you why I brought home a green orange it is just as good and a lot more efficient for me to say it looked like a lime to me than to tell a story about wavelengths. Here my purpose is to get you to see how I saw it, not why I saw it that way.

[43] Williams cannot use shareability as the *criterion* of independence, because this leads to a form of idealism and he is trying to argue for a form of realism. That is, he thinks that the world is in his phrase what is 'there *anyway*' and not that it is simply that which all observers share.

science, like Nagel's about ethics, is really just a statement of his confidence in the subject. In that case it is of course subject to the same criticism as far as meeting *sceptical* worries is concerned. If someone has fallen into doubt about whether 'wavelengths' have any more to do with what the world is really like than 'colours' it will not help to tell him that science explains colours in terms of wavelengths. That science tells us what the world is really like is *exactly* what he is doubting. But as I said earlier, for now I prefer to set this worry aside.

2.3.4

The best sort of convergence in science is convergence guided by the way the world really is. Now consider what the parallel would be in ethics. Here too we must deal with a possible objection, namely that there is nothing analogous to perceptual judgments in ethics. Seeing the facts is one thing, and evaluating them in a certain way is another. This sort of argument was popular among early and mid-twentieth-century emotivists and prescriptivists. To counter it, Williams notices, we may appeal to the existence of what he calls 'thick' as opposed to 'thin' ethical concepts. Thin ethical concepts – like right and good and ought – do not appear to be world-guided, in the sense that their application does not appear to be guided by the facts. Pure in their normativity, they are like those little gold stars you can stick on anything. But thick ethical concepts (Williams's examples are coward, lie, brutality, and gratitude) are world-guided and action-guiding at the same time.[44] Only an action which is motivated in some way by fear can be called cowardly, and yet to call an action cowardly is to suggest that it ought not to be done.[45]

Of course the prescriptivist or emotivist has his own account of these concepts. He thinks that their world-guidedness is one

---

[44] Williams, *Ethics and the Limits of Philosophy*, pp. 140–141.
[45] Williams says that thick concepts often provide reasons for action (or refraining) but of course strictly speaking this is not true of 'cowardly'. To say that an action is cowardly is to suggest that there is a reason not to do it but not to mention what that reason is. Something in the situation is worth overcoming human fearfulness for, but the term doesn't tell us what. This is because courage is a so-called executive virtue. Williams's other examples are of more directly reason-providing concepts.

thing and that their action-guidingness is another. The facts tell us which actions are motivated by fear, and when we disapprove of those actions or want to discourage others from doing them, we project our pejorative feelings on to them. So the word 'cowardly' is just a pejorative way of describing an act motivated by fear, used when we want to express our feelings or influence our neighbours.

The difficulty with this analysis is that it suggests that it would be possible to use a thick ethical concept with perfect accuracy even if you were completely incapable of appreciating the value which it embodies. Williams argues that this is implausible. Of course he does not mean that we can only use evaluative concepts when we ourselves actually endorse the values in question. But we apply such concepts by entering imaginatively into the world of those who have the values, not merely by applying a set of factual criteria.[46] We have to see the world through their eyes. This makes it natural to think of judgments employing thick ethical concepts as perceptual ones. And that in turn makes it natural to think that, like other perceptual judgments, they are a kind of knowledge.

2.3.5

I say that the sky is blue, and my visitor from Mars says that it makes a humming noise. Are we agreeing? Certainly we don't *mean* the same thing, since I am talking about how the sky looks and he is talking about how it sounds. Yet when we reflect on these views we find that the things we both say have implications which are expressible in terms of a more absolute concept, that of wavelengths. And when we look at those implications our judgments are found to converge. Here we find grounds for confidence that both of our perceptions are guiding us rightly: they are ways of knowing about the world. Now take this case. The medicine man says that killing the black snake will charm away the evil spirit. And we take 'charming away the evil spirit' to have implications expressible in terms of what *we* take to be a more absolute concept, let's say that

---

[46] Williams, *Ethics and the Limits of Philosophy*, pp. 141–142.

of curing an illness. And probably we think he is wrong: killing snakes is not a way of curing illnesses.[47]

What would the parallels be in ethics? They might look something like this. The Monk says that lying is sinful, and the Knight says that it is dishonourable. Certainly they do not *mean* exactly the same thing, for the Monk is saying something about the lie's effect on his soul, and about how it relates him to his God, while the Knight is saying something about the lie's effect on his reputation – on his 'character' in the older, more public sense of the word – and how it relates him to his social world. But we take both of their remarks to have implications for what *we* think is a more absolute concept – the lie is wrong, and ought not to be told – and here we find they converge. And we may think, in this case, that the convergence shows that their concepts are guiding them towards what we take to be a moral truth; or that they correctly reflect a moral reality: say, that there are certain kinds of actions which you cannot do without being personally diminished or disfigured, and that this is related to their wrongness.

On the other hand, suppose the Knight says he will be dishonoured unless he fights a duel with the man who has insulted him. If we take this to have the implication that trying to kill someone who has hurt your feelings is required, or even all right, we shall have to disagree. But now this is a conclusion which we should be uncomfortable with, and this is precisely because there is a world-guided side to the idea of dishonour. The Knight's reputation, his position in his social world, may be damaged in *exactly* the ways that he foresees and has in mind when he says he will be dishonoured. What is *for him* his identity may be diminished and disfigured just as it would have been by telling the lie. Facts of this sort should give us pause about whether he is, after all, using the idea of dishonour in a way that has implications for what is morally right or wrong in *our* sense of those words.

---

[47] He *might* be right, of course. There might be some story to tell about placebo effects – perhaps killing the black snake really works because the patient believes it will. Or perhaps the patient knows that if killing the black snake doesn't work the medicine man will try to frighten the evil spirit off by doing something dreadful to the patient, and this prospect frightens the patient into getting well. We don't know enough about medicine to know, and all that matters for the point is that we know roughly how such stories would have to go in order for us to be convinced by them.

2.3.6

Thinking about such cases may lead us to conclude that after all the analogy with the scientific case doesn't hold. We may see the medicine man as trying to cause health, but we should not see the Knight as trying to figure out what it is morally right to do. We should not even, according to Williams, assume that we share with the Knight any general sense of what it is right or all right to do, about which our views and the Knight's both have implications. Instead Williams propose a different way in which we might look at the ethical beliefs of others:

On the other model we shall see their judgments as part of their way of living, a cultural artifact they have come to inhabit (although they have not consciously built it). On this, nonobjectivist, model, we shall take a different view of the relations between that practice and critical reflection. We shall not be disposed to see the level of reflection as implicitly already there, and we shall not want to say that their judgments have, just as they stand, these implications [that is, implications about what it is right or all right to do].[48]

The proposal is that we should see their values not as their best approximations of the truth about rightness, but rather as a kind of *habitation*. Their values form a part of the structure of the social world in which they live.

But this does not mean that we cannot make any evaluative judgments about their values. We can ask whether their social world, that is, the world that is made of those values, is a good place for human beings to live. This is still, in a broad sense, an ethical question, but our resources for answering it are not tied to any particular system of values. Questions about the suitability of a habitat are answered with reference to the health and flourishing of the creatures who live in it. Williams suggests that a theory of human nature, drawing on the resources of the social as well as the physical sciences, could guide our reflections about what makes for human flourishing. And those reflections in turn could enable us to assess whether a given system of values promoted human

---

[48] Williams, *Ethics and the Limits of Philosophy*, p. 147.

flourishing.[49] Williams mentions psychoanalytic theory as one such resource, and of course it is impossible not to think of Freud in this context, with his gloomy view that 'the cultural superego . . . does not trouble itself enough about the facts of the mental constitution of human beings'.[50] It does seem natural to say that societies in which girls wish passionately that they had been born boys, or in which suicide motivated by feelings of personal worthlessness is common, or in which large segments of the population are sexually dysfunctional, are suffering from their values.

Williams proposes that if we find that a social world promoted the best life or at least a flourishing life for human beings, this would justify the values embodied in that social world. The structure of justification would be very different from the realist structure he thinks we can find in the case of scientific belief. The justification would not be that we find upon reflection that the values are true, or that they are reliable guides to the truth about morally right action the way colours are reliable guides to the truth about wavelengths. Williams suggests that the only ethical belief that might survive at the reflective level would be the belief 'that a certain kind of life was best for human beings'.[51] The justification of other ethical beliefs would be that it is good for human beings to lead a life that is guided and governed by those beliefs.

2.3.7

So far, in detailing Williams's view, I have been talking, as Williams does, as if from the point of view of an outside observer of an alien society. But when we imagine this same reflective exercise being carried out by a member of the society in question, it becomes clear that the structure of justification here is one of reflective endorsement. Hume, as we saw earlier, reverses the realist ordering of things, and argues that vice is bad because we disapprove of it. In a similar way, Williams thinks that ethical value is projected on to the world by our ethical beliefs. Both would deny that it is coherent to ask whether our values are true independently of our own

[49] Williams, *Ethics and the Limits of Philosophy*, pp. 45ff., 152–153.
[50] Williams, *Ethics and the Limits of Philosophy*, p. 45; Freud, *Civilization and Its Discontents*, p. 90.
[51] Williams, *Ethics and the Limits of Philosophy*, p. 154.

moral or ethical sentiments. The only question left to ask is whether it is good for us to have those sentiments, and that question must be answered from the perspective of the other practical claims our nature makes on us. Where Hume establishes normativity by showing that morality is congruent with self-interest, Williams asserts that it would have to be established by congruence with human flourishing.

2.3.8

Like Hume, Williams entertains the possibility that this will not be the result. But the prospect is in one way a more alarming one for Hume. Hume believes that he is talking about a set of evaluative concepts that are deeply grounded in human nature and human psychology. He supposes that if reflection yielded the result that morality is bad for the individual, the truth would have to be sunk in 'eternal silence and oblivion' in the interests of social order. Williams, by contrast, supposes that different cultures provide us with different sets of values. He sees the reflective test more as a method for choosing among them. When cultures come into what he calls 'real confrontation', their members, forced by that confrontation to reflect on the value of their values, may lose confidence in them, and come to the conclusion that some other values would lead to a better way of life.[52] The result will not be that they will decide that their old beliefs were false, or even that after all they did not know what, say, sin or honour was. It will be that they will stop using those concepts altogether.

In one case, a case of our own, this description of changing values rings true. Consider the uneasy fate of the evaluative concepts 'masculine' and 'feminine'. People who have fallen into doubt about the values embodied in these concepts and the way of life to which they once led us do not argue about whether they track the ethical truth. People who have already decided against these values do not run around telling us that masculinity and femininity are false or wrong. If someone says that aggressiveness is not feminine the response to him will not be that aggressiveness *is* feminine

---

[52] Williams, *Ethics and the Limits of Philosophy*, pp. 160ff.

or that aggressiveness is great. The response is 'let's not talk that way'. The complaint that has been launched against these values is not that they were false or misleading but that they were strait-jackets, stunting everybody's growth. It is that people who hold themselves and others to these ideals do not flourish. They must therefore be abandoned or revised.

2.3.9

There is even an element of *reflexivity* in Williams's view. Williams borrows the idea that morality is a projection of human dispositions from Aristotle rather than from Hume. Now Aristotle assumed that an ethically good life must be good for the person whose life it is. And Aristotle, again like Hume, has been accused of harbouring some form of egoism under this assumption. Defending Aristotle against this charge, Williams says:

The answer to this problem lies in the vital fact that the Aristotelian accounts puts substantive ethical dispositions into the content of the self. I am, at the time of mature reflection, what I have become, and my reflection, even if it is about my dispositions, must at the same time be expressive of them. I think about ethical goods *from* an ethical point of view that I have already acquired and that is part of what I am.[53]

As Williams points out, Aristotle's question is not whether an ethically good life serves some set of interests which are defined independently of the person's ethical nature. The Aristotelian agent asks about ethical value from an ethical point of view. Or, if he does try to reflect on his ethical dispositions from a point of view outside of those dispositions, from the point of view of his other needs and capacities, the important question will be:

whether there is anything in the view of things he takes from the outside that conflicts with the view of things he takes from the inside. For Aristotle, the virtuous agent would find no such conflict. He could come to understand that the dispositions that gave him his ethical view of the world were a correct or full development of human potentiality . . . Also, this perfection could be displayed harmoniously, so that the

---

[53] Williams, *Ethics and the Limits of Philosophy*, p. 51.

development of those ethical capacities would fit with other forms of human excellence. Aristotle's theory means that when the agent reflects, even from the outside, on all his needs and capacities, he will find no conflict with his ethical dispositions.[54]

Again, the conclusion is that our ethical dispositions are judged good from every point of view which makes practical claims on us, including their own point of view. And in this way normativity is established.

JOHN STUART MILL

2.4.1

John Stuart Mill provides us with a third, although slightly aberrant, case of a philosopher who uses the reflective endorsement method. Before I discuss the similarities, I want to say why the case is aberrant. The two philosophers I have been discussing so far both deny any form of substantive moral realism, and believe that morality, including moral motivation, is grounded in human dispositions. Whether those dispositions are natural, as Hume supposes, or cultivated by life in a particular social world, as Williams thinks, the question of their normativity is simply whether they are reinforced or undermined by reflection. The answer, as we have seen, is that reflection supports them if they nurture or at least harmonize with the other dispositions that make practical claims on us. If morality harmonizes with and promotes these, then we have reason to be glad we have a moral nature, and not to try to cast it away. If not, we might come to regard morality as a sort of sickness that humanity should get over, as Freud and Nietzsche sometimes seemed to do.[55]

But Mill, unlike Hume and Williams, is most naturally read as a kind of moral realist, a naturalistic realist who thinks that the desirable is the good. In chapter 4 of *Utilitarianism*, Mill provides us

---

[54] Williams, *Ethics and the Limits of Philosophy*, p. 52.
[55] I do not think that this is the final position of either Freud or Nietzsche. Instead they think that our moral nature needs to be reformed and modified in certain ways in order to prevent it from making us ill, or, in Nietzsche's case, to return it to the form of strength from which it originated. I say a little more about this in lecture 4, 4.3.14.

with what is supposed to be a 'proof' of the principle of utility. The proof assumes the truth of consequentialism, and therefore takes questions of what to do to be tantamount to questions of what is good. These in turn are questions about what is desirable, and Mill undertakes to prove the principle of utility by showing that pleasure and the absence of pain are the only things that are desirable.[56] It is natural, and not altogether wrong, to understand this as implying that Mill thinks that desire is the source of normativity, in the sense that all reasons for action ultimately spring from it.[57]

But Mill does not suppose that acceptance of this proof, all by itself, will motivate anyone to the practice of utilitarianism. This is clear from the previous chapter, where Mill discusses the 'sanctions' that bind us to moral practice. He argues there that there are two kinds of sanctions to moral practice, external and internal. External sanctions are provided by rewards and punishments, the love of others (and of God) with its consequent desire to please them, and so on. An internal sanction is 'a feeling in our own mind, a pain, more or less intense, attendant on violation of duty, which in properly cultivated moral natures rises, in the more serious cases, into shrinking from it as an impossibility'.[58] Some people think such conscientious feelings serve as a divine guide to moral conduct. But according to Mill, internal sanctions are not intrinsically connected to any particular principle of conduct, any more than external ones are. Instead, human experience shows that by 'a sufficient use of the external sanctions and of the force of early impressions' the internal sanctions or conscientious feelings can be

---

[56] More properly speaking, pleasure and the absence of pain are the characteristics that make all desirable things desirable, since Mill wants to insist that we desire many different things for their own sake. See *Utilitarianism*, pp. 35–37.

[57] Alternatively, we might suppose that Mill thinks that pleasure and pain are the sources of normativity, perhaps the more usual utilitarian view. For in one place, in startling anticipation of Sidgwick, Mill says:

If there be anything innate in the matter, I see no reason why the feeling which is innate should not be regard to the pleasures and pains of others. If there is any principle of morality which is intuitively obligatory, I should say it must be that. If so, the intuitive ethics would coincide with the utilitarian, and there would be no further quarrel between them. (p. 29)

Whether we suppose Mill thinks the desirable or the pleasant is the source of normativity, this passage shows how close to the realist tradition Mill sometimes comes.

[58] Mill, *Utilitarianism*, p. 27.

'cultivated in almost any direction'. Indeed, Mill says, 'there is hardly anything so absurd or so mischievous that it may not, by means of these influences, be made to act on the human mind with all the authority of conscience'.[59] Since neither sort of sanction is intrinsically connected to any particular moral principle, and each can be connected to any principle of conduct, Mill concludes that 'there is no reason why [the principle of utility] might not have . . . all of the sanctions which belong to any other system of morals'.[60] One can be trained to be a conscientious utilitarian as well as anything else.

2.4.2

Mill's separation of the proof of the principle of utility from his account of its sanctions is not exactly the same as Hume's separation of theoretical from practical philosophy. But it can leave you with the same odd impression that the question of normativity has fallen between the cracks. The bare fact that you accept the proof doesn't seem to obligate you to utilitarian conduct, at least if we suppose that obligation requires the presence of a motive. Mill apparently thinks that motives are instilled by training and education, not aroused by argument. On the other hand, the bare fact that you have been trained to have conscientious feelings which motivate you to utilitarian conduct doesn't seem to obligate you to such conduct either, since Mill admits that you might have such feelings about anything, no matter how 'absurd or mischievous'. Where then does the obligation come from? Careful reading only adds to the puzzle, for within a single paragraph he identifies 'the source of obligation' and the 'binding force' of morality with the sanctions and motives we have for practising it, and yet he also suggests that morality 'derives its obligation' from the principle of utility.[61] And yet for him these

---

[59] Mill, *Utilitarianism*, p. 30.   [60] Mill, *Utilitarianism*, p. 27.
[61] Chapter 3, paragraph one. The latter remark comes in the context of an explanation why the ordinary person is inclined to challenge the obligatory force of utilitarianism. This ordinary person supposes that customary morality is 'in itself obligatory' and 'when asked to believe that this morality derives its obligation from some general principle around which custom has not thrown the same halo, the assertion is to him a paradox . . .' (p. 26). The general principle referred to is of course that of utility.

two things are separate and so it seems that they cannot both be the source of obligation.

At this point it may be helpful to bring in a piece of contemporary jargon, and to situate this discussion towards the debate which it invokes. So far, almost all of the philosophers whom I have been discussing are (or at least aspire to be) what we would now call 'internalists', in the general sense that they believe that moral considerations necessarily have some power to motivate us. Internalists believe that when a person has a duty, say, or knows that she has, she *ipso facto* has a motive for doing that duty.[62] And up until now, I have been more or less operating under two assumptions in these lectures: first, that internalism in this general sense is correct, and second, that internalism in this general sense does not exhaust the question of normativity. Once we see what the motives morality provides us with are – how moral ideas are able to motivate us in a given case – we can still ask whether we endorse those motives.

Now Mill's separation of the proof of the principle of utility from its sanctions suggests that he is an externalist. He does not expect the proof by itself to motivate us to the practice of utilitarianism. The motives for moral practice do not come from moral knowledge or understanding, nor do they necessarily accompany the correct application of moral concepts. Instead they come from an upbringing which has supplied us with the relevant internal sanctions. If morality does not of itself provide us with motives then the way in which I have been asking the normative question – which is, roughly, 'should we allow ourselves to be moved by the motives which morality provides?' – seems slightly out of order. Actually, something like this is also true of the early twentieth-century rational intuitionists, who thought of the motive of duty as something like a natural desire that takes duty for its object, rather than as a motive inevitably connected with the thought of duty, and who therefore are strictly speaking externalists. Yet this does not seem to matter, for we can ask the normative question this way: 'should we allow ourselves to be moved by such motives as may be

---

[62] See Nagel, *The Possibility of Altruism*, chapter II; my 'Skepticism about Practical Reason', and the other works I refer to there.

provided for morality (either by nature or by training)?' with the same effect. And that, as we are about to see, is exactly what Mill does.[63]

Hume's answer, as we have seen, was that normativity emerges when the two sides of philosophy can work together in a certain way. The anatomy of morality is lovely enough to withstand our gaze, and so the practical philosopher need only paint the truth. Mill's answer, in a similar way, is that morality is normative when reflection on our moral concepts leads us to be glad that moral motives have been instilled in us. What we have so far imagined taking place within philosophical reflection is what Mill imagines happening within the maturing individual. Internal sanctions, as we have seen, can and have been connected to any sort of conduct, including that which is wholly arbitrary. But, Mill says:

> moral associations which are wholly of artificial creation, when the intel-lectual culture goes on, yield by degrees to the dissolving force of analysis; and if the feeling of duty, when associated with utility, would appear equally arbitrary . . . it might happen that this association also, even after it had been implanted by education, might be analyzed away.[64]

Utilitarian motivation would come to seem arbitrary, according to Mill:

> if there were no leading department of our nature, no powerful class of sentiments, with which that association would harmonize, which would make us feel congenial and incline us not only to foster it in others (for which we have abundant interested motives), but also to cherish it in our-selves . . .[65]

---

[63]   In spite of what I have just said, I should confess that I think that, at least if internalism is formulated in a certain way, it can be argued that no externalist theory has a chance of establishing normativity. Such an argument is in the background of my 'Kant's Analysis of Obligation: The Argument of *Foundations* I'. I have not chosen to take that line in these lectures for two reasons. First of all, the kind of argument I have in mind eliminates too many traditional theories from the contest for normative success too quickly and without stopping to examine their own proposals for establishing normativity. Leaving the inter-nalism requirement out of the argument allows us to listen to philosophers like Mill and Prichard a little longer, to see what they do have to say. Second, there is at present so much disagreement in the literature about what internalism is, which of its characteristics are definitive, and what it implies that introducing the issue has become almost a guaranteed way of introducing confusion.

[64]   Mill, *Utilitarianism*, p. 30.   [65]   Mill, *Utilitarianism*, p. 30.

But, he continues:

> there *is* this basis of powerful natural sentiment; and this it is which, when once the general happiness is recognized as the ethical standard, will constitute the strength of the utilitarian morality. This firm foundation is that of the social feelings of mankind – the desire to be in unity with our fellow creatures, which is already a powerful principle in human nature, and happily one of those which tend to become stronger, even without express inculcation, from the influences of advancing civilization . . .[66]

2.4.3

Suppose someone has been brought up in some puritanical religion, and has been taught from childhood onward that it is wrong to dance. His education, along with the more brutal forms of training, have instilled in him a horror of the activity, so that he 'shrinks from it as an impossibility'. As he grows older, the natural onset of reflection, helped along by exposure to others who do not share his view, causes him to call this view and the motives that support it into question. Mill does not say exactly what sort of analysis he has in mind, but I do not think we need to imagine the agent investigating the philosophical grounds of the wrongness of dancing. We may imagine him to be, as so many people are, a kind of primitive and unconscious intuitionist, so that the question he asks himself is not 'why after all is dancing wrong?' but simply 'is dancing really wrong?' There he sits, watching his friends whirling away: unable not to enjoy the beauty of the music, feeling its rhythm in his feet, hungering for the sheer pleasure of the physical activity, attracted by the erotic and social character of the scene. Everything in him that is natural, physical, and sociable protests against what is an unnatural and arbitrary restriction. Once out of the range of his parents and their sanctions, what could be easier, and more natural, than for him to say to himself 'I do not see what's wrong with this' and to join in the dance?

But suppose instead that he has been taught that it is his duty to promote the happiness of others, and to shrink from hurting them as an impossibility. Now some occasion comes along in

[66] Mill, *Utilitarianism*, pp. 30–31.

which he could promote his own interests at the expense of someone else. He's seen the advertisement first and he would like to buy the house. He wouldn't live in it, but it is near the college and it would bring in a good rent. But he knows how much she loves that house; it was her parents' home before they went bankrupt and she has always hoped it would go on the market so that she could buy it back. Still, he did see the advertisement first, and all is fair in love and the market. Would it really be wrong just to buy it and not tell her? But this time sympathy, sociability, and the desire to be in unity with his fellows rise up against the question. He can imagine her disappointment later when she learns the opportunity has come and gone, and his sympathy goes out to her. He can imagine her confronting him with what he has done – 'you knew how much I wanted it, and you could at least have given me the chance to make a bid' – and he shrinks from the thought of her anger and of the contention between them. He shrinks just as much from the idea of trying to keep his ownership secret, and having to look away in embarrassment when she wonders aloud whether those people will ever sell. His social feelings, his desire to be in unity with others, are all on the side of his conscience. Mill writes:

This feeling in most individuals is much inferior in strength to their selfish feelings, and is often wanting altogether. But to those who have it, it possesses all the characters of a natural feeling. It does not present itself to their minds as a superstition of education or a law despotically imposed by the power of society, but as an attribute which it would not be well for them to be without. This conviction is the *ultimate sanction* of the greatest happiness morality.[67]

On reflection we would be glad to find ourselves to be people who shrink from hurting others as an impossibility. Although the motives which obligate us to utilitarian conduct are the effect of training, it is training which we think it would not be well for us to be without. The utilitarian sense of obligation, being in harmony with our social and sympathetic nature, is sustained by reflection, and therefore it is normative.

---

[67] Mill, *Utilitarianism*, p. 33, my emphasis.

THE REFLECTIVE AGENT

2.5.1

But on reflection, it is really very obscure what Mill thinks this argument can accomplish. That is, what effect is it supposed to have on his reader? If you have been raised as a utilitarian, I suppose it might provoke exactly the sort of reflections it describes, and so in this roundabout way help you to sustain your sense of obligation. But most of Mill's intended audience had not been so raised. *Utilitarianism* was written to persuade people to become utilitarians, not to belay the sceptical worries of utilitarians in danger of lapse. But if you have not been raised as a utilitarian, is this argument supposed to help motivate you to become one? In that case it looks as if arguments *can* motivate us after all, and we do not need to have the sanctions instilled by training and education as Mill apparently thinks. But then why doesn't the 'proof' of the principle of utility do that job? On the other hand, if these arguments cannot motivate the reader to become a utilitarian then how can it show that utilitarianism is normative? What the argument about the sanction actually seems to do is to prove that if there were any utilitarians then their morality would be normative for them. But why on earth should Mill's readers care about that? Are we to imagine that they would like to become utilitarians but are afraid that it would not be normative? How could they have got into *that* predicament? If they have already endorsed utilitarianism presumably they already find it normative. So what does Mill think he is doing?

Mill does have a sort of answer to this question. Mill thinks that common sense morality is really based on the principle of utility, since he thinks that ordinary moral rules are something like inductive generalizations from many particular calculations of utility. So ordinary morality is really implicitly utilitarian. But Mill cannot appeal to that argument here, since his reader doesn't acknowledge that his own morality is really based on utility, and part of the *reason* he doesn't acknowledge it is that he doesn't see how utilitarianism can be obligatory.

Mill has lost track of an essential point. The normative question must be answered in a way that addresses the *agent* who asks it. And according to Mill's own theory this argument cannot address the agents it is meant for. If they are not utilitarians, it cannot matter to them that utilitarianism would seem normative to people who had been brought up to it. So Mill misses his target altogether.

2.5.2

Reflection, Bernard Williams tells us, can destroy knowledge.[68] History illustrates the point, for when Bentham reflected on Hume's theory of the virtues, he became a utilitarian.[69] Unfortunately, it looks as if there is a route from Hume to Bentham. And it is a route that leads through reflection, and in particular, through the reflection of *agents*.

We have seen that in Hume's theory just actions are done from the motive of obligation. Sympathy with the public interest inspires us with a sentiment of disapproval when we think of injustice, and this motivates us to avoid it ourselves. Now let us consider a slightly more attractive version of Hume's sensible knave. Our knave is the lawyer for a rich client who has recently died, leaving his money to medical research. In going through the client's papers the lawyer discovers a will of more recent date, made without the lawyer's help but in due form, leaving the money instead to the client's worthless nephew, who will spend it all on beer and comic books. The lawyer could easily suppress this new will, and she is tempted to do so. She is also a student of Hume, and believes the theory of the virtues that we find in *A Treatise of Human Nature*. So what does she say to herself?

Well, she says to herself that she would disapprove of herself if she did this. She hates unjust actions and the people who perform them. But since the lawyer knows Hume's theory she also knows *why* she would disapprove of herself. She would disapprove of herself because unjust actions have a general tendency to bring

---

[68] Williams, *Ethics and the Limits of Philosophy*, p. 148.

[69] This is by Bentham's own report. In a well-known footnote in *A Fragment on Government* (1776), Bentham reports that when he read Hume's *Treatise*, 'I felt as if the scales had fallen from my eyes' (p. 50 n.2). What he learned from Hume was 'that *utility* was the test and measure of all virtue; . . . and that the obligation to minister to general happiness, was an obligation paramount to and inclusive of every other' (p. 51 n.2).

down the system of justice. But she also knows that her distaste for such actions is caused by their *general* tendency, not their *actual* effects. As Hume has shown, our moral sentiments are influenced by 'general rules'. And our lawyer knows that this particular unjust action will have no actual effects but good ones. It will not bring down the system of justice, and it will bring much-needed money to medical research.[70]

The lawyer believes that her disapproval of this action depends on the fact that actions of this kind usually have bad effects which this one does not have. It is almost inconceivable that believing this will have no effect on her disapproval itself. Her own feeling of disapproval may seem to her to be, in this case, poorly grounded, and therefore in a sense irrational. And this may lead her to set it aside, or if she can't, to resist its motivational force. She may say to herself: since I approve of just actions because they are, generally speaking, useful, why not simply do what will be useful? And then of course she is not a Humean any more; she is a utilitarian.[71]

Hume has a defence against this point, but it is a defence of the wrong kind. Consider once more the original sensible knave. What does he lose by his knavery? According to Hume, he loses his character with himself, his pleasing sense of self-worth. As I argued earlier, this does not depend on his moral beliefs, or on whether he endorses the claims of morality. Since sympathy makes him see himself through the eyes of others, who would disapprove of him for his injustice, it will happen anyway. But that is exactly the problem. To see this, it might help to recall the case with which I began, the evolutionary theory of morality. One possibility I considered in connection with that theory was that our moral instincts would be so strong that they could move us, or at least make us miserable, even if we decided that their claims on us were illegitimate. The theory might then explain moral conduct, including the

---

[70] In the footnote in *A Fragment of Government* immediately prior to the famous one discussed in n. 69 above, Bentham describes book III of Hume's *Treatise* and his own reaction to it this way: 'That the foundations of all *virtue* are laid in *utility*, is there demonstrated, after a few exceptions made, with the strongest force of evidence: but I see not . . . what need there was for the exceptions' (p. 50 n.1).

[71] There might be arguments of a familiar rule-utilitarian kind against the action she is considering, but if she is moved by those arguments she is still now a utilitarian and not a Humean, at least not in the sense of the *Treatise*.

conduct of people who know the theory. But it would not be normative, because the people themselves would not think that their
conduct was justified. If they could cure themselves of their
instincts they would. And that is the trouble here. If Hume is right,
the lawyer may find that she cannot destroy a valid will without
intense feelings of humility or self-hatred. These may or may not
be strong enough to cause her to desist. But even if they are there
will have been normative failure. The lawyer does not believe that
the claims her moral feelings make on her in this case are well-
grounded. If she could cure herself of them then that is what she
would do.

2.5.3

The difficulty in this case is not, strictly speaking, a difficulty with
the reflective endorsement strategy. It arises most immediately
from something particular to Hume's view: the fact that the moral
sentiments are supposed to be influenced by 'general rules', rules
which do not hold in every case. Such rules cause us to disapprove
of certain dispositions or character traits, which are themselves
tendencies of a general kind. But that disapproval will be trans-
ferred to each and every exercise of the disposition in question only
if we forget that the rules that cause it are merely general.

But the difficulty does show us something important about the
reflective endorsement method. Consider again the knavish
lawyer. She has asked herself whether her feeling of disapproval is
really a *reason* – and now I mean a normative reason – not to do the
action, and in this case she has found that it is not. She only dis-
approves of injustice because it is usually counterproductive. But
this act, isolated and secret, will be useful in every way. So now she
thinks she has a reason to do it.

Or does she? Why should her reflection stop there? We said that
she was a convinced Humean, so she rejects realism. She therefore
does not think the fact that an action is useful is in and of itself a
reason for doing it, that is, she does not think that utility is an intrinsically normative consideration. So why should she be moved by
utility, any more than by disapproval? Perhaps she now finds that
she is *inclined* to be moved by the thought of utility, but that is no

more a reason than the fact that she was *inclined* to be moved by disapproval before. She can also ask whether this new inclination is really a reason for action. What is to stop her from continuing to ask that question, from pushing reflection as far as it will go?

If the reflective endorsement of our dispositions is what establishes the normativity of those dispositions, then what we need in order to establish the normativity of our more particular motives and inclinations is the reflective endorsement of those. That after all is the whole point of using the reflective endorsement method to justify morality: we are supposing that when we reflect on the things which we find ourselves inclined to do, we can then accept or reject the authority those inclinations claim over our conduct, and act accordingly.

But what I have just described is exactly the process of thought that, according to Kant, characterizes the deliberations of the autonomous moral agent. According to Kant, as each impulse to action presents itself to us, we should subject it to the test of reflection, to see whether it really is a *reason* to act. Since a reason is supposed to be intrinsically normative, we test a motive to see whether it is a reason by determining whether we should allow it to be a *law* to us. And we do that by asking whether the maxim of acting on it can be willed as a law.

Hume and Williams see the test of reflective endorsement as a philosophical exercise, used to establish the normativity of our moral dispositions and sentiments. But according to Kant, it is not merely that. The test of reflective endorsement is the test used by actual moral agents to establish the normativity of all their particular motives and inclinations. So the reflective endorsement test is not merely a way of justifying morality. *It is morality itself.* In the next lecture, I will elaborate this view.

The authority of reflection

Christine Korsgaard

Shall I not reckon among the perfections of the human understanding that it can reflect upon itself? Consider its habits as dispositions arising from past actions? Judge which way the mind inclines? And direct itself to the pursuit of what seems fittest to be done? Our mind is conscious to itself of all its own actions, and both can and often does observe what counsels produced them; it naturally sits a judge upon its own actions, and thence procures to itself either tranquillity and joy, or anxiety and sorrow. In this power of the mind, and the actions thence arising consists the whole force of conscience, by which it proposes laws to itself, examines its past and regulates its future conduct.   Richard Cumberland[1]

INTRODUCTION

3.1.1

Over the course of the last two lectures I have sketched the way in which the normative question took shape in the debates of modern moral philosophy. Voluntarists try to explain normativity in what is in some sense the most natural way: we are subject to laws, including the laws of morality, because we are subject to lawgivers. But when we ask why we should be subject to those lawgivers, an infinite regress threatens. Realists try to block that regress by postulating the existence of entities – objective values, reasons, or obligations – whose intrinsic normativity forbids further questioning. But why should we believe in these entities? In the end, it seems, we

---

[1] Cumberland, *Treatise of the Laws of Nature*, 1672, in Schneewind I, pp. 146–147.

will be prepared to assert that such entities exist only because – and only if – we are already confident that the claims of morality are justified.

The reflective endorsement theorist tries a new tack. Morality is grounded in human nature. Obligations and values are projections of our own moral sentiments and dispositions. To say that these sentiments and dispositions are justified is not to say that they track the truth, but rather to say that they are good. We are the better for having them, for they perfect our social nature, and so promote our self-interest and our flourishing.

But the normative question is one that arises in the heat of action. It is as agents that we must do what we are obligated to do, and it is as agents that we demand to know why. So it is not just our dispositions, but rather the particular motives and impulses that spring from them, that must seem to us to be normative. It is this line of thought that presses us towards Kant. Kant, like the realist, thinks we must show that particular actions are right and particular ends are good. Each impulse as it offers itself to the will must pass a kind of test for normativity before we can adopt it as a reason for action. But the test that it must pass is not the test of knowledge or truth. For Kant, like Hume and Williams, thinks that morality is grounded in human nature, and that moral properties are pro-jections of human dispositions. So the test is one of reflective endorsement.

3.1.2

In this lecture and the next I will lay out the elements of a theory of normativity. This theory derives its main inspiration from Kant, but with some modifications which I have come to think are neces-sary. What I say will necessarily be sketchy, and sketchily argued. In this lecture, I will argue for two points: first, that autonomy is the source of obligation, and in particular of our ability to obligate ourselves; and second, that we have *moral* obligations, by which I mean obligations to humanity as such. However, it will be no part of my argument – quite the contrary – to suggest either that *all* obligations are moral, or that obligations can never conflict, and at the end of this lecture, I will say a little about that.

In lecture 4, I will respond to some natural objections to the argument of this lecture and, in so doing, I will develop the view further. In particular, some readers will think that the argument of this lecture shows only (or at most) that an individual has obligations to his own humanity, not that of others. In answering this worry I will be led to address the question of the scope of our obligations. I will argue first, that in the same way that we can obligate ourselves, we can be obligated by other people, and second, that we have obligations both to, and with regard to, other living things.

I will have little to say about the content of any of these obligations. I believe that the view suggests, although it does not completely settle, what that content should be, but I have made no attempt to work that out here. My aim is show where obligation comes from. Exactly which obligations we have and how to negotiate among them is a topic for another day.

Finally I will address another worry. The argument of this lecture is intended to show that if we take anything to have value, then we must acknowledge that we have moral obligations. Because that conclusion is conditional, you might think that I have not answered the sceptic. At the end of the lecture 4, I will discuss this objection.

THE PROBLEM

3.2.1

The human mind is self-conscious. Some philosophers have supposed that this means that our minds are somehow internally luminous, that their contents are completely accessible to us – that we can always be certain what we are thinking and feeling and wanting – and so that introspection yields certain knowledge of the self. Like Kant, and many philosophers nowadays, I do not think that this is true. Our knowledge of our own mental states and activities is no more certain than anything else.

But the human mind *is* self-conscious in the sense that it is essentially reflective. I'm not talking about being *thoughtful*, which of course is an individual property, but about the structure of our minds that makes thoughtfulness possible. A lower animal's attention is fixed on the world. Its perceptions are its beliefs and its desires are its will. It is engaged in conscious activities, but it is not conscious *of* them. That is, they are not the objects of its attention. But we human animals turn our attention on to our perceptions and desires themselves, on to our own mental activities, and we are conscious *of* them. That is why we can think *about* them.

And this sets us a problem no other animal has. It is the problem of the normative. For our capacity to turn our attention on to our own mental activities is also a capacity to distance ourselves from them, and to call them into question. I perceive, and I find myself with a powerful impulse to believe. But I back up and bring that impulse into view and then I have a certain distance. Now the impulse doesn't dominate me and now I have a problem. Shall I believe? Is this perception really a *reason* to believe? I desire and I find myself with a powerful impulse to act. But I back up and bring that impulse into view and then I have a certain distance. Now the impulse doesn't dominate me and now I have a problem. Shall I act? Is this desire really a *reason* to act? The reflective mind cannot settle for perception and desire, not just as such. It needs a *reason*. Otherwise, at least as long as it reflects, it cannot commit itself or go forward.

If the problem springs from reflection then the solution must do so as well. If the problem is that our perceptions and desires might not withstand reflective scrutiny, then the solution is that they might.[2] We need reasons because our impulses must be able to withstand reflective scrutiny. We have reasons if they do. The normative word 'reason' refers to a kind of reflective success. If 'good' and 'right' are also taken to be intrinsically normative words,

---

[2] As the quotation from Cumberland at the beginning of this lecture shows, the idea that a moral motive is one approved in reflection did not originate with Kant. It is carried on the surface of the relation between the words 'consciousness' and 'conscience', as well as their Greek predecessor 'syneidesis' [συνείδησις] all of which mean, roughly, 'to know in common with' and which came to have the interesting meaning 'to know in common with oneself' and so 'to be able to bear witness for or against oneself'. (I draw here on Potts, *Conscience in Medieval Philosophy*, pp. 1–2). In modern moral philosophy, the idea of the reflective endorsement of motives was brought into prominence by the work of Shaftesbury (*An Inquiry Concerning Virtue or Merit*, treatise IV of *Characteristics*) who thought of the moral sense as a kind of automatic approval or disapproval of our motives. Shaftesbury in turn was drawing on Locke's notion of an 'idea of reflection', one that arises from the mind's observation of its own activity.

names for things that automatically give us reasons, then they too must refer to reflective success. And they do. Think of what they mean when we use them as *exclamations*. 'Good!' 'Right!' There they mean: I'm satisfied, I'm happy, I'm committed, you've convinced me, let's go. They mean the work of reflection is done.

Scepticism about the good and the right is not scepticism about the existence of intrinsically normative entities. It is the view that the problems which reflection sets for us are insoluble, that the questions to which it gives rise have no answers. It is the worry that nothing will count as reflective success, and so that the work of reflection will never be done. It is the fear that we cannot find what Kant called 'the unconditioned'.

3.2.2

The problem can also be described in terms of freedom. It is because of the reflective character of the mind that we must act, as Kant put it, under the idea of freedom. He says 'we cannot conceive of a reason which consciously responds to a bidding from the outside with respect to its judgments'.[3] If the bidding from outside is desire, then the point is that the reflective mind must endorse the desire before it can act on it, it must say to itself that the desire is a reason. As Kant puts it, we must *make it our maxim* to act on the desire. Then although we may do what desire bids us, we do it freely.

Occasionally one meets the objection that the freedom that we discover in reflection is a delusion. Human actions are causally determined. The philosopher's bugbear, the Scientific World View, threatens once more to deprive us of something we value. When desire calls we think we can take it or leave it, but in fact someone could have predicted exactly what we will do.

But how can this be a problem? The afternoon stretches before me, and I must decide whether to work or to play. Suppose first that *you can predict* which one I am going to do. That has no effect on me at all: I must still decide what to do. I am tempted to play but worried about work, and I must decide the case on its merits.

---

[3] Kant, *Foundations of the Metaphysics of Morals*, p. 448; in Beck's translation, p. 66.

Suppose next *I believe that you can predict* which one I'm going to do. You've done it often enough before. What then? I am tempted by play but worried about work, and I must decide the case on its merits.

The worry seems to be that if we were sure we were determined or knew how we were determined then either we could not act or we would not act, or else we would act differently. But why is this supposed to happen? Having discovered that my conduct is predictable, will I now sit quietly in my chair, waiting to see what I will do? Then I will not do anything but sit quietly in my chair. And that had better be what you predicted, or you will have been wrong. But in any case why should I do that, if I think that I ought to be working? Well, suppose that you tell me *what* you predict I am going to do. If you predict that I am going to work, and I think that I should work, then there is no problem. Or do I now have to do it less freely? If you predict that I am going to play, and I think that I should work, I am glad to have been forewarned. For if I am about to do what I think I have good reason not to do, then a moment of weakness or self-deception must be in the offing, and now I can take precautions against it. And then perhaps I will work after all.

If you are going to tell me what you predict I will do, then your prediction must take into account the effect on me of knowing your prediction, because otherwise it will probably be wrong. Of course it *can* happen, in a specific kind of case, that knowing the sort of thing I am usually determined to do diminishes my freedom. If I see that I often give in to temptation, I might become discouraged, and fight against it even less hard. But there is no reason to think that this kind of discouragement would be the *general* result of understanding ourselves better. Or if there is, it must come from some pessimistic philosophy of human nature, not from the Scientific World View. If predictions can warn us when our self-control is about to fail, then they are far more likely to increase that self-control than to diminish it. Determinism is no threat to freedom.

Now it will be objected that this is not what philosophers mean when they claim that determinism is a threat to freedom. They aren't talking about a practical problem – that knowledge could somehow take away our freedom – but about a theoretical one –

that knowledge would show us we weren't free after all. But how is it supposed to do that? By showing that we could not have done otherwise?

That might show that we aren't responsible.[4] But it is a different question whether determinism is a threat to responsibility. Freedom is the capacity to do otherwise, not the capacity to have done otherwise. No one has *that* capacity, because you cannot change the past. That sounds like a joke but I mean it. The freedom discovered in reflection is not a theoretical property which can also be seen by scientists considering the agent's deliberations third-personally and from outside. It is from within the deliberative perspective that we see our desires as providing suggestions which we may take or leave. You will say that this means that our freedom is not 'real' only if you have defined the 'real' as what can be identified by scientists looking at things third-personally and from outside.

The point here is the same as the point I made in lecture 1 against the argument that reasons are not real because we do not need them for giving scientific explanations of what people think and do. That is not, in the first instance, what we need them for, but that does not show that they are not real. We need them because our reflective nature gives us a choice about what to do. We may need to appeal to the existence of reasons in the course of an explanation of why human beings experience choice in the way that we do, and in particular, of why it seems to us that there are reasons. But that explanation will not take the form 'it seems to us that there are reasons because there really are reasons'. Instead, it will be just the sort of explanation which I am constructing here: reasons exist because we need them, and we need them because of the structure of reflective consciousness, and so on.

In the same way, we do not need the concept of 'freedom' in the first instance because it is required for giving scientific explanations of what people do, but rather to describe the condition in which we find ourselves when we reflect on what to do. But that doesn't mean that I am claiming that our experience of our freedom is scientifically inexplicable. I am claiming that it is to be explained in terms

---

[4] Actually, I don't think it does. See my 'Creating the Kingdom of Ends: Reciprocity and Responsibility in Personal Relations'.

of the structure of reflective consciousness, not as the (possibly delusory) *perception* of a theoretical or metaphysical property of the self.

The Scientific World View is a description of the world which serves the purposes of explanation and prediction. When its concepts are applied correctly it tells us things that are true. But it is not a *substitute* for human life. And nothing in human life is more real than the fact we must make our decisions and choices 'under the idea of freedom'.[5] When desire bids, we can indeed take it or leave it. And that is the source of the problem.

3.2.3

'Reason' means reflective success. So if I decide that my desire is a reason to act, I must decide that on reflection I endorse that desire. And here we run into the problem. For how do I decide that? Is the claim that I look at the desire, and see that it is intrinsically normative, or that its object is? Then all of the arguments against realism await us. Does the desire or its object inherit its normativity from something else? Then we must ask what makes that other thing normative, what makes it the source of a reason. And now of course the usual regress threatens. What brings such a course of reflection to a successful end?

Kant, as I mentioned, described this problem in terms of freedom. He defines a free will as a rational causality which is effective without being determined by any alien cause. Anything outside of the will counts as an alien cause, including the desires and inclinations of the person. The free will must be entirely self-determining. Yet, because the will is a causality, it must act according to some law or other. Kant says: 'Since the concept of a causality entails that of laws . . . it follows that freedom is by no means lawless . . .'[6] Alternatively, we may say that since the will is

---

[5] Kant himself says that 'People who are accustomed merely to explanations by natural sciences' refuse to acknowledge the existence of freedom and its imperatives because 'they are stirred by the proud claims of speculative reason, which makes its power so strongly felt in other fields, to band together in a general call to arms, as it were, to defend the omnipotence of theoretical reason.' Kant, The *Metaphysics of Morals*, p. 378; in Gregor's translation, pp. 183–184.

[6] *Kant, Foundations of the Metaphysics of Morals*, p. 446; in Beck's translation, p. 65.

practical reason, it cannot be conceived as acting and choosing for no reason. Since reasons are derived from principles, the free will must have a principle. But because the will is free, no law or principle can be imposed on it from outside. Kant concludes that the will must be autonomous: that is, it must have its *own* law or principle. And here again we arrive at the problem. For where is this law to come from? If it is imposed on the will from outside then the will is not free. So the will must make the law for itself. But until the will has a law or principle, there is nothing from which it can derive a reason. So how can it have any reason for making one law rather than another?

Well, here is Kant's answer. The categorical imperative, as represented by the Formula of Universal Law, tells us to act only on a maxim which we could will to be a law. And *this*, according to Kant, *is* the law of a free will. To see why, we need only compare the problem faced by the free will with the content of the categorical imperative. The problem faced by the free will is this: the will must have a law, but because the will is free, it must be its own law. And nothing determines what that law must be. *All that it has to be is a law.* Now consider the content of the categorical imperative, as represented by the Formula of Universal Law. The categorical imperative merely tells us to choose a law. Its only constraint on our choice is that it has the form of a law. And nothing determines what the law must be. *All that it has to be is a law.*

Therefore the categorical imperative is the law of a free will. It does not impose any external constraint on the free will's activities, but simply arises from the nature of the will. It describes what a free will must do in order to be what it is. It must choose a maxim it can regard as a law.[7]

3.2.4

Now I'm going to make a distinction that Kant doesn't make. I am going to call the law of acting only on maxims you can will to be

---

[7] This is a reading of the argument Kant gives in *Foundations of the Metaphysics of Morals*, pp. 446–448; in Beck's translation, pp. 64–67; and in *Critique of Practical Reason* under the heading 'Problem II, p. 29; in Beck's translation, pp. 28–29. It is defended in greater detail in my 'Morality as Freedom'.

laws 'the categorical imperative'. And I am going to distinguish it from what I will call 'the moral law'. The moral law, in the Kantian system, is the law of what Kant calls the Kingdom of Ends, the republic of all rational beings. The moral law tells us to act only on maxims that all rational beings could agree to act on together in a workable cooperative system. Now the Kantian argument which I just described establishes that *the categorical imperative* is the law of a free will. But it does not establish that *the moral law* is the law of a free will. Any law is universal, but the argument I just gave doesn't settle the question of the *domain* over which the law of the free will must range. And there are various possibilities here. If the law is the law of acting on the desire of the moment, then the agent will treat each desire as a reason, and her conduct will be that of a wanton.[8] If the law ranges over the agent's whole life, then the agent will be some sort of egoist. It is only if the law ranges over every rational being that the resulting law will be the moral law.

Because of this, it has sometimes been claimed that the categorical imperative is an empty formalism. And this has in turn been conflated with another claim, that the moral law is an empty formalism. Now that second claim is false.[9] Kant thought that we could test whether a maxim could serve as a law for the Kingdom of Ends by seeing whether there is any contradiction in willing it as a law which all rational beings could agree to act on together. I do not think this test gives us the whole content of morality, but it is a mistake to think that it does not give us any content at all, for there are certainly some maxims which are ruled out by it. And even if the test does not completely determine what the laws of the

[8] I have a reason for saying that her behaviour will be that of a wanton rather than simply saying that she will be a wanton. Harry Frankfurt, from whom I am borrowing the term, defines a wanton as someone who has no second-order volitions. An animal, whose desire is its will, is a wanton. I am arguing here that a person cannot be like that, because of the reflective structure of human consciousness. A person must act on a reason, and so the person who acts like a wanton must be treating the desire of the moment as a reason. That commits her to the principle that the desire of the moment is a reason, and her commitment to that principle counts as a second-order volition. See Frankfurt, 'Freedom of the Will and the Concept of a Person', especially the discussion on pp. 16–19. The affinity of my account with Frankfurt's should be obvious.

[9] I argue for this in 'Kant's Formula of Universal Law'. There however I do not distinguish the categorical imperative from the moral law, and my arguments claim to show that the categorical imperative has content when actually they show only that the moral law has content.

Kingdom of Ends would be, the moral law still could have content. For it tells us that our maxims must qualify as laws for the Kingdom of Ends, and that is a substantive command as long as we have *some* way of determining what those laws would be. And there are other proposals on the table about how to do that: John Rawls's to name only one.

But it is true that the argument that shows that we are bound by the categorical imperative does not show that we are bound by the moral law. For that we need another step. The agent must think of *herself* as a Citizen of the Kingdom of Ends.

THE SOLUTION

3.3.1

Those who think that the human mind is internally luminous and transparent to itself think that the term 'self-consciousness' is appropriate because what we get in human consciousness is a direct encounter with the self. Those who think that the human mind has a reflective structure use the term too, but for a different reason. The reflective structure of the mind is a source of 'self-consciousness' because it forces us to have a *conception* of ourselves. As Kant argued, this is a fact about what it is *like* to be reflectively conscious and it does not prove the existence of a metaphysical self. From a third-person point of view, outside of the deliberative standpoint, it may look as if what happens when someone makes a choice is that the strongest of his conflicting desires wins. But that isn't the way it is *for you* when you deliberate. When you deliberate, it is as if there were something over and above all of your desires, something which is *you*, and which *chooses* which desire to act on. This means that the principle or law by which you determine your actions is one that you regard as being expressive of *yourself*. To identify with such a principle or way of choosing is to be, in St Paul's famous phrase, a law to yourself.[10]

---

[10] Romans 2:14. This paragraph is lifted with modifications from my 'Personal Identity and the Unity of Agency: a Kantian Response to Parfit', 111. I believe there are resources in this line of thought for dealing with the problem of personal identity, and some of them are explored in that paper.

An agent might think of herself as a Citizen of the Kingdom of Ends. Or she might think of herself as someone's friend or lover, or as a member of a family or an ethnic group or a nation. She might think of herself as the steward of her own interests, and then she will be an egoist. Or she might think of herself as the slave of her passions, and then she will be a wanton. And how she thinks of herself will determine whether it is the law of the Kingdom of Ends, or the law of some smaller group, or the law of egoism, or the law of the wanton that will be the law that she is to herself.

The conception of one's identity in question here is not a theoretical one, a view about what as a matter of inescapable scientific fact you are. It is better understood as a description under which you value yourself, a description under which you find your life to be worth living and your actions to be worth undertaking. So I will call this a conception of your practical identity. Practical identity is a complex matter and for the average person there will be a jumble of such conceptions. You are a human being, a woman or a man, an adherent of a certain religion, a member of an ethnic group, a member of a certain profession, someone's lover or friend, and so on. And all of these identities give rise to reasons and obligations. Your reasons express your identity, your nature; your obligations spring from what that identity forbids.

Our ordinary ways of talking about obligation reflect this connection to identity. A century ago a European could admonish another to civilized behaviour by telling him to act like a Christian. It is still true in many quarters that courage is urged on males by the injunction 'be a man!' Duties more obviously connected with social roles are of course enforced in this way. 'A psychiatrist doesn't violate the confidence of her patients.' No 'ought' is needed here because the normativity is built right into the role. But it isn't only in the case of roles that the idea of obligation invokes the conception of practical identity. Consider the astonishing but familiar 'I couldn't live with myself if I did that.' Clearly there are two selves here, me and the one I must live with and so must not fail. Or consider the protest against obligation ignored: 'Just who do you think you are?'

The connection is also present in the concept of integrity.

Etymologically, integrity is oneness, integration is what makes something one. To be a thing, one thing, a unity, an entity; to be anything at all: in the metaphysical sense, that is what it means to have integrity. But we use the term for someone who lives up to his own standards. And that is because we think that living up to them is what makes him one, and so what makes him a person at all.

It is the conceptions of ourselves that are most important to us that give rise to unconditional obligations. For to violate them is to lose your integrity and so your identity, and to no longer be who you are. That is, it is to no longer be able to think of yourself under the description under which you value yourself and find your life to be worth living and your actions to be worth undertaking. It is to be for all practical purposes dead or worse than dead. When an action cannot be performed without loss of some fundamental part of one's identity, and an agent could just as well be dead, then the obligation not to do it is unconditional and complete. If reasons arise from reflective endorsement, then obligation arises from reflective *rejection*.

3.3.2

Actually, all obligation is unconditional in the sense that I have just described. An obligation always takes the form of a reaction against a threat of a loss of identity. But there are two important complications, and both spring from the complexity of human identity. One is that some parts of our identity are easily shed, and, where they come into conflict with more fundamental parts of our identity, they should be shed. The cases I have in mind are standard: a good soldier obeys orders, but a good human being doesn't massacre the innocent. The other complication, more troublesome, is that you can stop being yourself for a bit and still get back home, and in cases where a small violation combines with a large temptation, this has a destabilizing effect on the obligation. You may know that if you always did this sort of thing your identity would disintegrate, like that of Plato's tyrant in *Republic* IX, but you also know that you can do it just this once without any such result. Kant points out that when we violate the laws of the Kingdom of Ends we must be making exceptions of ourselves, because we cannot coherently will their universal violation.[11] In one sense, a commitment to your own identity – that is, to your integrity – is supposed to solve that problem. But as we have just seen, the problem reiterates within the commitment to your own integrity. The problem here does not come from the fragility of identity, but rather from its stability. It can take a few knocks, and we know it. The agent I am talking about now violates the law that she is to herself, making an exception of the moment or the case, which she knows she can get away with.

This is why it is best if we love our values as well as having them. But lest you think that I am about to make the same mistake of which I have accused Hume, let me admit that I think this argument establishes an authentic limit to the *depth* of obligation.[12] Obligation is always unconditional, but it is only when it concerns really important matters that it is *deep*. Of course, since we can see that the shallowness of obligation could give rise to problems, we must commit ourselves to a kind of second-order integrity, a commitment to not letting these problems get out of hand. We cannot make an exception 'just this once' every time, or we will lose our identities after all. But the problem will reiterate within that commitment, and so on up the line.

That, by the way, is why even people with the most excellent characters can *occasionally* knowingly do wrong.

3.3.3

To get back to the point. The question how exactly an agent *should* conceive her practical identity, the question which law she should be to herself, is not settled by the arguments I have given. So moral obligation is not yet on the table. To that extent the argument so far is formal, and in one sense empty.

But in another sense it is not empty at all. What we have established is this. The reflective structure of human consciousness requires that you identify yourself with some law or principle

---

[11] Kant, *Foundations of the Metaphysics of Morals*, p. 424; in Beck's translation, p. 42.

[12] I mean the objection at the end of lecture 2. Hume forgot that knowing that our hatred of injustice was based on general rules would have a destabilizing effect on the obligation always to be just.

which will govern your choices. It requires you to be a law to your-self. And that is the source of normativity.[13] So the argument shows just what Kant said that it did: that our autonomy is the source of obligation.

It will help to put the point in Joseph Butler's terms, the distinc-tion between power and authority. We do not always do what upon reflection we would do or even what upon reflection we have already decided to do. Reflection does not have irresistible power over us. But when we do reflect we cannot but think that we ought to do what on reflection we conclude we have reason to do. And when we don't do that we punish ourselves, by guilt and regret and repentance and remorse.[14] We might say that the acting self concedes to the thinking self its right to government. And the thinking self, in turn, tries to govern as well as it can.[15] So the reflective structure of human consciousness establishes a relation here, a relation which we have to ourselves.[16] And it is a relation not of mere power but rather of *authority*. And *that* is the authority that is the source of obligation.

Notice that this means that voluntarism is true after all. The source of obligation is a legislator. The realist objection – that we need to explain why we must obey that legislator – has been answered, for this is a legislator whose authority is beyond question and does not need to be established. It is the authority of your own mind and will. So Pufendorf and Hobbes were right. It is not the bare fact that it would be a good idea to perform a certain action

---

[13] What I am saying here is that the categorical imperative is the general principle of normativity in the practical sphere. In 'Reason and Politics in the Kantian Enterprise', Onora O'Neill argues that the categorical imperative is the supreme principle of reason in general, which in my language means it is the supreme principle of normativity in general. It will become apparent in the course of this lecture and the next that I agree with that, although of course the idea is not completely defended here.

[14] In lecture 4, 4.3.8, I present a further account of these moral emotions and how they are related to autonomy.

[15] The distinction between the thinking self and the acting self is very close to Kant's dis-tinction between *Wille* (will) and *Willkür* (choice). See *The Metaphysics of Morals*, pp. 213–214; in Gregor's translation, pp. 41–43.

[16] In *The Metaphysics of Morals*, Kant says that all duties must be grounded in duties to the self, and yet that duties to the self are only intelligible if there are two aspects to the self. He calls them 'homo noumenon' and 'homo phenomenon' (pp. 417–418; in Gregor's translation, pp. 214–215). Notice the strange alternation of one and two here: duties must arise within one, rather than between two, and yet for them to arise that one must be two. The idea of the reflective character of human consciousness, together with the thesis that obligation springs from autonomy, explains why it has to be this way.

that obligates us to perform it. It is the fact that we *command ourselves* to do what we find it would be a good idea to do.

3.3.4

With that in mind, let me return to the example I used in lecture 1 to illustrate the voluntarist conception of the motive of duty: the example of a student who takes course because it is a required. In lecture 1 I said that acting on the motive of duty as Pufendorf and Hobbes understood it seems appropriate in this kind of case. Although the student might appreciate the reasons why it is a good idea that the course should be required, it would be a little odd to say that that is his motive, since he has a decisive reason for taking the course whether he understands those reasons or not. I had in mind a story like this: you are visiting some other department, not your own, and fall into conversation with a graduate student. You discover that he is taking a course in some highly advanced form of calculus, and you ask him why. With great earnestness, he begins to lay out an elaborate set of reasons. 'Philosophers since the time of Plato', he says, 'have taken mathematics to be the model for knowledge: elegant, certain, perfect, beautiful, and utterly *a priori*. But you can't really understand either the power of the model or its limits if you have an outsider's view of mathematics. You must really get in there and do mathematics if you are to fully appreciate all this . . .' And just when you are about to be really impressed by this young man's commitment and seriousness, another student comes along smiling and says 'and anyway, calculus is required in our department'.

In that story, the first student seems like a phony. Since he has *that* motive for taking the course, all the rest seems a little irrelevant. But now I am saying that when we are autonomous, we bind ourselves to do what it seems to us to be a good idea to do. So isn't the first student, after all, more autonomous than the student who takes the course merely because it's required? And isn't the first student's action therefore more authentically an action from duty?

If he weren't required to take the course, and he took it for the reasons he gives you, then in one sense he would be more autonomous than the student who takes it merely because it is required. He would be guided by his own mind, not that of another. But if he is required to take it, the reasons he gives should not be his motive. This may seem odd, since in a sense they are better reasons. But even if he understands them, they are excluded by his practical identity. Because his practical identity, in this case, is being a student. And this has two implications. First, to the extent that you identify yourself as a student, you *do* act autonomously in taking a course that is required. And second, it is an essential part of the idea of being a student that you place the right to make some of the decisions about what you will study in the hands of your teachers. And that means that when one of those decisions is in question, you are not free to act on your own *private* reasons any more, no matter how good those reasons are in themselves.[17]

This is not just because there is an inherent element of subordination in the position of a student. For exactly similar reasons, a good citizen cannot pay her taxes because she thinks the government needs the money. She can *vote* for taxes for that reason. But once the vote is over, she must pay her taxes because it is the law. And that is again because citizenship is a form of practical identity, with the same two implications. To be a citizen is to make a certain set of decisions in company with the other citizens – to participate in a general will. In so far as you are a citizen, you do act autonomously in obeying the law. And for exactly that reason, in so far as you are a citizen, you aren't free to act on your own private reasons any more.

Some will be tempted to say that the student who understands the reasons why a course is required, and who therefore would take it even if it weren't required, is somehow *more* autonomous than the student who takes the course *just* because it is required. If a student understands why the course is required, his taking it is endorsed both from the point of view of his identity as a student and from the point of view of his identity as a rational being with a mind of his own. So he seems to be more autonomous. But we shouldn't be too quick to jump to the conclusion that this is the way things work in general. The student's autonomy may be augmented in this case,

---

[17] By 'private reasons' here I mean reasons arrived at by thinking through the problem yourself. In lecture 4 I deny that 'private reasons' in another sense, reasons that have normative force only for one person, exist. That's not what I mean here.

because his understanding of the reasons for the requirement also helps him to make sense to himself of his *being* a student. It helps him to endorse his identity as a student, for it gives him confidence in his teachers' judgment. But other cases are different. The reason for participating in a general will, and so for endorsing one's identity as a citizen, is that we share the world with others who are free, not that we have confidence in their judgment. A citizen who acts on a vote that has gone the way she thinks it should may in one sense be more wholehearted than one who must submit to a vote that has not gone her way. But a citizen in whom the general will triumphs *gracefully* over the private will exhibits a very special kind of autonomy, which is certainly not a lesser form. Autonomy is commanding yourself to do what you think it would be a good idea to do, but that in turn depends on who you think you are. That's what I've been saying all along.

3.3.5

One more step is necessary. The acting self concedes to the thinking self its right to govern. But the thinking self in turn must try to govern well. It is its job to make what is in any case a good idea into law. How do we know what's a good idea or what should be a law? Kant proposes that we can tell whether our maxims should be laws by attending not to their matter but to their form.

To understand this idea, we need to return to its origins, which are in Aristotle. According to Aristotle, a thing is composed of a form and a matter. The matter is the material, the parts, from which it is made. The form of a thing is its functional arrangement. That is, it is the arrangement of the matter or of the parts which enables the thing to serve its purpose, to do whatever it does. For example the purpose of a house is to be a shelter, so the form of a house is the way the arrangement of the parts – the walls and roof – enables it to serve as a shelter. 'Join the walls at the corner, put the roof on top, and that's how we keep the weather out.' That is the form of a house.[18]

---

[18] These views are found throughout Aristotle's writings, but centrally discussed in books VII–IX of *Metaphysics* and in *On the Soul*.

Next consider the maxim of an action. Since every human action is done for an end, a maxim has two parts: the act and the end. The form of the maxim is the arrangement of its parts. Take for instance Plato's famous example of the three maxims:[19]

1 I will keep my weapon, because I want it for myself.
2 I will refuse to return your weapon, because I want it for myself.
3 I will refuse to return your weapon, because you have gone mad and may hurt someone.

Maxims one and three are good: maxim two is bad. What makes them so? Not the actions, for maxims two and three have the same actions; not the purposes, for maxims one and two have the same purposes. The goodness does not rest in the parts; but rather in the way the parts are combined and related; so the goodness does not rest in the matter, but rather in the form, of the maxim. But form is not merely the arrangement of the parts; it is the *functional* arrangement – the arrangement that enables the thing to do what it does. If the walls are joined and roof placed on top *so that* the building can keep the weather out, then the building has the form of a house. So: if the action and the purpose are related to one another *so that* the maxim can be willed as a law, then the maxim is good.

Notice what this establishes. A good maxim is good in virtue of its internal structure. Its internal structure, its form, makes it fit to be willed as a law. A good maxim is therefore an *intrinsically normative entity*. So realism is true after all, and Nagel, in particular, was right. When an impulse presents itself to us, as a kind of candidate for being a reason, we look to see whether it really is a reason, whether its claim to normativity is true.

But this isn't an exercise of intuition, or a discovery about what is out there in the world. The test for determining whether an impulse is a reason is whether *we* can will acting on that impulse as a law. So the test is a test of endorsement.

3.3.6

I've just claimed that realism is true after all. Realists believe that ethics is grounded in intrinsically normative entities, and a good

---

[19] Plato, *Republic*, I, 331c., p. 580.

maxim, I've just claimed, is exactly that – an 'entity' whose intrinsic properties, or internal structure, renders it normative. I want to make two points about how this form of realism is related to the more familiar views I discussed in lecture 1.

The first point concerns these questions: in virtue of what does a thing have intrinsic value or normativity, and how do we know that it does? Here we find a distinction between ancient and modern approaches to the question. Modern philosophers have tended to hold that if you can say *why* something is valuable, that *ipso facto* shows that the thing is *extrinsically* valuable. If I say that a hammer is good for pounding nails I am assigning it a merely instrumental and so an extrinsic value: the hammer gets its value from some further purpose that it serves. If I say that fine weather is good because today we have planned a picnic, or even just because it gives us pleasure, I do not make the weather a mere instrument, but the value still seems derivative from something outside the weather itself – namely, human purposes, interests, and capacities for enjoyment. If we extend the lesson of these cases, we may come to think that if you can say why a thing is valuable, then it does not have its value in itself. And this metaphysical view leads to an epistemological one, namely, that intrinsic values must be known by intuition. For if we cannot give a reasoned account of *why* something is valuable, then we cannot arrive at the knowledge *that* the thing is valuable by working out the reasons why it is so. So we must just 'see' that the thing is intrinsically good.

That Plato thought otherwise is suggested by the way he proceeds in the *Republic*. In *Republic* II, Glaucon and Adeimantus challenge Socrates to show that justice is intrinsically good and injustice bad by showing 'what each of them is in itself, by its own inherent force, when it is within the soul of the possessor . . .', that is, what value there is in being just apart from any outward consequences it might have.[20] Socrates of course replies by showing that justice is a *form* of the soul – that is, an arrangement of its parts – that makes its possessor both happy and master of himself.

Those steeped in the modern way of looking at things sometimes suppose that Plato is making a mistake here. If we give reasons why

[20] Plato, *Republic* II, 366e, p. 613.

justice is good, then it is only extrinsically good – good because it has these consequences, happiness and self-mastery, for the person who has it. Inward consequences may be less superficial than outward ones, and more essentially related to justice itself, but they are consequences all the same.[21] But there is a different way to understand what is going on here. First, Plato wants to show that justice is a virtue, and a virtue makes *the thing which has it* good. So it is the just soul, not justice itself, which Plato aims to show is intrinsically good. And he thinks that for a thing to have intrinsic value is for it to have an internal structure that makes it good. That's what he tries to show about the just soul in the rest of the *Republic*: that its internal structure makes it good. If we approach the matter this way then, as Plato thinks, we *can* say why a thing is good, even when its value is intrinsic.

Now it may be objected that this is not a rival conception of intrinsic value, but simply a different conception, namely the conception of virtue. For to say that something has an internal structure that makes it good must be to say that it has an internal structure that makes it good at being what it is. It is to make a claim about the thing being good at its function (its [ἔργον]), about its having the virtues that are proper to it. At least this is what Plato seems to mean, for Plato has Socrates argue that living and acting are the functions of the soul, and justice makes it good at those, good at living and acting. In that sense, we could say that justice gives the soul intrinsic value. But in exactly the same sense, we could say that since cutting is the function of a knife, a sharp blade gives a knife intrinsic value. But that's just a misleading way of talking: when we say that something has intrinsic value, we do not mean merely that it has the virtues of its kind, for its kind may be of no value at all. And Plato clearly means to argue more than *merely* that justice is a virtue, for Socrates already did that in *Republic* I, before Glaucon and Adeimantus utter their challenge. Plato also means to show that it is good to have justice and the other virtues. His argument is meant to show that a just soul is *good to have for its own sake* in virtue of its internal properties.

I'll come back to Plato; I now want to approach the question from another angle. Elsewhere I have argued that it is important not to

---

[21] See for instance Prichard, in 'Duty and Interest'.

confuse two distinctions in goodness: the distinction between final and instrumental value on the one hand, and the distinction between intrinsic and extrinsic value on the other.[22] The distinction between final and instrumental value concerns our reasons for valuing something: whether we value it for its own sake or for the sake of some other end which it serves. The distinction between intrinsic and extrinsic value concerns the source of its value: whether it has its value in itself or gets its value from some outside source. Both final value and intrinsic value may seem to be in a certain way ultimate, or foundational. Which kind of value, or of normativity more generally, does the realist really need for his argument? That is, which kind of value brings a course of reflection about how an action might be completely justified to a satisfactory end?

On the one hand, it seems like it has to be a final good, or, if you will allow the expression, a final right: an end sought or an action undertaken for its own sake alone. For if the object is sought or the action undertaken for the sake of something else, then we do have a further question to ask: what about this other thing? Is it in turn really good, right, necessary or whatever? Yet on the other hand, it seems like it has to be an intrinsic good, or an intrinsic right, for an essentially similar reason: if the normativity comes from some other source, we can then raise a question about that source. This, as we saw in lecture 1, is the thought that drives realism in the first place. And we might think that the realist needs an intrinsic value for another reason as well. At least if we are to get anything like *morality* out of this line of thought, that is, if we are going to get *categorical* duties out of it, the value in terms of which we justify action must be independent of people's particular desires and interests. And final goods are not, in that way, necessarily independent: what you value for its own sake at least sometimes depends on particular things about you, your own desires and interests.

The answer is that the *intrinsically normative entity* that serves the purposes of realism, the entity that brings a regress of justification to a satisfactory end, must *combine* these two conceptions. It must be something that is *final*, good or right for its own sake, *in virtue of its intrinsic properties*, its intrinsic structure. And we don't need to dis-

---

[22] Korsgaard, 'Two Distinctions in Goodness'.

cover such values by intuition, if we can show that a thing's intrinsic properties *make it* a final good.[23] Now this is what Plato tries to show about the just soul in the *Republic*: that its intrinsic properties make it a final good, a thing worth having for its own sake. In the same way, a maxim is an entity whose intrinsic properties make it a final reason for action, a final 'right'. Something which has the form of a law, that is, which is a law by virtue of its internal structure, is *intrinsically* suited to answer the question why the action it dictates is necessary. In this sense, a good maxim is *exactly* the sort of entity which the realist argument requires.

The second clarification in a way follows from the first, and concerns the criticisms I levelled against substantive realism in lecture 1. Values are not discovered by intuition to be 'out there' in the world. Good maxims are intrinsically normative entities, but they are also the products of our own legislative wills. In that sense, values are created by human beings. Of course we discover that the maxim is fit to be a law; but the maxim isn't a law until we will it, and in that sense create the resulting value. This is what Pufendorf means when he says that moral entities are produced by imposition, and that imposition in turn is a matter of making laws.[24] The form of realism I am endorsing here is procedural rather than substantive realism: values are constructed by a procedure, the procedure of making laws for ourselves.

3.3.7

This completes the first part of my argument, so let me sum up what I've said. What I have shown so far is why there is such a

---

[23] In 'Two Distinctions in Goodness' I argue that part of the problem with G. E. Moore's idea that we recognize intrinsic values by the intuitions we have when we view certain 'organic unities' in isolation is that it conceals the fact that an organic unity has value in virtue of its structure, of the internal relations of its parts (pp. 193–195). Moore did insist that for a thing to have value its parts have to be combined in just the right way – that is the whole point of the doctrine of organic unities – and this suggests that he shares Plato's sense – and Kant's – that a thing has intrinsic value in virtue of its internal structure. But he did not think that we could say anything about *how* the structure gives the thing intrinsic value: we just have to recognize, by intuition, that it does so. This is where I think he goes wrong. Now I am making a similar point against Nagel and about reasons. We do not recognize reasons by intuition but by examining their internal structure – that is, of course, the internal structure of the maxims of acting on them.

[24] See lecture 1, 1.3.1; and Pufendorf, *The Law of Nature of Nations*, in Schneewind 1, p. 171.

thing as obligation. The reflective structure of human consciousness sets us a problem. Reflective distance from our impulses makes it both possible and necessary to decide which ones we will act on: it forces us to act for reasons. At the same time, and relatedly, it forces us to have a conception of our own identity, a conception which identifies us with the source of those reasons. In this way, it makes us laws to ourselves. When an impulse – say a desire – presents itself to us, we ask whether it could be a reason. We answer that question by seeing whether the maxim of acting on it can be willed as a law by a being with the identity in question. If it can be willed as a law it is a reason, for it has an intrinsically normative structure. If it cannot be willed as a law, we must reject it, and in that case we get obligation.

A moment ago I said that realism is true after all. But that could be misleading. What I have established so far is that obligation in general is a reality of human life. That we obligate ourselves is simply a fact about human nature, and our maxims can be seen as intrinsically normative entities. But there is still a deep element of relativism in the system. For whether a maxim can serve as a law still depends upon the way that we think of our identities. And as I've said already, different laws hold for wantons, egoists, lovers, and Citizens of the Kingdom of Ends. In order to establish that there are particular ways in which we *must* think of our identities, and so that there are *moral* obligations, we will need another step.

MORAL OBLIGATION

3.4.1

There is another way to make the points I have been making, and in approaching the problem of relativism it will be helpful to employ it. We can take as our model the way Rawls employs the concept/conception distinction in *A Theory of Justice*. There, the *concept* of justice refers to a problem, or, if you prefer, refers in a formal way to the solution of that problem. The problem is what we might call the distribution problem: people join together in a cooperative scheme because it will be better for all of them, but they must decide how its benefits and burdens are to be distributed. A *conception* of justice is a principle that is proposed as a solution to the distribution problem. How are we to distribute the benefits and burdens of cooperative living? 'So that aggregate happiness is maximized' is the utilitarian conception of justice. 'So that things are as good as possible for the least advantaged, in so far as that is consistent with the freedom of all' is Rawls's. The concept names the problem, the conception proposes a solution. The normative force of the conception is established in this way. If you recognize the problem to be yours, and the solution to be the best one, then the solution is binding upon you.[25]

In the same way, the most general normative concepts, the right and the good, are names for problems – for the normative problems that spring from our reflective nature. 'Good' names the problem of what we are to strive for, aim at, and care about in our lives. 'Right' names the more specific problem of which actions we may perform.[26] The 'thinness' of these terms, to use Bernard Williams's language, comes from the fact that they are, so far, only concepts, names for whatever it is that solves the problems in question. We need *conceptions* of the right and the good before we know what to do.

---

[25] At least until a better solution is proposed. See Rawls, *A Theory of Justice*, section 9.

[26] The distinction between the right and the good is a delicate one which it is a little difficult to articulate clearly. One way to put it would be to say that 'rightness' refers to the way action relates us to the people with whom we interact, whereas goodness, at least as applied to action, refers to the way in which it relates us to our goals and the things we care about. It would not follow from the fact that an action was good, in the sense that it related us correctly to what we aim for and care about, that it was right: its rightness has to do also with its acceptability to those with whom we interact. But this way of describing the difference might be misleading in two ways. First, it might make it sound as if right and wrong refer only to actions which relate us to others and not to those which concern only ourselves. That is not what I mean: we can wrong ourselves, but this is because we can interact with ourselves. I know that this sounds paradoxical. But look: someone who becomes addicted to a drug is not just failing to do what will best serve his future interests. He is hurting *himself*. He is making himself weaker, less free, and less competent, and his future self will be in a sense cornered by what he is doing now. So he is not treating himself with respect; he is using himself as a mere means. Its effects on his interests makes the addiction *bad*; its effects on himself, and the self-disrespect that imposing those effects expresses, makes it *wrong*. The second way in which this formulation of the distinction might be misleading is that the way I've put it might make it sound as if being rightly related to other people is not among the things we aim for and care about. Of course it is, and for this reason right actions are normally also good.

3.4.2

How do we get from concepts to conceptions? As suggested above, what mediates is a conception of practical identity. This conception both embodies the problem and serves as an aid in finding the solution. For example, in Rawls's argument, we move from concept to conception by taking up the standpoint of the pure liberal citizen, who has only the attributes shared by all the citizens of a well-ordered liberal state: a willingness to abide by whatever principles of cooperation may be chosen in the original position, and her own conception of the good.[27] We ask what laws such a citizen has reason to adopt. And in so far as we regard ourselves as such citizens, those are laws which we have reason to accept. In Kant's argument, we move from concept to conception by taking up the standpoint of a legislative Citizen in the Kingdom of Ends, and asking what laws that kind of citizen has reason to adopt. Again, in so far as we regard ourselves as Citizens of the Kingdom of Ends, those laws are ones we have reason to accept. Citizen of the Kingdom of Ends is a conception of practical identity which leads in turn to a conception of the right.

3.4.3

If this is correct, then Williams is wrong to say that reflection is not inherent in, or already implied by, what he calls 'thick ethical concepts'.[28] Thick ethical concepts stand to thin ones as conceptions to concepts. Since they are normative, they are essentially reflective, and that means they embody a view about what is right or good.

And there is another implication. Williams concluded that our ethical concepts, unlike the ones we employ in the physical sciences, need not be shared with members of other cultures. But our thin ethical concepts, although not necessarily our thick ones, will be shared, even with the alien scientific investigators that his argument invokes.[29] For the fact that they are scientific investigators

---

[27] Rawls, *A Theory of Justice*, section 2, p. 8; and section 4, p. 19; and 'Kantian Constructivism in Moral Theory', 524ff.
[28] See lecture 2, 2.3.6.
[29] See lecture 2, 2.3.2.

means that they have asked themselves what they ought to believe, and that they have decided that the question is worth pursuing. And that in turn means that they are rational and social beings, who face normative problems like our own, and sometimes solve them. The exact shape of their problems may be different from ours, and so they may have different conceptions.[30] But they will have views about what is right and what is good, and their language will have terms in which these views are expressed. So we will be able to translate our own terms into their language, and to talk to them about the right and the good. And if we can come at least to see their conceptions as solutions to the normative problems that *they* face, there will even be a kind of convergence.

But neither the fact that we will share thin ethical concepts with the aliens nor the way in which reflection is inherent in thick ones suggests that we are converging on an *external* world of objectively real values. Value is grounded in rational nature – in particular in the structure of reflective consciousness – and it is projected on to the world. So the reflection in question is practical and not theoretical: it is reflection about what to do, not reflection about what is to be found in the normative part of the world.

3.4.4

But this does not eliminate the element of relativism that Williams has sought to preserve. The mediation between concepts and

---

[30] There are, I think, at least two ways in which this could happen. One is that the aliens' psychology might be quite different from ours. Perhaps we can imagine that nature equipped them to deal with danger by some mechanism other than the emotion of fear, for example, so that they will not need courage. (Some people think that they might have no emotions at all, although this is less obviously imaginable than it seems at first sight. Some sort of affect which will direct attention in useful ways is absolutely requisite to getting around in the world at all.) A more interesting possibility is that their identities might be constructed quite differently from ours. Some of the possibilities explored in both science fiction and the personal identity literature might be true of them: they might be 'series people' (see Parfit, *Reasons and Persons*, pp. 289–293) or exist in clone clusters or have no genders, so that the relationship between their practical lives and their physical lives would really be very different from ours. These exotic possibilities may actually more closely resemble the cultural differences we really find among human beings. Human beings – indeed all animals – have strong psychological resemblances, but our identities are constructed in very different ways. For instance, not being able to conceive yourself except as a member of a certain family might be like being a series person or a member of a clone cluster.

conceptions comes by way of practical identity. A view of what you ought to do is a view of who you are. And human identity has been differently constituted in different social worlds. Sin, dishonour, and moral wrongness all represent conceptions of what one cannot do without being diminished or disfigured, without loss of identity, and therefore conceptions of what one must not do. But they belong to different worlds in which human beings thought of themselves and of what made them themselves in very different ways. Where sin is the conception my identity is my soul and it exists in the eyes of my God. Where dishonour is the conception my identity is my reputation, my position in some small and know-able social world. The conception of *moral* wrongness as we now understand it belongs to the world *we* live in, the one brought about by the Enlightenment, where one's identity is one's relation to humanity itself. Hume said at the height of the Enlightenment that to be virtuous is to think of yourself as a member of the 'party of humankind, against vice and disorder, its common enemy'.[31] And that is now true. But we coherently can grant that it was not always so.

3.4.5

But this is not to say to say that there is nothing to be said in favour of the Enlightenment conception. This sort of relativism has its limits, and they come from two different but related lines of thought.

We have already seen one of them set forward by Bernard Williams. We could, with the resources of a knowledge of human nature, rank different sets of values according to their tendency to promote human flourishing. If values are associated with ways of conceiving one's identity, then the point will be that some ways of thinking of our identity are healthier and better for us than others. The basic claim here would be that it is better for us to think of ourselves, and more essentially to value ourselves, just as human beings than, say, as men or women, or as members of certain religious or ethnic groups, or as the possessors of certain talents. Or at

---

[31] Hume, *Enquiry Concerning the Principles of Morals*, p. 275.

least it is better if these other conceptions are governed by a value one places on oneself as simply human, a member of the party of humanity.

Obviously, without the resources of psychoanalytic and sociological theory we cannot envision what this kind of argument would look like in any detail. But it is a striking fact that philosophers who promote the adoption of Enlightenment liberal ideas have often appealed to arguments of this kind. In *The Subjection of Women*, for example, Mill points out the damaging effects on *men* of identifying themselves in terms of gender.[32] In *A Theory of Justice*, Rawls argues that the view of human talents as a kind of shared social resource, which he thinks would result from the just society he envisions, would make it easier for people to maintain a sense of self-worth.[33] Both of these arguments are meant to show that societies which accord equal value to human beings as such are better *for* people and that this is one reason to have them.

Of course there are also different ways of thinking of what it means to be valuable as a human being, or as a member of the party of humanity. Citizen of the Kingdom of Ends, participant in a common happiness, species being, one among others who are equally real, are different conceptions of the human-being-as-such among which further sorting would have to be done.

3.4.6

But it is also important to remember that no argument can preserve any form of relativism without on another level eradicating it. This is one of the main faults with one well-known criticism of liberalism, that the conception of the person which is employed in its arguments is an 'empty self'.[34] It is urged by communitarians that people need to conceive themselves as members of smaller communities, essentially tied to particular others and traditions. This is an argument about how we human beings need to constitute our practical identities, and if it is successful what it establishes

---

[32] Mill, *The Subjection of Women*. See especially chapter IV, pp. 86–88.
[33] Rawls, *A Theory of Justice*, especially sections 67 and 81.
[34] See for instance Michael Sandel, *Liberalism and the Limits of Justice*.

is a *universal* fact, namely that our practical identities must be constituted in part by particular ties and commitments.[35] The liberal who
wants to include everyone will now argue from that fact. And the
communitarian himself, having reflected and reached this conclusion, now has a conception of his own identity which is universal:
he is an animal that needs to live in community.

And there is a further implication of this which is important.
Once the communitarian sees himself this way, his particular ties
and commitments will remain normative for him only if this more
fundamental conception of his identity is one which he can see as
normative as well. A further stretch of reflection requires a further
stretch of endorsement. So he must endorse this new view of his
identity. He is an animal that needs to live in community, and he
now takes *this* to be a normative identity. He treats it as a source of
reasons, for he argues that it matters that he gets what he needs.[36]

And this further stretch of endorsement is exactly what happens.
Someone who is moved to urge the value of *having* particular ties
and commitments has discovered that part of their normativity
comes from the fact that human beings need to have them. He
urges that our lives are meaningless without them. That is not a
reason that *springs from* one of his own particular ties and commitments. It is a plea on behalf of all human beings, which he makes
because he now identifies in a certain way with us all. And that
means that he is no longer immersed in a normative world of particular ties and commitments. Philosophical reflection does not
leave everything just where it was.

---

[35] Ideas along these lines are developed in the first chapter of Scott Kim's unpublished dissertation, *Morality, Identity, and Happiness: an Essay on the Kantian Moral Life*. Kim works out a
position on the relation between particular commitments and moral commitment which
he is then able to use in an effective argument against those who criticize Kantian ethics
on the grounds that it is too impartial and leaves no room for particular commitments. I
have been deeply influenced by Kim's dissertation and our conversations about these
issues.

[36] We can see this as the kind of argument Nagel appeals to in *The Possibility of Altruism* (see
especially chapter XI). The communitarian now has two views of himself. Subjectively, he
feels essentially tied to this particular community. But when he looks at himself more
objectively, he sees himself as an animal that needs to be tied to some community or
other. In order to prevent dissociation between these two views of his identity, he now
needs to accord normativity to the more objective view if he is going to retain it for the
more subjective one.

3·4·7

So we may begin by accepting something like the communitarian's point. It is necessary to have *some* conception of your practical identity, for without it you cannot have reasons to act. We endorse or reject our impulses by determining whether they are consistent with the ways in which we identify ourselves. Yet most of the self-conceptions which govern us are contingent. You are born into a certain family and community, perhaps even into a certain profession or craft. You find a vocation, or ally yourself with a movement. You fall in love and make friends. You are a mother of some particular children, a citizen of a particular country, an adherent of a particular religion, because of the way your life has fallen out. And you act accordingly – caring for your children because they are your children, fighting for your country because you are its citizen, refusing to fight because you are a Quaker, and so on.

Because these conceptions are contingent, one or another of them may be shed. You may cease to think of yourself as a mother or a citizen or a Quaker, or, where the facts make that impossible, the conception may cease to have practical force: you may stop caring whether you live up to the demands of a particular role. This can happen in a variety of ways: it is the stuff of drama, and perfectly familiar to us all. Conflicts that arise between identities, if sufficiently pervasive or severe, may force you to give one of them up: loyalty to your country and its cause may turn you against a pacifist religion, or the reverse. Circumstances may cause you to call the practical importance of an identity into question: falling in love with a Montague may make you think that being a Capulet does not matter after all. Rational reflection may bring you to discard a way of thinking of your practical identity as silly or jejune.[37]

What is not contingent is that you must be governed by *some* conception of your practical identity. For unless you are committed

---

[37] I have not mentioned giving up a practical conception of your identity (or deciding that you aren't free to give one up) for moral reasons here. This is not because I don't think that happens, of course, but because this argument is supposed to explain why moral identity has a special status. Until that conclusion is established, conflict between morality and other forms of identity just counts as one case of conflict between identities.

to some conception of your practical identity, you will lose your grip on yourself as having any reason to do one thing rather than another – and with it, your grip on yourself as having any reason to live and act at all. But *this* reason for conforming to your particular practical identities is not a reason that *springs from* one of those particular practical identities. It is a reason that springs from your humanity itself, from your identity simply as *a human being*, a reflective animal who needs reasons to act and to live. And so it is a reason you have only if you treat your humanity as a practical, normative, form of identity, that is, if you value yourself as a human being.

But to value yourself just as a human being is to have moral identity, as the Enlightenment understood it. So this puts you in moral territory. Or at least, it does so if valuing humanity in your own person rationally requires valuing it in the persons of others. There's an objection to that idea, which I will take up in the next lecture. For now, I will assume that valuing ourselves as human beings involves valuing others that way as well, and carries with it moral obligations.

If this is right, our identity as moral beings – as people who value themselves as human beings – stands behind our more particular practical identities. It is because we are human that we must act in the light of practical conceptions of our identity, and this means that their importance is partly derived from the importance of being human. We must conform to them not merely for the reasons that caused us to adopt them in the first place, but because being human requires it. You may give up one of your contingent practical roles. But so long as you remain committed to a role, and yet fail to meet the obligations it generates, you fail yourself as a human being, as well as failing in that role. And if you fail in all of your roles – if you live at random, without integrity or principle, then you will lose your grip on yourself as one who has any reason to live and to act at all.

Most of the time, our reasons for action spring from our more contingent and local identities. But part of the normative force of those reasons springs from the value we place on ourselves as human beings who need such identities. In this way all value depends on the value of humanity; other forms of practical identity matter in part because humanity requires them. Moral identity and the obligations it carries with it are therefore inescapable and pervasive. Not every form of practical identity is contingent or relative after all: moral identity is necessary.

3.4.8

This is just a fancy new model of an argument that first appeared in a much simpler form, Kant's argument for his Formula of Humanity.[38] The form of relativism with which Kant began was the most elementary one we encounter – the relativism of value to human desires and interests. He started from the fact that when we make a choice we must regard its object as good. His point is the one I have been making – that being human we must endorse our impulses before we can act on them. He asked what it is that makes these objects good, and, rejecting one form of realism, he decided that the goodness was not in the objects themselves. Were it not for our desires and inclinations – and for the various physiological, psychological, and social conditions which gave rise to those desires and inclinations – we would not find their objects good. Kant saw that we take things to be important because they are important to us – and he concluded that we must therefore take ourselves to be important. In this way, the value of humanity itself is implicit in every human choice. If complete normative scepticism is to be avoided – if there is such a thing as a reason for action – then humanity, as the source of all reasons and values, must be valued for its own sake.

3.4.9

The point I want to make now is the same. In this lecture I have offered an account of the source of normativity. I have argued that human consciousness has a reflective structure that sets us normative problems. It is because of this that we require reasons for action, a conception of the right and the good. To act from such a conception is in turn to have a practical conception of your identity, a

---

[38] Kant, *Foundations of the Metaphysics of Morals*, pp. 427–428; in Beck's translation, pp. 45–47. I am here summarizing the interpretation of this argument I give in 'Kant's Formula of Humanity'.

conception under which you value yourself and find your life to be worth living and your actions to be worth undertaking. That conception is normative for you and in certain cases it can obligate you, for if you do not allow yourself to be governed by any conception of your identity then you will have no reason to act and to live. So a human being is an animal who needs a practical conception of her own identity, a conception of who she is which is normative for her.

But you are a human being and so if you believe my argument you can now see that that is *your* identity. You are an animal of the sort I have just described. And that is not merely a contingent conception of your identity, which you have constructed or chosen for yourself, or could conceivably reject. It is simply the truth. It is because we are such animals that our practical identities are normative for us, and, once you see this, you must take this more fundamental identity, being such an animal, to be normative as well. You must value your own humanity if you are to value anything at all.

Why? Because now that you see that your need to have a normative conception of yourself comes from your human identity, you can query the importance of that identity. Your humanity requires you to conform to some of your practical identities, and you can question this requirement as you do any other. Does it really matter whether we act as our humanity requires, whether we find some ways of identifying ourselves and stand by them? But in this case you have no option but to say yes. Since you are human you *must* take something to be normative, that is, some conception of practical identity must be normative for you. If you had no normative conception of your identity, you could have no reasons for action, and because your consciousness is reflective, you could then not act at all. Since you cannot act without reasons and your humanity is the source of your reasons, you must value your own humanity if you are to act at all.

It follows from this argument that human beings are valuable. Enlightenment morality is true.

3.4.10

The argument I have just given is a transcendental argument. I might bring that out more clearly by putting it this way: rational action exists, so we know it is possible. How is it possible? And then by the course of reflections in which we have just engaged, I show you that rational action is possible only if human beings find their own humanity to be valuable. But rational action is possible, and we are the human beings in question. Therefore we find ourselves to be valuable. Therefore, of course, we are valuable.

You might want to protest against that last step. How do we get from the fact that we find ourselves to be valuable to the conclusion that we are valuable? When we look at the argument this way, its structure seems to be like that of Mill's argument, which proved that if there were any utilitarians, they would find their morality to be normative, and invited us to think that therefore utilitarianism is normative.

But my argument, unlike Mill's, will not fail to find its target. For Mill's readers were not already utilitarians, or did not acknowledge themselves to be so, but you are already human beings, and do acknowledge yourself to be so.

And there's a good reason why the argument must take this form after all. Value, like freedom, is only directly accessible from within the standpoint of reflective consciousness. And I am now talking about it externally, for I am describing the nature of the consciousness that gives rise to the perception of value. From this external, third-person perspective, all we can say is that when we are in the first-person perspective we find ourselves to be valuable, rather than simply that we are valuable. There is nothing surprising in this. Trying to actually see the value of humanity from the third-person perspective is like trying to see the colours someone sees by cracking open his skull. From outside, all we can say is why he sees them.[39]

Suppose you are now tempted once more to say that this shows that value is unreal just as colour is unreal. We do not need to posit the existence of colours to give scientific explanations of why we see them. Then the answer will be the same as before. The Scientific World View is no substitute for human life. If you

---

[39] This is why Prichard, in 'Does Moral Philosophy Rest on a Mistake?' says that when we fall into doubt about whether we have obligations the remedy is to place or imagine ourselves in a situation where we are really obligated (pp. 16–17). The normative force of reasons, obligations, and values, is a force that is felt by a deliberating agent and is imperceptible from outside of the deliberative perspective.

think colours are unreal, go and look at a painting by Bellini or Olitski, and you will change your mind. If you think reasons and values are unreal, go and make a choice, and you will change your mind.

MORALITY, PERSONAL RELATIONSHIPS, AND CONFLICT

3.5.1

The argument I have just given is, as I said a moment ago, a transcendental argument. What it is really intended to show is this: that if you value anything at all, or, if you acknowledge the existence of any practical reasons, then you must value your humanity as an end in itself. Or, I might put it, if you are to have any practical identity at all, you must acknowledge yourself to have moral identity – human identity conceived as a form of normative practical identity – as well. And this identity like any other carries with it obligations.

I take this argument to show that any reflective agent can be led to acknowledge that she has moral obligations. What makes morality special is that it springs from a form of identity which cannot be rejected unless we are prepared to reject practical normativity, or the existence of practical reasons, altogether – a possibility about which I will say more in the next lecture. Our other practical identities depend for their normativity on the normativity of our human identity – on our own endorsement of our human need to be governed by such identities – and cannot withstand reflective scrutiny without it. We must value ourselves as human.

But I do not take the argument to show that all obligations are moral, or that moral obligations always trump others. In fact the argument requires – and our nature requires – that we do have some more local and contingent identities, which provide us with most of our reasons to live and to act. Moral identity does not swamp other forms of identity: no one is simply a moral agent and nothing more. Bernard Williams is right when he says that if morality demanded that of us, it would be incoherent.[40] But it

---

[40] See Williams, 'Persons, Character, and Morality' and 'Moral Luck'.

would be wrong to conclude that therefore either moral obligation, or our other obligations, can't be unconditional. To conclude that would not be to affirm the possibility of conflict, but rather to remove its sting. Conflicting obligations can both be unconditional; that's just one of the ways in which human life is hard.

To clarify the point, we should distinguish between two kinds of conflict. One may have a practical identity that is in and of itself contradictory to the value of humanity – say, the identity of an assassin. Or, one may have a practical identity that is not by its nature contrary to moral value, but that leads to a conflict with it in this or that case. The first kind of identity, and the conflicts it generates, is, I think, ruled out by the course of reflection I have tried to describe. In so far as the importance of having a practical identity comes from the value of humanity, it does not make sense to identify oneself in ways that are inconsistent with the value of humanity. But the second kind of conflict cannot be ruled out in this way. Conflict between the specific demands of morality and those of some more contingent form of identity may still exist.

3.5.2

One source of this second kind of conflict deserves special mention, though I cannot give it a full treatment here: personal relationships. Autonomy-based views of the sort I am advocating here are often thought to be unduly individualistic, or even to exclude deep forms of affiliation with others. In this section I want to explain why I think my view does not do this, and also why I think personal relationships can give rise to a special kind of conflict.

To do this, it will be helpful to contrast the view of personal relationships which I take to be correct with another view which is popularly assumed, although usually not fully articulated, in the philosophical literature. According to this other view, a personal relationship is an affectional tie – one loves or likes the other, where that is thought of as being some sort of an emotion. The emotion either consists in or causes two characteristic desires: you want to be around this other person, and you desire his happiness or more generally his good. This view is supposed to have three important implications. First, since having personal relationships is a matter of having certain desires and feelings, even an egoist can have such relationships. One does not need moral character to sustain them. Second, and relatedly, personal relationships are quite different in kind from moral ones. Moral relationships are governed by reason and supposedly demand that we be relentlessly impartial; personal relationships are governed by affection and pull us towards partiality. Third, and as a consequence, there is an inherent tension between personal relationships and morality, and that in two senses. First, treating someone as a friend is quite different from treating him morally, and may in a certain way exclude treating him morally. Being motivated by a sense of duty is at odds with being motivated by affection. Second, personal relationships draw us to forms of partiality and favouritism which morality supposedly frowns on.

I think that this view is mostly nonsense. In the first place, the contrast on which it draws – the contrast between being motivated by reason and being motivated by affection – is, on my view, incoherent. To be motivated 'by reason' is normally to be motivated by one's reflective endorsement of incentives and impulses, including affections, which arise in a natural way.[41] More importantly, the account completely leaves out the essential element of willed commitment. On the Kantian account which I favour, by contrast, a personal relationship is a reciprocal commitment on the part of two people to take one another's views, interests, and wishes into account. This kind of reciprocity leads to what Kant called 'a unity of will', for the two parties must, at least in the areas their relationship is concerned with, deliberate as one.[42] Personal relationships are therefore *constitutive* of one's practical identity. One is a member of the party of humanity, a Citizen of the Kingdom of Ends, but one is a member of many smaller and more local communities as well. A personal relationship is a Kingdom of Two – two who are committed to being in a special degree ends for one another.

[41] It is only in cases of reflective rejection that the impulse to act or refrain has to 'come from reason'. For example, when I discover that my impulse to break a burdensome promise must be reflectively rejected, that discovery itself must be the source of a new impulse, an impulse to keep the promise. This second impulse is strictly speaking what Kant called 'respect for law'. But respect for law more generally is expressed by the standing commitment to act only on morally endorsable impulses.

[42] Kant, *Lectures on Ethics*, p. 167.

On this view, personal relationships are structurally just like moral ones, except that they normally involve more fully realized forms of reciprocity. Friends do not merely refrain from making one another unhappy, but actively pursue each other's interests, for example. The virtues called upon by personal relationships are the same as those called upon by moral ones: charity and respect. A real diehard egoist could not be a friend, but this is not exactly because you have to be moral to be a friend. It is imaginable that someone might stand in this relationship of shared life and deliberation with a few select persons while scorning humanity, and exercise the virtues of charity and respect only towards those few. For the reasons I have been laying out in this lecture, I think that position is reflectively unstable, but it is still possible. More importantly, however, even those who do acknowledge their obligations to humanity at large will see their obligations to particular others as having independent force. Thus personal relationships are not completely subsumed under morality, but they are not affectional ties of a wholly different kind either.[43]

Personal relationships, then, as a form of practical identity, are independent *sources* of obligation, like moral obligations in their structure but not completely subsumed under them. And the thought of oneself as a certain person's friend or lover or parent or child can be a particularly deep form of practical identity. There is no obvious reason why your relationship to humanity at large should always matter more to you than your relationship to some particular person; no general reason why the laws of the Kingdom of Ends should have more force than the laws of a Kingdom of Two. I believe that this is why personal relationships can be the source of some particularly intractable conflicts with morality.

CONCLUSION

3.6.1

In this lecture I have tried to establish two points. First, the reflective structure of human consciousness gives us authority over our-

---

[43] These views are spelled out in a little more detail in my 'Creating the Kingdom of Ends: Reciprocity and Responsibility in Personal Relations'.

selves. Reflection gives us a kind of distance from our impulses which both forces us, and enables us, to make laws for ourselves, and it makes those laws normative. To make a law for yourself, however, is at the same time to give expression to a practical conception of your identity. Practical conceptions of our identity determine which of our impulses we will count as reasons. And to the extent that we cannot act against them without losing our sense that our lives are worth living and our actions are worth undertaking, they can obligate us.

Being human, we may at any point come to question the normativity of one or another of our practical identities, to ask why we must live up to them and conform to their laws. Why should it matter whether I live up to the demands imposed upon me by citizenship, or motherhood, or my profession? Most of the ways in which we identify ourselves are contingent upon our particular circumstances, or relative to the social worlds in which we live. How can we be bound by obligations which spring from conceptions of our identity which are not in themselves necessary?

This leads to the second point. The course of reflection to which this kind of question gives rise leads us to recognize the form of identity which stands behind the others: our identity as human, that is, as reflective animals who need to have practical conceptions of our identity in order to act and to live. To treat your human identity as normative, as a source of reasons and obligations, is to have what I have been calling 'moral identity'.

In one sense, moral identity is just like any other form of practical identity. To act morally is to act a certain way simply because you are human, to act as one who values her humanity should. Among the many things that you are, you are a member of the party of humanity, or a Citizen of the Kingdom of Ends. And this identity like any other carries certain obligations. But moral identity also stands in a special relationship to our other identities. First, moral identity is what makes it necessary to have other forms of practical identity, and they derive part of their importance, and so part of their normativity, from it. They are important in part because we need them. If we do not treat our humanity as a normative identity, none of our other identities can be normative, and then we can have no reasons to act at all. Moral identity is therefore inescapable. Second, and for that reason, moral identity exerts a kind of governing role over the other kinds. Practical conceptions of your identity which are fundamentally inconsistent with the value of humanity must be given up.

The views as I have presented it so far leaves three important worries unaddressed. First, you may think that I have shown only (or at most) that you must place a value on your own humanity, but not yet that you therefore have obligations to other human beings. Valuing your own humanity does not require valuing the humanity of others. Second, you may object that moral concern should not be limited to human beings at all: animals and other parts of nature should have moral standing. And third, you may worry that I have not really answered the sceptic, for I have several times said that we must value our humanity if we are to value anything at all, but I have not said why we must value anything at all. In the next lecture, I will develop my account further by responding to these objections.

The origin of value and the scope of obligation

Christine Korsgaard

If suicide is allowed then everything is allowed.

If anything is not allowed then suicide is not allowed.

This throws a light on the nature of ethics, for suicide is, so to speak, the elementary sin . . .

. . . Or is suicide in itself neither good nor evil?

Wittgenstein[1]

INTRODUCTION

4.1.1

In this lecture I address three apparently unconnected worries to which my argument in the last lecture gives rise. First, I will discuss a familiar objection to the type of argument which I have offered: the objection that valuing your own humanity does not commit you to valuing that of others. I will argue that this objection does not hold. It is based upon a false view about reasons, the view that they are private mental entities. This response, which invokes Wittgenstein's ideas, will lead me into a discussion of the question of the normative status of pain, and that will put me in a position to address another familiar objection to Kantian theories: the objection that basing all value upon the value of humanity gives no moral standing to the other animals. I will argue that the other animals do have moral standing and that a natural extension of the

---

[1] Wittgenstein, *Notebooks 1914–1916*, p. 91.

sort of argument I have been presenting can accommodate that fact. That argument in turn will lead me to some reflections about the natural and in particular biological sources of value, and I will move from those to a discussion of the question of normative scepticism.

OBLIGATING ONE ANOTHER

4.2.1

In the last lecture I argued that we must value our own humanity, and so that we must treat our human identity as a form of practical, normative identity. There, I took it for granted that this places us under moral obligations: that is, that valuing one's humanity amounts to having what I called 'moral identity'. The exact form that moral obligations will take depends on how we cash out the idea of moral identity, whether it is, say, as Citizen of the Kingdom of Ends, participant in a common happiness, species being, one among others who are equally real, or in some other way. But valuing your own humanity will require conceiving yourself in one of these ways only if we can conclude that valuing humanity in your own person somehow implies, entails, or involves valuing it in that of others.

There is a familiar objection to this conclusion, which is based in turn on a view about how it is reached. Some background will help to explain what the objection is. The project of justifying morality, or showing each person that she has a reason to 'be moral', has taken a certain characteristic shape in recent Anglo-American moral philosophy. In the simplest versions, the individual is thought to be self-interested, or, at least, self-interest is taken to be an uncontroversial source of rational norms. Rational justifications of morality must then show that self-interest gives the individual some reason to participate in a moral system. Hobbes, as he is traditionally interpreted, as well as contemporary heirs of that interpretation such as Gauthier, produce arguments of this kind.[2] Now some neo-Kantian justifications proceed, or anyway might be

---

[2] See Gauthier, *Morals by Agreement*.

thought to proceed, in a similar way. These neo-Kantian justifications characteristically begin by showing that you are rationally
committed to a certain normative conception of yourself, or to
valuing certain features of yourself. They then try to move from
that conclusion to the further conclusion that you must hold the
same normative conception of others, or value the same features in
them, on pain of contradiction. Since I regard my humanity as
source of value, I must in the name of consistency regard your
humanity that way as well. So I must value the things that you
value. Or, to put it another way since I think my humanity is what
makes my desires into normative reasons, I must on pain of contradiction suppose that the humanity of others makes their desires
into normative reasons as well. Gewirth, for instance, makes an
argument that looks like this in *Reason and Morality*. Thomas Nagel's
argument, in *The Possibility of Altruism*, may be read in this way as
well, although I think it should not be.

What such neo-Kantian arguments (or neo-Kantian arguments
so interpreted) and the Hobbesian arguments have in common is
this: both assume that an individual agent has private reasons, that
is, reasons that have normative force for her, and they try to argue
that those private reasons give the individual some reason to take
the (private) reasons of other people into account. Either the individual's private reasons are served by attention to other people's
reasons, as in the neo-Hobbesian arguments; or the individual's
private reasons are found logically to commit her to taking other
people's reasons into account, as in the neo-Kantian arguments. If
public reasons are reasons which have normative force for everybody, then we can see these arguments as trying to *construct* the
public character of reasons, starting from the assumption that
reasons are private.[3] If I have reason to take your reasons into
account and you have reason to take my reasons into account, then
we have reason to share our reasons, and we could just as well call
them all *our* reasons: public reasons. So the public character of
reasons is as it were *created* by the reciprocal exchange of inherently

---

[3] What I am calling 'private' and 'public' reasons are roughly what in contemporary jargon
are called 'agent-relative' and 'agent-neutral' reasons. My reason for switching terminol-
ogy will become apparent as my argument proceeds.

private reasons, where that in turn is forced on us by the content of the private reasons themselves.

Yet arguments that try to move us from private reasons to public ones in this way suffer from certain standard defects. Prichard pointed out that the self-interest arguments are at least in danger of being completely irrelevant, since moral conduct by definition is not conduct motivated by self-interest. These arguments also inevitably encounter interference from the free-rider problem. The neo-Kantian arguments are said to be logically flawed. Consistency can force me to grant that your humanity is normative for you just as mine is normative for me. It can force me to acknowledge that your desires have the status of reasons for you, in exactly the same way that mine do for me. But it does not force me to share in your reasons, or make *your* humanity normative for me.[4] It could still be true that I have my reasons and you have yours, and indeed that they leave us eternally at odds. Human beings may still be egoistic, not in the sense of being concerned only about themselves, but in the sense defined by Nagel in *The Possibility of Altruism*. We each act on our own private reasons, and we need some special reason, like friendship or contract, for taking the reasons of others into account.

In one sense, this last objection is correct. If reasons *were* essentially private, consistency would not force me to take your reasons into account. And even if it did, it would do it in the wrong way. It should show that I have an obligation *to myself* to treat you in ways that respect the value which I place on you. It would show that I have duties with respect to you, about you, but not that there are things I owe *to* you. But some duties really are owed *to* others: we may be obligated by others, I will argue, in much the same way that we may be obligated by ourselves.

All of these objections have something in common. They are all ways of saying that private reasons will remain forever private, that the gap from private reasons to public ones cannot be bridged by argument. In one sense, this is just what we should expect. We cannot know what an argument *does* until after we know whether the reasons it employs are private or public.

The solution to these problems must be to show that reasons are

---

[4] See for instance Williams's criticism of Gewirth in chapter IV of *Ethics and the Limits of Philosophy*.

not private, but public in their very essence. This would almost, although not quite, amount to showing that morality does not need a justification. Prichard would be right after all: moral philosophy would indeed rest on a mistake, if moral philosophy is the attempt to argue us from having private reasons into having public ones. But there are in turn two ways to go about showing that reasons are inherently public. One is to try to defend some form of substantive moral realism. Reasons are public because they are derived from or refer to certain objective features of the public world, namely objective values. We might call this view 'publicity as objectivity'. As the reference to Prichard reminds us, this is not so much a way of arguing for morality as it is of insisting that it need not be done: the project of justifying morality to the individual by making some kind of appeal to the individual's private reasons is rejected as unnecessary, since the individual's reasons could never have been private in the first place. G. E. Moore's rejection of egoism is perhaps the argument that deploys this strategy most explicitly. Moore argued that the idea that my own good could be good for me and nobody else is simply incoherent; to say that something is good for me is just to say that it is objectively good that I should have it, and that is a goodness that exists for everybody.[5]

The other way retains one element of the picture I began with. The public character of reasons is indeed created by the reciprocal exchange, the sharing, of the reasons of individuals. But it acknowledges the point made by the criticisms made above. If these reasons really were essentially private, it would be impossible to exchange or to share them. So their privacy must be incidental or ephemeral; they must be inherently shareable. We might call this view 'publicity as shareability'. I take this to be equivalent to another thesis, namely, that what both enables us and forces us to share our reasons is, in a deep sense, our *social nature*.

Although it is universally acknowledged that human beings are in fact social animals, modern moral philosophers have usually not considered it allowable to help themselves to this fact in arguments aimed at justifying morality. Our sociability seems to be too biological or contingent a fact to play a role in rational arguments.

---

[5] Moore, *Principia Ethica*, pp. 97–105.

Perhaps we may think that we can imagine other rational beings who are not social or even human beings who would choose not to participate in social life. Or, alternatively, we may think that the sense in which we are social is merely that we need to cooperate in order to get the things we want as individuals, that we have private reasons to be social. In that case, arguments for morality cannot appeal to our social nature because our social nature is, roughly speaking, what they are trying to prove.

But if our social nature is deep, in the sense that it is the nature of our reasons that they are public and shareable, then justifications of morality can and should appeal to it. So the kind of argument we need here is not one that shows us that our private reasons somehow commit us to public ones, but one that acknowledges that our reasons were never more than incidentally private in the first place. To act on a reason is already, essentially, to act on a consideration whose normative force may be shared with others.[6] Once that is in place, it will be easy to show how we can get someone who acknowledges the value of his own humanity to see that he has moral obligations.

4.2.2

What obligates me is reflection. I can obligate myself because I am conscious of myself. So if you are going to obligate me I must be conscious of you. You must be able to intrude on my reflections – you must be able to get under my skin. People suppose that practical reasons are private because they suppose that reflection is a private activity. And they suppose that, in turn, because they believe in the privacy of consciousness. So what we need here is some help from Wittgenstein.

4.2.3

Consider the private language argument. As Wittgenstein defines it, a private language would be a language that referred to something essentially private and incommunicable, say for instance a

---

[6] See my 'The Reasons We Can Share' for a slightly different approach to this problem than the one that follows here.

sensation that is yours alone, and cannot be described in any other way than by a name that you give it. You can't even call it a tickle or an itch, for then it would be communicable. So you just call it 'S'. And whenever you experience it, you say to yourself, 'That was S'.[7] Wittgenstein argued that there couldn't be any such language. One way to understand his argument goes like this: meaning is relational because it is a *normative* notion: to say that X means Y is to say that one ought to take X for Y; and this requires two, a legislator to lay it down that one must take X for Y, and a citizen to obey. And the relation between these two is not merely causal because the citizen can disobey: there must be a possibility of misunderstanding or mistake. Since it is a relation, in which one gives a law to another, it takes two to make a meaning. So you cannot peer inwardly at an essentially private and incommunicable sensation and say 'that is what I mean by S' and so in that way mean something. For if that is what you mean by S, then when you call something S it must be *that*, and if you call something else S you must be wrong. But if what you call S is just that sensation which makes you feel like saying 'S', and it cannot be identified in any other way, then you cannot be wrong. As Wittgenstein puts it:

But 'I impress it on myself' [that is, I impress upon my self that 'S' will be my name for this sensation] can only mean: this process brings it about that I remember the connection *right* in the future. But in the present case I have no criterion of correctness. One would like to say: whatever is going to seem right to me is right. And that only means that here we cannot talk about 'right'.[8]

So the idea of a private language is inconsistent with the normativity of meaning.

If we read Wittgenstein that way, there is an obvious similarity between the kind of normativity which he thinks characterizes language and the kind of normativity which I have been attributing to practical reasons. We could make a parallel argument against private reasons: reasons are relational because reason is a normative notion: to say that R is a reason for A is to say that one should do

---

[7] Wittgenstein, *Philosophical Investigations*, sections 243ff., pp. 88ff.
[8] Wittgenstein, *Philosophical Investigations*, section 258, p. 92.

A because of R; and this requires two, a legislator to lay it down, and a citizen to obey. And the relation between them is not just causal because the citizen can disobey: there must be a possibility of irrationality or wrongdoing. Since it is a relation, and indeed a relation in which one gives a law to another, it takes two to make a reason. And here the two are the two elements of reflective consciousness, the thinking self and the acting self: what I have been talking about all along is how you can make laws and reasons for your self.[9]

4.2.4

There are two important points here. The first point is that the mistake involved in thinking that a meaning is a mental entity is exactly like that involved in thinking that a reason is a mental entity. To talk about values and meanings is not to talk about entities, either mental or Platonic, but to talk in a shorthand way about relations we have with ourselves and one another. The normative demands of meaning and reason are not demands that are made on us by objects, but are demands that we make on ourselves and each other.[10] 'Bring me a slab!' It is no accident that Wittgenstein starts from the way we use language in scenes of command and obedience.

The second point, which follows from the first, concerns privacy. The private language argument does not show that I could not have my own personal language. But it shows that I could not have a language which is in principle incommunicable to anybody else. When I make a language, I make its meanings normative for me. As Wittgenstein puts it, I *undertake* to use words in certain ways.[11] And however I go about binding myself to those meanings, however I 'bring it about that I remember the connection *right* in

---

[9] It may look as if there is a disanalogy here. The private language argument shows that you cannot mean a certain sensation by 'S' just now and never again, because then you could not be wrong. The remark I just made makes it look as if you could have a reason just now and never again – the thinking self could bind the acting self to act a certain way just now. Actually however I do not think that is a possibility, since the acting self cannot coherently be taken to exist just at a particular moment. See my 'Personal Identity and the Unity of Agency: a Kantian Response to Parfit', 113–114; and pp. 229–230 of this volume.

[10] This is consistent with my earlier claim that a maxim is an intrinsically normative entity. A maxim is a demand we make on ourselves: the relation is built into its nature.

[11] Wittgenstein, *Philosophical Investigations*, section 262, p. 93.

the future', it must be possible for me to bind another in exactly the same way.[12]

4.2.5

If I say to you 'Picture a yellow spot!' you will. What exactly is happening? Are you simply cooperating with me? No, because at least without a certain active resistance, you will not be able to help it. Is it a causal connection then? No, or at least not merely that, for if you picture a *pink* spot you will be mistaken, wrong. Causal connections cannot be wrong. What kind of necessity is this, both normative and compulsive? It is *obligation*.

4.2.6

Philosophers have been concerned for a long time about how we understand the meanings of words, but we have not paid enough attention to the fact that it is so hard not to. It is nearly impossible to hear the words of a language you know as mere noise.[13] And this has implications for the supposed privacy of human consciousness. For it means that I can always intrude myself into your consciousness. All I have to do is talk to you in the words of a language you know, and in that way I can force you to think. The space of

---

[12] Derek Parfit's views on personal identity in part III of *Reasons and Persons*, are of use here, because they help reduce the sense that my relationship to myself is unique, and in particular that I am unified and continuous with myself in a unique way. We might put his arguments about memory and intention this way: however memory brings it about that I get the past *right*, it must be possible for it to bind another in just the same way. However my intentions bind me to certain actions in the future, they could bind someone else in just the same way. Parfit's arguments help to show that even an individual human consciousness needs some sort of cement to hold it together. The physical bases of consciousness do part of this work, but, as I argue in 'Personal Identity and the Unity of Agency: a Kantian Response to Parfit', the construction of practical identity is also required to make an individual unified. One might say that normativity holds our inner world together in something like the way causality holds the outer world together. That is why we have always thought that the soul and value have something special to do with each other.

[13] One philosopher has at least noticed it. In the *Dialogues Concerning Natural Religion*, Hume has Cleanthes argue that you can no more really doubt that the teleological organization of the world is an expression of intelligence than you could doubt that a voice from the sky, which spoke to you in your own language, was an expression of intelligence (part II, pp. 152–153). This analogy depends on the impossibility of hearing the words of a language you know as mere noise.

linguistic consciousness is essentially public, like a town square. You might happen to be alone in yours, but I can get in anytime. Wittgenstein says: 'Think in this connection how singular is the use of a person's name to *call* him!'[14]

4.2.7

If I call out your name, I make you stop in your tracks. (If you love me, I make you come running.) Now you cannot proceed as you did before. Oh, you can proceed, all right, but not just as you did before. For now if you walk on, you will be ignoring me and slighting me. It will probably be difficult for you, and you will have to muster a certain active resistance, a sense of rebellion. But why should you have to rebel against me? It is because I am a law to you. By calling out your name, I have obligated you. I have given you a reason to stop.

Of course that's overstated: you don't have to stop. You have reasons of your own, and you might decide, rightly or wrongly, that they outweigh the one I have given you. But that I have given you a reason is clear from the fact that, in ordinary circumstances, you will feel like giving me one back. 'Sorry, I must run, I'm late for an appointment.' We all know that reasons must be met with reasons, and that is why we are always exchanging them.

4.2.8

When we experience a desire or an impulse, we consider whether to treat it as a reason, whether to make it our maxim to act on it. We may or may not, though in ordinary cases, we will, so long as there is no reason why not. In that sense, our ordinary impulses have standing with us, an automatic right at least to be heard.

So the first point here is that the reasons of others have something like the same standing with us as our own desires and impulses do.[15] We do not seem to need a reason to take the reasons

---

[14] Wittgenstein, *Philosophical Investigations*, section 27, p. 13.
[15] I thank Ulrike Heuer for supplying this comparison.

of others into account. We seem to need a reason not to. Certainly we do things because others want us to, ask us to, tell us to, all the time. We give each other the time and directions, open doors and step aside, warn each other of imminent perils large and small. We respond with the alacrity of obedient soldiers to telephones and doorbell and cries for help. You could say that it is because we want to be cooperative, but that is like saying that you understand my words because you want to be cooperative. It ignores the same essential point, which is that it is so hard not to.

Now the egoist may reply that this does not establish that other people's reasons are reasons for me. I am merely describing a deep psychological fact – that human beings are very susceptible to one another's pressure. We tend to cave in to the demands of others. But nothing I have said so far shows that we really have to treat the demands of others as *reasons*.

4.2.9

Doesn't it? Consider an exchange of reasons. A student comes to your office door and says: 'I need to talk to you. Are you free now?' and you say 'No, I've got to finish this letter right now, and then I've got to go home. Could you possibly come around tomorrow, say about three?' And your student says 'Yes, that will be fine. I'll see you tomorrow at three then.'

What is happening here? On my view, the two of you are reasoning together, to arrive at a decision, a single shared decision, about what to do. And I take that to be the natural view. But if egoism is true, and reasons cannot be shared, then that is not what is happening. Instead, each of you backs into the privacy of his practical consciousness, reviews his own reasons, comes up with a decision, and then re-emerges to announce the result to each other. And the process stops when the results happen to coincide, and the agents know it, because of the announcements they have made to each other.

Now consider an exchange of ideas, of meanings, rather than an exchange of practical reasons. Here we do not find these two possibilities. If meanings could not be shared, there would be no point in announcing the results of one's private thinking to anybody else.

If they can be shared, then it is in principle possible to think the issues through together, and that is what people do when they talk. But if we have to grant that meanings can be shared, why not grant that practical reasons can be shared too?

The egoist may reply that I am leaving out an option. The student/teacher relation is a personal one. People who enter into particular personal relationships have special reasons to take each other's reasons into account. So the exchange I've just described takes place against a background agreement that the parties involved will take each other's reasons into account. The egoist is someone who acts on his own reasons, not someone who has no concern for others. So you and your student reason together because you have tacitly agreed to, but this does not show that this is what usually happens.

But the objection re-emerges within this framework. How are we to understand this personal relationship? If reasons are still private then it goes like this: each of you has a private reason to take the reasons of the other into account. A personal relationship is then an interest in one another's interests. I've already explained, in lecture 3, why I think this isn't right. But in any case this wouldn't change the shape of the deliberation – you still back into your private deliberative spaces and then re-emerge to announce the results. This only shows why you think there's a point in the exercise at all, why you hope to reach a convergence.

But if you are really reasoning together, if you have joined your wills to arrive at a single shared decision – well, then that can happen, can't it? And why shouldn't it be what usually happens? Why shouldn't language force us to reason practically together, in just the same way that it forces us to think together?

4.2.10

Now how do we get from here to moral obligation? This is where Thomas Nagel's argument, from *The Possibility of Altruism*, comes into its own.

Suppose that we are strangers and that you are tormenting me, and suppose that I call upon you to *stop*. I say: 'How would you like it if someone did that to you?' And now you cannot proceed as you did before. Oh, you can proceed all right, but not just as you did before. For I have obligated you to stop.

How does the obligation come about? Just the way Nagel says that it does. I invite you to consider how you would like it if someone did that to you. You realize that you would not merely dislike it, you would resent it. You would think that the other has a reason to stop, more, that he has an obligation to stop. And that obligation would spring from your own objection to what he does to you. You make yourself an end for others; you make yourself a law to them. But if you are a law to others in so far as you are just human, just *someone*, then the humanity of others is also a law to you. *By making you think these thoughts*, I force you to acknowledge the value of *my* humanity, and I obligate you to act in a way that respects it.

There is an appeal to consistency in this argument; it is meant to remind you of what the value of humanity requires. But it is not what makes you take my reasons into account, or bridges the gap between your reasons and mine, for there is no gap to bridge. Of course it's true that, as Nagel observes, the argument would not go through if you failed to see yourself, to identify yourself, as just someone, a person, one person among others who are equally real. The argument invites you to change places with the other, and you could not do that if you failed to see what you and the other have in common. Suppose you could say 'someone doing that to *me*, why that would be terrible! But then I am *me*, after all.' Then the argument would fail of its effect, it would not find a foothold in you. But the argument never really fails in *that* way.

For it to fail in that way, I would have to hear your words as mere noise, not as intelligible speech. And it is impossible to hear the words of a language you know as mere noise. In hearing your words as *words*, I acknowledge that you are *someone*. In acknowledging that I can hear them, I acknowledge that I am *someone*. If I listen to the argument at all, I have already admitted that each of us is *someone*.

Nagel characterized the egoist as a practical solipsist and of course he was right. And no form of solipsism is an option for us. You can no more take the reasons of another to be mere pressure than you can take the language of another to be mere noise.

4.2.11

You can try, of course. She says, 'My career is just as important to me as yours is to you, you know. I have ambitions too.' He says, 'It isn't the same thing for a woman.' What isn't the same? Does 'career' mean something different to her? Does 'ambition'? How about 'important'? Or (let's get down to brass tacks) how about 'I?'

In Hume's *Dialogues Concerning Natural Religion*, Demea suggests that when we use the names of human characteristics, like 'intellect' and 'will', to describe the Deity, they don't mean quite the same thing that they mean when we apply them to ourselves, since divine attributes are beyond our understanding. And Cleanthes replies that unless these words mean the same thing that they mean in our own case, they don't mean anything at all. They're just noise.[16]

She's trying to obligate him; he's trying to block it. So he tries to tell her, and he tries to tell himself, that she's just making noise.

4.2.12

I believe that the myth of egoism will die with the myth of the privacy of consciousness. Now you may object that the way in which I have argued against the privacy of consciousness – by showing that we can think and reason together – has nothing to do with what philosophers mean when they discuss that privacy. What they mean by privacy is that you don't always know what someone else is thinking or feeling. The way in which you have access to the contents of another person's mind – through words and expressions and other such forms of evidence – doesn't allow you to look around in it freely, and make sure that you know what's there and what's not.

But that's not an issue about privacy. If you accept the thesis that consciousness is reflective rather than internally luminous, then you must admit that you don't have access to your own mind in *that* way. So that doesn't mark a difference between the kind of relationship you have to yourself and the kind that you have to others. All we've got here is a matter of degree. You know some people

---

[16] Hume, *Dialogues Concerning Natural Religion*. For Demea's remarks, see part II, pp. 141–142; for Cleanthes's reply, see part IV, pp. 158–159; and again part XI, p. 203.

better than others; if you're honest and lucky, you know yourself pretty well.

Human beings are social animals in a deep way.[17] It is not just that we go in for friendship or prefer to live in swarms or packs. The space of linguistic consciousness – the space in which meanings and reasons exist – is a space that we occupy together.

THE ORIGIN OF VALUE AND THE VALUE OF LIFE

4.3.1

Pain is an objection. Interestingly, it is an objection to several of the views which I have discussed here. First, for many, pain is the biggest stumbling block to accepting Wittgenstein's views about our mental lives. It seems to them that pain is a sensation and that it is in the mind and therefore that what it is to be in pain is to have a sensation in your mind. And it seems to them that there could be a pain, otherwise indescribable but recognizable upon repetition, that was private in just the sense that Wittgenstein denied. Second, for many, pain is the biggest temptation to some form of naturalistic realism about normativity. One can have doubts about pleasure, for there are pleasures we deplore, but pain seems obviously to be a kind of normative fact. And third, if that is so, pain is an objection to Kantian ethics, or to any ethics which makes the value of humanity the foundation of all value. For the other animals suffer pain, and if pain is intrinsically normative, then it matters that they do. Animals just as such should have moral standing.

4.3.2

The first two objections are related. Wittgenstein's argument against a private language deploys one of the standard objections

---

[17] Another powerful account of our social nature can be found in Hume. Hume's argument about why virtue is its own reward, which I discussed in lecture 2 in connection with the problem of the sensible knave, can be seen as an argument against the privacy of consciousness. It shows how we live in each other's eyes. To that extent it does some of the same work as Wittgenstein's argument. It may also serve as a useful supplement to Wittgenstein's, since it helps to show why we continue to live in each other's eyes even when we are not actually talking.

against any form of normative naturalism – that you cannot be wrong. Hobbes said you could only be obligated by the law if the sovereign is able to punish you. But if you break the law and get away with it, then the sovereign was not after all able to punish you and so you were not wrong. Hume says that your reason is your strongest desire. But if you always act from your strongest desire, then you always do what you have reason to do, and you cannot be wrong. Wittgenstein says that if a word just refers to the very sensation that makes you feel like saying that word, then you cannot be wrong.

But both the opponent of Wittgenstein and the normative realist point to pain, and more generally to sensation, as a case of where it seems to be no objection to say that we cannot be wrong. In fact it creates a foundation. The utilitarian claims that pleasure and pain are facts which are also values, a place where the natural and normative are one, and so where ethics can find a foundation in the natural world. And this is exactly analogous to the epistemological claim that our sensations are the place where the natural and the normative are one, and so where knowledge can find a foundation in the world. Sensations are seen to be intrinsically normative entities, about which we cannot be wrong.

4.3.3

But can't we? 'I cannot be wrong about whether I am seeing red.' If you mean that the object before you is red, you can certainly be wrong. 'No, I mean that I am having a red sensation.' And what is that? It is the sensation that makes you feel like saying that a thing is red. You are not describing a condition that explains what you are inclined to say. You are simply announcing what you are inclined to say. In the same way, someone who says he is in pain is not describing a condition which gives him a reason to change his condition. He is announcing that he has a *very* strong impulse to change his condition.

Now that way of putting it, inspired by Wittgenstein, has a problem. People have thought that Wittgenstein was making a point about *language*, to the effect that when people talk about their own inner states and sensations they must be using language expressively, as if 'I am in pain' could only be a cry of pain, and you could not simply be reporting your condition. Of course you can report your condition; once you've mastered the language, you can do anything you like. His point is rather about mental activities, and whether a way of talking leaves anything for them to *be*. If 'I see something red' *means* 'I am having a red sensation' then one can never perceive; one can only announce the results of a perception that has already taken place. For what is this 'having'? Did the little person in your mind perceive the red sensation? Wittgenstein is attacking a certain picture of what it is like to be conscious, which reduces all mental activity to the contemplation of sensations and ideas. And the language of 'having' supports this picture. Does 'I am in pain' mean 'I am having a horrible sensation'? What here is the form of the 'having'? Are you contemplating it? What would be so horrible about that?

4.3.4

But surely, you will reply, a *physical* pain is not just an impulse to change your condition? It *is* a sensation of a certain character. Now I am not denying that when we are in pain part of what is going on is that we are having sensations of a certain character. I am however denying that the painfulness of pain consists entirely in the character of those sensations. The painfulness of pain consists in the fact that these are sensations which we are inclined to fight. You may want to ask: why are we inclined to fight them if they are not horrible in themselves? In some cases we are biologically wired this way; pain could not do its biological job if we were not inclined to fight it. When nature equipped us with pain she was giving us a *way* of taking care of ourselves, not a *reason* to take care of ourselves. Why do you thrash? Is it as if you were trying to hurl your body away from itself? Why do you say 'as if'? Pain really is less horrible if you can curb your inclination to fight it. This is why it helps, in dealing with pain, to take a tranquillizer or to lie down. Ask yourself how, if the painfulness of pain rested just in the character of the sensations, it could help to lie down? The sensations do not change. Pain wouldn't hurt if you could just relax and enjoy it.

If the painfulness of pain rested in the character of the sensations rather than in our tendency to revolt against them, our belief that physical pain has something in common with grief, rage and disappointment would be inexplicable. For that matter, what physical pains have in common with each other would be inexplicable, for the sensations are of many different kinds. What do nausea, migraine, menstrual cramps, pinpricks, and pinches have in common, that makes us call them all pains? (Don't say they're all horrible; that's just repeating yourself.) What emotional pains have in common with physical ones is that in these cases too we are in the grip of an overwhelming urge to do battle, not now against our sensations, but against the world. Stoics and Buddhists are right in thinking that we could put an end to pain if we could just stop fighting. The person who cared only for his own virtue, if there could be such a person, would be happy on the rack.[18] They are wrong if they conclude that we should therefore stop fighting. Many pains are worth having; one may even say that they are true. Pain is not the condition that is a reason to change your condition, the condition in which the natural and the normative are one. It is your *perception* that you have a reason to change your condition.[19]

4.3.5

When you feel pity for someone, why does it strike you as a reason to help him? Why don't you just take a tranquillizer? Hutcheson says

[18] Of course there could not be such a person, or at least, he could not *have* the virtues which were the only things he cared about. To have the virtues is in part to care about certain external things.

[19] Some will want to say that physical pain would be just as bad even if it were not a perception of our body's condition. Imagining physical pain apart from our body's condition is like imagining colour apart from coloured objects. In *Philosophical Investigations*, section 276, p. 96, Wittgenstein says that our suspicions ought to be aroused by the idea that we can detach the colour impression from the object, like a membrane. In the same way, it ought to be aroused by the idea that we can detach the sensation of pain from the bodily state of which it is a perception. In response to an earlier version of this footnote, more than one person suggested to me that a headache is a pain that does not seem to be a perception of any sort of bodily condition. In section 314, p. 104, Wittgenstein says 'It shews a fundamental misunderstanding, if I am inclined to study the headache I have now in order to get clear about the philosophical problem of sensation.' I am not exactly sure what he means, but it *certainly* ought to arouse our suspicion about this example that headaches occur in the *head*. I agree with Wittgenstein that it is a mistake to take this kind of case as the central one to study, but I do address it in section 4.3.11 below.

'If our sole Intention, in Compassion or Pity, was the Removal of our Pain, we should run way, shut our Eyes, divert our Thoughts from the miserable Object, to avoid the Pain of Compassion, which we seldom do . . .'[20] The point is reiterated by Nagel: 'Sympathy is not, in general, just a feeling of discomfort produced by the recognition of distress in others, which in turn motivates one to relieve their distress. Rather, it is the pained awareness of their distress as *something to be relieved.*'[21] Wittgenstein says 'How am I filled with pity *for this man*? How does it come out what the object of my pity is? (Pity, one may say, is a form of conviction that someone else is in pain.)'[22] Pity is painful because it is the perception of *another's* pain, and so the perception that there is a reason to change *his* condition.

4.3.6

Pain is the perception of a reason. Since animals have pain, and up until now I have seemed to suggest that only human beings have reasons, this will take a moment to explain.

The best account of what an animal is comes from Aristotle. We have already seen that Aristotle thought that the form of a thing is the organization or arrangement of its parts that allows it to be what it is, to do what it does, to do its job. Now Aristotle thought that a *living* thing is a thing with a special kind of form. A living thing is so designed as to maintain and reproduce itself. It has what we might call a self-maintaining form. So it is its own end; its job is just to keep on being what it is. Its business in life is to preserve its own *identity*. And its organs and activities are arranged to that end.[23]

If a living thing is an animal, if it is conscious, then part of the way it preserves its own identity is through its sensations. And this is

---

[20] This passage is from the 1726 edition of Hutcheson's *Inquiry* and is not in Raphael; one may find it in Selby-Bigge, *British Moralists*, p. 93. Raphael used the 1738 edition, which contains a passage parallel to this one on p. 276.

[21] *The Possibility of Altruism*, p. 80 n.1.

[22] *Philosophical Investigations*, section 287, p. 98.

[23] This is not a piece of teleological metaphysics that we need to give up, or that is inconsistent with the Scientific World View. It is an account of what a living thing is, not an account of why there are such things. In so far as the process of natural selection accounts for the existence of living things, it is perfectly clear why they are 'designed' to maintain and reproduce themselves.

where pain comes in. When something is a threat to its physical existence, or would be if it went on long enough, the animal perceives that fact, and revolts against it. The animal is moved to take action to fix what is wrong. Suppose for instance the animal needs nourishment. It perceives that by getting hungry. It finds this unpleasant and is moved to get something to eat. Don't be confused here: it is not that the pain is an unpleasant sensation which gives the animal a reason to eat. The animal has a reason to eat, which is that it will die if it does not. It does not know that it has that reason, but it does perceive it. The sensation in question is the sensation of hunger, not of pain. But an animal is designed to perceive and revolt against threats to the preservation of its identity, such as hunger. When it does that, it is in pain.

4.3.7

Now consider this comparison:

1 A human being is an animal whose nature it is to construct a practical identity which is normative for her. She is a law to herself. When some way of acting is a threat to her practical identity and reflection reveals that fact, the person finds that she must reject that way of acting, and act in another way. In that case, she is obligated.

2 A living thing is an entity whose nature it is to preserve and maintain its physical identity. It is a law to itself. When something it is doing is a threat to that identity and perception reveals that fact, the animal finds that it must reject what it is doing and do something else instead. In that case, it is in pain.

Obligation is the reflective rejection of a threat to your identity. Pain is the *unreflective* rejection of a threat to your identity. So pain is the *perception* of a reason, and that is why it seems normative.

4.3.8

There is a point, and an important one, at which these two ideas come together. It concerns the negative moral emotions. In lecture 1, when I was explaining the voluntarist conception of the motive of duty, I argued that according to Hobbes and Pufendorf, sanctions are essential to the legislator's authority. Although we are not supposed to do our duty out of the fear of punishment or the hope of reward, no one who cannot impose sanctions on us is in a position to *require* anything of us. In lecture 3, I argued that we are in a position to require things of ourselves, that we have legislative authority over ourselves. And I also argued that a person's own mind does indeed impose sanctions on her: that when we don't do what we should, we punish ourselves, by guilt and regret and repentance and remorse.

But do I mean to say that the authority of your own mind over your conduct is in any case inevitable, or do I mean to say that it depends on your mind's capacity to punish you? If you didn't experience regret or remorse when you acted against your own mind's command, would you then be free to ignore your mind's command?[24]

The answer lies in what I have just said. Pain is the perception of a reason: that applies when we look back as well as at the present and when we look ahead.[25] Someone who recalls failing to do what she was obligated to do *will* experience pain, and that is what remorse and regret are. The mind's authority does not depend upon the experience of the negative moral emotions, but it absolutely implies it. A mind that could not perceive its reasons, after all, could not function as a mind at all.[26]

---

[24] I thank Andrews Reath for pointing this problem out to me.

[25] For the view that regret and the moral emotions (especially resentment) are backwards-looking responses to reasons, see Nagel, *The Possibility of Altruism*.

[26] What I say here is modelled on Kant's account of respect, the forward-looking or present-tense moral emotion of an agent who is morally obligated to act. Respect is our awareness of the activity of moral reason in our own minds: this awareness has the character of a feeling because being motivated by reason has an effect on feeling – it thwarts inclination (producing pain) and strikes down self-conceit (producing humiliation). (*Critique of Practical Reason*, pp. 71–76; in Beck's translation, pp. 74–79.) Kant's account of respect, as well as the argument I give here, show the artificiality of supposing that accounts of the moral emotions are either completely separable from or only contingently related to accounts of moral reason. If the mind must be percipient of its activities, and if pleasure and pain as well as the emotions that grow out of them are among its perceptions of its activities, then emotions *must* play an essential role in moral life even on the most rationalistic theory. More generally, those who suppose that we can imagine completely emotionless rational beings tend to have in mind violent emotions like the passions of love or rage and to forget that these are continuous with the low-level forms of affect that more quietly pervade mental life – for example, the phenomenon of being interested in something. It seems to me to be extremely doubtful that we can imagine a sensible creature that lacks these forms of affect. See also lecture 3, note 30.

4.3.9

John Balguy, an eighteenth-century British rationalist, wrote:

It may . . . be questioned, whether *Pleasure* can, in Strictness, be called the *ultimate End* of a sensible Agent. Considered as *Sensible*, he seems to be rather *himself* his own ultimate End. He pursues it for *his own Sake*, regards it always with Reference to *himself*, and all his Views about it terminate *in himself*.[27]

It is 'considered as *Sensible*', that a person is his own end. But animals are sensible too and that means they are their own ends too. This is the view of pleasure and pain that I am advocating here. They are expressive of the value that an animal places on itself.

It sounds funny to say that an animal places value on itself, because *for us* that is an exercise of reflection, so it sounds as if it means that the animal thinks itself to be of value. Of course I don't mean that. I am just talking about the kind of thing that it is. As Aristotle said it is its own end. Valuing itself just is its nature.

To say that life is a value is almost a tautology. Since a living thing is a thing for which the preservation of identity is imperative, life is a form of morality. Or to put the point less strangely and in a way that has been made more familiar to us by Aristotle, morality is just the form that *human life* takes.

4.3.10

From here the argument proceeds as it did in the case of other people. I won't spell out the details here. Roughly it will look like this: I first point out to you that your animal nature is a fundamental form of identity on which the normativity of your human identity, your moral identity, depends. It is not just as human but considered as sensible, considered as an animal, that you value yourself and are your own end. And this further stretch of reflection requires a further stretch of endorsement. If you don't value your animal nature, you can value nothing. So you must endorse its value. And the reasons and obligations to which your animal

---

[27] Balguy, *The Foundation of Moral Goodness*, part II, pp. 25–26.

identity gives rise are not private reasons. However you bind your-self by those reasons, you can bind and be bound by others as well. So the reasons of other animals are also reasons for you.

When you pity a suffering animal, it is because you are perceiv-ing a reason. An animal's cries express pain, and they mean that there is a reason, a reason to change its condition. And you can no more hear the cries of an animal as mere noise than you can the words of a person. Another animal can obligate you in exactly the same way another person can. It is a way of being *someone* that you share.[28] So of course we have obligations to animals.

4.3.II

In some cases, pain is a *misperception* of a reason: there is no underly-ing malfunction or identity-threatening condition that it signals. In others, there is one, but there is nothing we can do about it: the person, or the animal, is beyond help or cure. Yet in these cases, we are still concerned to alleviate the pain. Someone is dying of an incurable disease; or an animal must be killed – we want to make things as painless as possible for them. If a pain is not a perception of a reason, or if we can do nothing about the reason that it does perceive, is there then no reason to alleviate it? Or if there is one, doesn't that show that I am wrong – that pain is after all intrinsi-cally bad?

A first point is that although such a pain may signal a threat to your physical identity, the pain *itself* threatens the other parts of your identity as well. It is hard to be yourself, to think and react normally, when you are in pain. And the dying (say) want to go on being themselves as long as possible. Here the imperative to pre-serve identity does give rise to a reason to alleviate pain in a straightforward way. But this answer appears to cover only certain cases, and to be primarily concerned with the human case. The real answer, I think, goes a little deeper.

I have suggested that the other animals do not have a reflective consciousness – that they are not, as we are, self-conscious. Nevertheless, it may be said that pain and reasons share a reflective

---

[28] We are, or should be, the most social of all the animals, since we are the ones who can form a conception of what all animals have in common.

structure. A reason is an endorsement of an impulse; a pain is a reaction to a sensation. And when a state has this sort of double structure, or reference to itself, it is *recursive*. An animal which is in pain is objecting to its condition. But it also objects to being in a condition to which it objects. *It is a pain to be in pain.* And that is *not* a trivial fact.

As it is impossible to think without saying to oneself 'I think' so it is nearly impossible to suffer without having the awareness of oneself as suffering. And we object to this as well as to the suffering itself. In the human case, at least, this recursive structure is perfectly clear. Earlier I suggested that as physical pain is a revolt against our sensations, so emotional pains like grief, rage, and disappointment are revolts against the world. And for us, physical pain is almost always accompanied by such emotional pains, for we revolt against the world in which we can be made to feel pain. We experience pain as an assault on the self, and may resent it as if it were an enemy. Now an animal does not quite in this way think about itself when it is in pain. But to the extent that it objects not only to its condition, but to being in an objectionable condition, it has itself in view. It too perceives pain as an assault on the self, and suffers from its suffering.

This is why pain is nearly always bad – because the creatures who suffer from it object to it. But it is important to see that this does not show that pain is an intrinsically bad sensation. For one thing, we don't always object to pain, and this on two levels. First, we don't always object to the sensations that we sometimes call 'pain'. An acute sensation, say, of effort or of appetite will be welcome in one context, unwelcome in another. The sensation of effort when we expect to be successful, or of appetite when we expect to be satisfied, gives relish to an activity; pretty much the same sensations, with no prospect of overcoming in view, may cause a certain panic, and then they will be pains. And sometimes we welcome, not just the sensations to which in other contexts we object, but even pain itself. No one, I suppose, would choose not to experience grief at the death of a loved one at all, although we are rightly afraid of finding it unbearable. We may object to a world in which our loved ones are taken away, but if they are taken away, we do not want to fail to experience the fact, to register it as an evil.

And that is related to the deepest point of all here. The impulse to think that pain is an intrinsically bad sensation springs from a fundamental error about the way in which value is related to consciousness. Value exists in the deliberative perspective, or anyway in the perspective of a conscious agent, but that does not mean that it must be in the mind rather than in the world. When I say that pain is not a reason but rather is the perception of a reason, the utilitarian takes that to mean that pain and pleasure simply bring us information about reasons which exist independently of consciousness and perception themselves. It is as if the utilitarian thinks we have to choose between two views of the relationship between consciousness and value: the utilitarian's own view which holds that value applies directly only to conscious states themselves; and a kind of instrumental view which says that conscious states like pleasure and pain merely bring us information about values which are out there in the world, and which we need only care about if we can do something about them. But both of these views are wrong.

I can only articulate what is wrong here by making a comparison. Being in a pain that signals a condition you can do nothing about is like looking at a picture of something horrifying – a snuff movie, concentration camp photographs. It is bad to look at a picture of something bad, although sometimes we have reason to do so, to face it – but as the case of grief shows, that's also true of pain. The badness of looking at the picture cannot be explained in terms simply of the value of the information that it brings us, for it is bad to look whether or not there is anything we can do about the bad situation which the picture portrays. And this badness normally gives us a reason not to look at the picture. Someone who felt free to enjoy watching a snuff movie, on the grounds that he could no longer do anything to save the person who dies in the movie anyway, would be making a terrible error. But this has no tendency, *none whatsoever*, to show that the badness of looking at the movie is *independent* of the badness of what is portrayed there. We turn away not merely because it pains us, but because of the evil which our pain perceives.[29]

---

[29] I thank Derek Parfit for prompting me to deal with this problem.

4.3.12

According to Aristotle, the soul comes in what we might think of as layers. All life has a nutritive and reproductive soul, a kind of plant soul; animals add a perceptive and locomotive soul; and we add to that a rational soul. Plants, although not sensible, are in a way organized to be their own end. Like animals they have a self-maintaining form. And it is also true that we find it natural to use the language of reason and action about plants. We say that a plant *needs* water, that it *turns* towards the light, even that it is not *happy* in that window and must be moved to another. So do we also have duties to plants?

I don't think so. Since a plant is not conscious, being a plant is not a way of being someone, so it is not a way of being someone that we share with them.[30] (I do not know how to defend that point further.) Still, I can't help thinking that the kind of thing Kant believed about our obligations with regard to natural objects generally is true of our obligations with regard to plants. Kant thought that we have no duty *to* other things found in nature, but that we have duties with regard to them, to treat them in ways that show a sensitivity to the fact that they are alive (in the case of plants and animals) and beautiful (Kant's example is 'beautiful crystal formations'). He thought that these duties are really grounded in a general duty not to do things which will have a bad effect on our own characters.[31] This is an inadequate account of our obligations to animals, but it seems to me to be right in the case of plants. Is it crazy to say that there is something amiss with someone who destroys plant life wantonly, or who can see a plant drooping but still alive without wanting to give it a drink? Such a person shows a lack of the reverence of life which is the basis of all value.[32]

---

[30] It may also matter that they are harder to individuate than animals: their criteria of identity are less well-defined.

[31] See Kant, *The Metaphysics of Morals*, pp. 442–443; in Gregor's translation, pp. 237–238; and the *Lectures on Ethics*, pp. 239–241.

[32] In the current climate of opinion it is worth mentioning that I do not take the claim that reverence for life is the basis of value to imply that abortion and euthanasia are always wrong. I cannot go into these complex topics here, although I will say something about suicide and by implication euthanasia in the final section.

4.3.13

Do the animals have obligations to us? The idea is absurd. They are not reflective, they do not construct or endorse their identities. They don't even know that they have them. They just have them. But now suppose we ask the question this way: can we obligate them? Then it is not so clear.

Your dog is sniffing around some other dog, and you don't want him to do that. So you call him. He looks at you, and then looks away, and goes on investigating the other dog. You then call him loudly, in a more commanding tone, and he comes. His reluctance is visible, but he comes. So what happened? He didn't want to come, and you didn't literally force him, say by dragging on the leash. Yet he had to come. Isn't this a case of obligation? Didn't he do what he didn't want to do, because you are a law to him?

Now you will want to protest that of course this is not a case of obligation. It is a case of domination. We know how this works. A dog is a social animal, who lives in a pack characterized by structures of hierarchy and domination. You train a dog by making him regard you as his pack leader. So it's not that you obligate him. It is just that you dominate him.

Now that is like saying that the reason we are inclined to do what other people ask us to do is that we are susceptible to social pressure. It isn't exactly false, but it's a completely external description of the situation. It's what the whole thing looks like from outside, not what it looks like from the animal's own point of view. From the person's own point of view, or the animal's own point of view, pressure and domination have a shape, a form. And that form is the form of normativity – it is the form of law.

4.3.14

The world of social animals is characterized by elaborate structures of hierarchy and domination. Although the ability to dominate does have to do with strength and prowess, it is not related to it in an obvious way. When two animals battle for dominance, the battle may be highly ritualized, and often the losing party is not at all injured. It is a battle of wills.

Both Nietzsche and Freud believed that morality and the special character of human consciousness emerged simultaneously in the evolution of our species. Since I have grounded morality in the special character of human consciousness – in particular, in its reflective nature – I take these accounts to be harmonious with my view. Both also believed that the special character of human consciousness arose when the impulse to dominate – the will to power, or the aggressive instincts – were deprived of any outlet and turned against the self.[33] An intelligent, wilful animal, held captive and punished by others, was not permitted to be aggressive. And having nothing else to dominate, it turned these instincts inward, and learned to dominate itself. And in that way reflective distance and the autonomy that goes with it came into being. Nietzsche describes it in this way:

All instincts that do not discharge themselves outwardly turn inward – this is what I call the *internalization* of man: thus it was that man first developed what was later called his 'soul'. The entire inner world, originally as thin as if it were stretched between two membranes, expanded and extended itself, acquired depth, breadth, and height, in the same measure as outward discharge was inhibited.[34]

The only way to prevent an aggressive animal from behaving aggressively is to punish it – that is, to inflict pain on it. And this is not like the pain that arises naturally in the life of an animal, when nature and circumstance threaten its physical identity, and it finds it must revolt against the threat. This pain is imposed from without, when the animal is acting naturally, that is, doing what is made imperative by the identity it naturally has. So this pain, the pain of punishment, forces the animal to revolt against its own identity. And then for the first time it says to itself: I should be different from what I am, and it experiences guilt. And that is the origin of normative thought. Nietzsche warns us:

One should guard against thinking lightly of this phenomenon merely on account of its initial painfulness and ugliness . . . this entire *active* 'bad conscience' . . . as the womb of all ideal and imaginative phenomena, also brought to light an abundance of strange new beauty and affirmation,

---

[33] See for example Nietzsche, *The Genealogy of Morals*, essay ii; and Freud, *Civilization and Its Discontents*, chapter vii.
[34] Nietzsche, *The Genealogy of Morals*, ii.16, p. 84.

and perhaps beauty itself – After all, what would be 'beautiful' if the contradiction had not first become conscious of itself, if the ugly had not first said to itself: 'I am ugly?'[35]

Despite this admonition, Nietzsche did think that the achievements of the bad conscience had been bought at a price, and Freud, who saw this process recapitulated in the life of every human child, agreed with him that there were grounds for concern. Roughly speaking, they both believed that the psychic structures that give rise to our ability to control our natural impulses are subject to a natural dynamic that causes guilt to escalate, so that the better we become, the more guilt we will feel. The morally good human being comes to feel guilty even about *having* natural impulses and *being* an animal. Eventually this leads to extreme self-hatred, which in turn produces a revolt against the world of nature, and a hatred of life itself, and finally ends in complete nihilistic collapse. If value begins with the fact that an animal is its own end and in a sense values itself, then the bad conscience that leads us to hate ourselves and our animal nature ends by undermining all value.[36]

But it is absurd to think that either Nietzsche or Freud supposed we could simply go back. The moral revolution that Nietzsche hoped and called for was not a return to the state of the aggressive brute, but a second internalization which would turn the bad conscience against itself the way the first internalization turned the animal against itself.[37] The result would be what Nietzsche called the superman, a being whose consciousness is as different from our own as ours is from that of the other animals, a being whose inner life we can no more imagine than they can imagine ours.

It is a strange proposal. I have not brought up these ideas in order to agree or disagree with Nietzsche and Freud's worries about humanity's ability to tolerate itself. Their specific claims about the natural dynamic of guilt would have to be examined in more detail, and perhaps in a more scientific way, than I can do here. They lived in priggish times, and the problem may have been more local than they thought. As I pointed out earlier, there are

[35] Nietzsche, *The Genealogy of Morals*, ii.18, pp. 87–88.
[36] This last is of course more Nietzsche than Freud; I think it is what he meant when he suggested that value might fail a self-critique.
[37] See especially *The Genealogy of Morals*, essay ii, section 24.

limits to the depth of obligation, because we know that we can maintain our identities in a general way without at each and every moment being ourselves. It is easy to imagine how this fact, properly deployed, could have therapeutic value. After all, we deploy it whenever we laugh at ourselves, and that has therapeutic value. Maybe a little distance is all we need to keep obligation from getting out of control.

That isn't exactly an alternative to Nietzsche's idea. In one way it is just what he had in mind – that we get a little control over our own self-control. Just as reflective distance gave us control over our animal nature, so maybe reflective distance from our self-control could give us control over it. So this is pretty much the same as Nietzsche's idea, only a more local and occasional version of it, and one which does not offer to turn us into supermen after all. You may think that a loss or a gain as you like.

What I wanted from these views was simply this. Nietzsche and Freud have provided us with a powerful account of how the distinctive features of human conscience and consciousness could have evolved in a natural world of animals. You can see them as trying to explain how obligation ever emerged, a source of normativity in a different, genealogical, sense. The account I have given of what obligation is and where it comes from is harmonious with theirs. And I take this to be a point in its favour.

SCEPTICISM AND SUICIDE

4.4.1

In one sense, the account of obligation which I have given in these lectures is naturalistic. It grounds normativity in certain natural – that is, psychological and biological – facts. I have traced the normativity of obligation to the fact of reflective consciousness and the apparent normativity of pain to the fact of simple consciousness, together with the nature of an animal. My account does not depend on the existence of supernatural beings or non-natural facts, and it is consistent with although not part of the Scientific World View. In that sense, it is a form of naturalism.

But in another sense it is not. In another sense, a naturalistic view identifies normative truth with factual truth. It says, for instance, that pain is intrinsically bad, and therefore the fact that someone is in pain is a reason to do something about it. I have not quite said that. Certainly I am not saying that reflective endorsement – I mean the bare *fact* of reflective endorsement – is enough to make an action right. For in one sense no human action can happen without reflective endorsement. When people skip reflection or stop too soon, that is a kind of endorsement, for it implies that the work of reflection is done. So if reflective endorsement made an action right, there would be a sense in which every action was right. This is once again the problem of normative naturalism. There is no normativity if you cannot be wrong.

When we describe pleasure, or pain, or reflective endorsement or rejection from outside of consciousness, third-personally, they are merely facts. It is in standpoint created by consciousness, when you are *in* pain, or find yourself obligated, that value lives. We *have* reasons in the way we *have* experiences and sensations, not as the possession of mental entities, but as a fact about what it is like to be conscious, about what it is like to be *us*. It is because the standpoint created by consciousness can be made public by language or sympathy that reasons and values can be shared. But that kind of publicity is still inside the reflective standpoint. From outside of that standpoint, we can recognize the fact of value, but we cannot recognize value itself.

So there is something left of the fact/value distinction, although it isn't much. The fact of value isn't value itself – it is merely a fact. But it is a fact of life. In fact, it is *the* fact of life. It is the natural condition of living things to be valuers, and that is why value exists.

4.4.2

If value is the fact of life, then a rejection of all value takes the form of a rejection of life. The most straightforward expression of complete practical normative scepticism would therefore be a form of suicide. Of course not every case of suicide is like this: I believe that there can be good reasons for committing suicide. As I mentioned at the beginning of these lectures, most people would rather die than completely lose their identities, and there are various ways to do that. Violating your own essential principles, failing to meet your deepest obligations, is the one that has been the subject of these lectures, but there are others over which we have less control. The ravages of severe illness, disability, and pain can shatter your identity by destroying its physical basis, obliterating memory or making self-command impossible. Suicide, in such cases, may be the only way to preserve your identity, and to protect the values for which you have lived.

But there is another kind of suicide, the kind I have in mind here, which people commit because they feel that they themselves are worthless and, as a result, that life has no meaning and nothing is of value. Some philosophers and religious thinkers have thought that this kind of suicide is immoral, but the immorality here, if we can even call it that, is deeper than the usual kind. For this kind of suicide is not the denial of this or that value, but rather the denial of value itself. And this is a thought that several of the thinkers who have occupied these pages have shared. In a discussion of the person who commits suicide because he can see neither reason nor meaning in anything, Bernard Williams says: 'I do not see how it could be regarded as a defeat for reason or rationality that it had no power against this man's state; his state is rather a defeat for humanity'.[38] The duty not to commit suicide is the very first and most basic duty of virtue Kant discusses in *The Metaphysics of Morals*, because 'To annihilate the subject of morality in one's own person is to root out the existence of morality itself from the world.'[39] In his *Notebooks*, Wittgenstein wrote that 'suicide is, so to speak, the elementary sin' because 'If suicide is allowed then everything is allowed. If anything is not allowed then suicide is not allowed'. A few lines later he adds, 'Or is even suicide in itself neither good nor evil?'[40] All of these philosophers give voice to the idea that remaining alive is not so much a value as a condition of all value; and suicide (of this type) is not so much a rejection of some particular value as it is a rejection of value itself. It is hard to say of one who commits such suicide that he has done wrong, for he has

[38] Williams, *Morality: an Introduction to Ethics*, p. 2.
[39] Kant, *The Metaphysics of Morals*, pp. 422–423; in Gregor's translation, pp. 218–219.
[40] Wittgenstein, *Notebooks, 1914–1916*, p. 91; the passage was pointed out to me by Peter Hylton.

violated no value in which he still believes. And yet the rest of us cannot hear of such a case without feeling betrayed, and we are right. It is, as Williams says, a defeat for us all.

In these lectures I have argued that moral obligation and moral value are a condition of all obligation and of all value. The price of denying that humanity is of value is complete practical normative scepticism. The argument is, if successful, a reply to the *moral* sceptic, one who thinks he can value *something* without acknowledging the force of moral obligation. But I have not shown that *complete* practical normative scepticism is impossible. Is there an argument against that kind of scepticism, a reason not to commit suicide? In one sense, the right reply is that there can't be, since life itself is the source of reasons. In another sense, the right reply is that this is not an issue to be settled by philosophical argument alone. It really does depend: it depends on what we do with our lives, as individuals, and on what we do with the world, as a species. There is no way to put the point that is not paradoxical: value only exists if life is worth living, and that depends on what we do.

Does the normative sceptic *have* to commit suicide? No, of course not. There is nothing the normative sceptic *has* to do. But it is worth remembering what an extreme position complete practical normative scepticism is. The normative sceptic has no reason for doing anything. He does have some desires and impulses, of course – those are to some extent supplied by nature – but he has no reason for acting on one rather than another. No doubt what he will do, if he goes on living, is to follow the desire of the moment, at least if such a thing is clearly discernible. It is obvious that he cannot be guided by categorical imperatives. And although it is less obvious, it is also true that he cannot be guided by hypothetical imperatives. A hypothetical imperative tells us to take the means to our ends, but the practical normative sceptic does not really have any *ends*, since his desires do not provide him with reasons. He does have *desires*, of course, and he may indeed be motivated to take the means to the satisfaction of the desire that prevails at the moment. But this is not, strictly speaking, to follow the hypothetical imperative, for desires, in the absence of reflective endorsement, do not, strictly speaking, determine ends in the sense needed for the hypothetical imperative – things we have reason to pursue. To see this, let's suppose that desires by themselves do determine ends. Then the hypothetical imperative tells you to do what will satisfy your desire, the desire that prevails at the moment. Now suppose that the hypothetical imperative tells you to do one thing, but that you have a desire to do something else instead. Then you will do that other thing, and you will not be wrong. For if your end is just the object of your prevailing desire, and all that the hypothetical imperative says to do is what will satisfy your prevailing desire – well, that's what you are doing. If ends are the objects of prevailing desires, then whatever you do will *count* as pursuing your end, and you cannot be wrong. But as I have argued repeatedly, there is no normativity if you cannot be wrong.[41] So the hypothetical imperative is not, for the sceptic, a normative principle. Since he cannot violate it, he cannot follow it either.

Practical normative scepticism is the view that there is no such thing as rational action. And there really is a sense in which, being human, and as long as we go on living, we *have to* engage in rational action. Animal action, unreflective action, is not open to us; and yet we must do something. So does the normative sceptic, after all, have to commit suicide? There is no way to put the point that is not paradoxical: yes and no.

CONCLUSION

4.5.1

I hope by now it is clear that all of the accounts of normativity which I have discussed in these lectures are true.

Voluntarists like Pufendorf and Hobbes held that normativity must spring from the commands of a legislator. A good legislator commands us to do only what is in any case a good idea to do, but the bare fact that an action is a good idea cannot make it a requirement. For that, it must be made law by someone in a position to command us.

As we saw, that view is true. What it describes is the relation in

---

[41] I think that this shows that the view that there are only hypothetical imperatives is not only false, but incoherent. I have argued for this at greater length in 'The Normativity of Instrumental Reason'.

which we stand to ourselves. The fact that we must act in the light of reflection gives us a double nature. The thinking self has the power to command the acting self, and it is only its command that can make action obligatory. A good thinking self commands the acting self only to do what is good, but the acting self must in any case do what it says.

4.5.2

Realists like Nagel think that reasons are intrinsically normative entities, and that what we should do when a desire presets itself is to look at it more objectively, to see whether it is such an entity. This view is also true. What it describes is the activity of the thinking self as it assesses the impulses that present themselves to us, the legislative proposals of our nature.

4.5.3

Reflection has the power to compel obedience, and to punish us for disobedience. It in turn is bound to govern us by laws that are good. Together these facts yield the conclusion that the relation of the thinking self to the acting self is the relation of legitimate authority. That is to say, the necessity of acting in the light of reflection makes us authorities over ourselves. And in so far as we have authority over ourselves, we can make laws for ourselves, and those laws will be normative. So Kant's view is also true. Autonomy is the source of obligation.

4.5.4

Once we see this, we can see that the reflective endorsement theory is true on another level as well. In the end, nothing can be normative unless we endorse our own nature, unless we place a value upon ourselves. Reflection reveals to us that the normativity of our values springs from the fact that we are animals of a certain kind, autonomous moral animals. That is, in the Aristotelian sense, our human form.

4.5.5

That means that realism is true on another level as well. To see this, recall once again John Mackie's famous 'argument from queerness'.[42] According to Mackie, it is fantastic to think that the world contains objective values, or intrinsically normative entities. For in order to do what values do, they would have to meet certain impossible criteria. They would have to be entities of a very strange sort, utterly unlike anything else in the universe. The way that we know them would have to be different from the way that we know other sorts of facts. Knowledge of them, Mackie said, would have to provide the knower with both a direction and a motive. For when you met an objective value, according to Mackie, it would have to be – and I'm nearly quoting now – able both to tell you what to do and make you do it. And nothing is like that.

But Mackie is wrong and realism is right. Of course there are entities that meet these criteria. It's true that they are queer sorts of entities, and that knowing them isn't like anything else. But that doesn't mean that they don't exist. John Mackie must have been alone in his room with the Scientific World View when he wrote those words. For it is the most familiar fact of human life that the world contains entities that can tell us what to do and make us do it. They are people, and the other animals.

[42] See lecture 1, section 1.4.5.

Reason, humanity, and the moral law

G. A. Cohen

I

You might think that, if you make a law, then that law binds you, *because* you made it. For, if you will the law, then how can you deny that it binds you, without contradicting your own will? But you might also think the opposite. You might think that, if you are the author of the law, then it *cannot* bind you. For how can it have authority over you when you have authority over it? How can it *bind* you when you, the law*maker*, can change it, at will, whenever you like?

Now, in that pair of arguments mutually contradictory conclusions are drawn from the selfsame premiss: the premiss that you make the law. So at least one of the arguments is invalid. But, even if they are *both* invalid, they might still be unignorable, because they might have elements of truth in them. They might be healthy argument-embryos out of which sound arguments could develop. And, whatever else is true, each of the arguments is sufficiently persuasive that, mutually contradictory though they are, each was affirmed in Hobbes's *Leviathan*, in much the form in which I just stated them.

There are, by my count, four arguments in Hobbes for the conclusion that the citizen is obliged to obey the law. Three of the arguments don't matter here.[1] The one that matters here has two premises, the first of which is that every act of the sovereign is an act of each citizen, since 'every man gives their common repre-

---

[1] They are: (1) the consequentialist argument that the state of nature is intolerable; (2) the argument of hypothetical consent: any rational person would agree to submit to government, and (3) the argument of actual consent: all citizens in fact agree to submit to government.

senter authority from himself in particular; and owning all the actions the representer doth, in case they give him authority without stint', and there is, of course, no stint in the authority Hobbesian people give their sovereign. Accordingly, 'the subject is the author of every act the Sovereign doth'.[2]

Having thus possessed himself of the premiss that I am the author of what the sovereign does, hence of each law he enacts, Hobbes now enters his second premiss, which is that it is absurd for me to object to what I myself do. Accordingly, it is absurd for me to object to any law that I pass, and I must therefore, on pain of absurdity, obey the sovereign's law.[3] I must obey it because I made it.

Now you might think that, if I am subject to the law *because* I make it, not, albeit, directly, but through my representative, then that representative himself, the sovereign, is equally or even *a fortiori* subject to the law, because *he* makes it, and, indeed, makes it more directly than I do. But that is not Hobbes's inference. Not only does Hobbes not infer, using the same reasoning that he used in the case of the citizen, which should, it seems also apply to the sovereign, that the latter *is* subject to the law he makes; but Hobbes concludes, oppositely, that the sovereign is *not* subject to the law. And the reason that Hobbes gives for that conclusion is the very same one as the reason that he gives for concluding that the citizen *is* subject to the law, to wit that he, the sovereign, *makes* the law. Here is what Hobbes says:

---

[2] *Leviathan*, pp. 221, 265, cf. p. 276.
[3] Step-wise, the argument runs as follows:
    What the sovereign does, I do.
But The sovereign makes the law.
So   I make the law.
Now, It is absurd to object to what I myself do.
So   I cannot object to the law.
So   I must obey the law.

In a different version of the argument, which Hobbes also gives, the further premiss is not that I cannot object to what I myself do but that I cannot 'injure' (that is, do an injustice to) myself. The argument then runs as follows:
    What the sovereign does, I do.
But A man cannot injured himself.
So   The sovereign does not injure me.
So   I cannot object to what the sovereign requires of me.
So   I must obey the sovereign.

to those laws which the Soveraign himselfe, that is, which the Common-wealth maketh, he is not subject. For to be subject to Lawes, is to be subject to the Common-wealth, that is to the Sovereign Representative, that is to himself; which is not subjection, but freedom from the Lawes.

The Sovereaign of a Common-wealth, be it an assembly, or one man, is not subject to the civil laws. For having power to make, and repeal laws, he may when he pleaseth, free himself from that subjection, by repealing those laws that trouble him, and making of new; and consequently he was free before. For he is free, that can be free when he will: Nor is it possible for any person to be bound to himself; because he that can bind, can release; and therefore he that is bound to himself only, is not bound.[4]

This argument says (in the fuller version of it to be found in the second quoted passage, and very slightly reconstructed):

The sovereign makes the law.
So The sovereign can unmake the law.
So The sovereign is not bound by the law that he makes.

Hobbes claims that, when the citizen violates the law, he contradicts his own will: he, in the person of the sovereign, made the law, and therefore cannot without absurdity violate it. Yet it is precisely because the sovereign makes the law that he is *not* bound by it: according to Hobbes, it is conceptually impossible for him to violate it.

There is no inconsistency in the idea that two make the one law, for one makes as author what the other makes as representative of that author. But it cannot follow from 'X makes the law' both that X is subject to it and that X is not subject to it. You cannot say both: because you make the law, you must obey it; and: because you make the law, it has no authority over you, so you need not obey it. The inference of the argument about the citizen requires the principle that, if I make the law, then I am bound by it. The inference of the argument about the sovereign requires the principle that, if I make the law, then I am not bound by it. At least one of those principles must be wrong.

Now, the truth of this whole matter is complicated, but the parts of it that concern us here seems to me to be this. I pass a law. Either

<hr />

[4] *Leviathan*, pp. 367, 313; and see *De Cive*, XII.4, XI.14.

the law says that everyone must act thus and so, or its scope is restricted to, say, everyone except me. If the latter is true, then I am clearly not obliged to obey the law: so the first point to make about the first argument is that the terms of the law need to be specified before the inference in that argument can be examined.

Suppose, then, that the law is indeed universal, or that it includes me within its scope by virtue of some other semantic or pragmatic feature of it. Then, if I had the authority to legislate it, it indeed binds me, as long as I do not repeal it. (It remains unclear, even then, that it binds me *because*, if I violate it, I contradict my will: so the kernel of truth in the first argument may be quite a small one.) The necessity to add that rider reflects the important element of truth in the argument about the sovereign, which is also incorrect in its unmodified form. The big mistake in that argument is the supposition that if I *can* repeal the law, then it fails to bind me even when I have not *yet* repealed it. Hobbes is wrong that, if you can free yourself at will, then you are already free, that 'he is free, that can be free when he will'. But other important things do follow from my being able to be free myself at will, for example, that I cannot complain about my unfreedom. And, more pertinently to our theme, although you may be bound by a law that you can change, the fact that you can change it diminishes the significance of the fact that you are bound by it. There's not much 'must' in a 'must' that you can readily get rid of.

2

In Christine Korsgaard's ethics, the subject of the law is also its author: and that is the ground of the subject's obligation – that *it* is the author of the law that obliges it. That sounds like Hobbes's first argument. So we should ask a question inspired by Hobbes's second argument, the one about the sovereign: how can the subject be responsible to a law that it makes and can therefore unmake? As we know, Korsgaard's answer relates to the circumstance that the subject has a practical identity.

Now Korsgaard's ethics descends from Kant, but it contrasts in important ways with Kant's ethics. Korsgaard's subject is unequiv-ocally the author of the law that binds it, for its law is the law of *its* practical identity, and the subject itself '*constructs*' that identity. But in Kant the position is more equivocal. We can say that the Kantian subject both is and is not the author of the law that binds it. There is an important duality with respect to the source of the law in the following characteristic text from the *Grundlegung*. In previous moral philosophy, Kant says:

Man was seen to be bound to laws by his duty, but it was not seen that he is subject to his own, *but still universal*, legislation, and that he is bound to act only in accordance with his own will, which is, however, *designed by nature to be a will giving universal law*. For if one thought of him as *only* subject to a law . . . this necessarily implied some interest as a stimulus or compulsion to obedience because the law did not arise from his own will. Rather his will had to be constrained by something else to act in a certain way. This might be his own interest or that of another, but in either case the imperative always had to be conditional, and could not at all serve as a moral command. The moral principle I will call the principle of *autonomy* of the will in contrast to all other principles which I accordingly count under *heteronomy*.[5]

Kant thought that if the moral law came *just* from my own will, then it would have no claim on me, rather as the law of the sovereign has none over the sovereign in Hobbes. If, on the other hand, the law was *just* externally imposed, and did *not* come from my own will, then it would be heteronomous slavery for me to obey it, and the challenging argument that Hobbes uses about the citizen, that he must obey the law because it is his *own* law, he must obey it on pain of inconsistency, would not be available. So the passage I've exhibited, while stating that man is subject to his *own* law, and bound to act only in accordance with his *own* will, is quick to add that man's legislation, though his own, is still universal, emanating from a will 'designed by nature to be a will giving universal law'. And that makes Kant's person different from Hobbes's sovereign. Kant's person indeed makes the law, but he cannot unmake it, for he is designed by nature to make it as he does, and what he is designed to make has the inherent authority of reason as such. So Hobbes's sovereignty argument does not apply, and Kant can stay with the citizen argument. He can give the citizen argument for

---

[5] *Foundations of the Metaphysics of Morals*, pp. 49–50, my emphases, except on 'autonomy' and 'heteronomy'. All further references below to the *Grundlegung* are signalled by 'Beck'.

obedience and rebut the sovereignty argument for freedom from law by pointing out that *this* law is *not* one that the agent can unmake. In the moral realm, we are, Kant says, 'subjects . . . not sovereigns'.[6]

So the Hobbesian reflection about the sovereign and the law sheds light on Kant's insistence that the imperative of morals must not come from *human* nature, nor even from human *reason*, should there be any respect in which human reason differs from reason as such. For it is reason as such that is sovereign over us, and that gives determinacy, stability, and authority to a law that would otherwise lack all that: 'the ground of obligation must not be sought in the nature of man . . . but a priori solely in the concepts of pure reason'.[7] 'For with what right could we bring into unlimited respect something that might be valid only under contingent human conditions?'[8] And

whatever is derived from the particular natural situation of man as such, or from certain feelings and propensities, or even from a particular tendency of human reason which might not hold necessarily for the will of every rational being (if such a tendency is possible), can give a maxim valid for us but not a law . . . This is so far the case that the sublimity and intrinsic worth of the command is the better shown in a duty the fewer subjective causes there are for it and the more there are against it.[9]

Since Kant was certain that to root the moral law exclusively in human nature was to derogate from its authority, Korsgaard is not entirely right when she says that

Kant, like Hume and Williams, thinks that morality is grounded in human nature, and that moral properties are projections of human dispositions.[10]

For Korsgaard, morality *is* grounded in human nature,[11] and that difference between her and Kant is consequential here, for Kant

---

[6] *Critique of Practical Reason*, p. 85:

> We are indeed legislative members of a moral realm which is possible through freedom and which is presented to us as an object of respect by practical reason; yet we are at the same time subjects in it, not sovereigns, and to mistake our inferior positions as creatures and to deny, from self-conceit, respect to the holy law is, in spirit, a defection from it even if its letter be fulfilled.

[7] *Foundations*, p. 5.   [8] *Ibid.*, p. 24.

[9] *Ibid.*, p. 42 cf. pp. 28, 65; and *Critique of Practical Reason*, p. 19.

[10] 3.1.1.   [11] See, for example, 4.4.1.

has a ready answer to Hobbes's argument about the sovereign, whereas Korsgaard may have no answer to it, because she has abandoned the element of Kant that transcends merely human nature. She appears to agree with the insistence she attributes to Pufendorf and Hobbes, that the only possible source of obligation, not of its being good or sensible or beneficial or desirable that you do something, but of your *having* to do it, is that you are ordered to do it by a lawgiver. No 'ought' without law and no law without a lawgiver. Korsgaard affirms all that,[12] but she adds that the only person 'in a position' to give that law is the self-commanding self. Accordingly, to secure the binding force of law, Korsgaard has to have a way of answering Hobbes's second argument, and she does not have Kant's way.

If Hobbes's position can be rendered consistent, if he can bind the citizen to obey while nevertheless freeing the sovereign from all duty of obedience, then legislating *qua* sovereign must for some reason *not* be self-binding whereas legislating through a sovereign representative *is*. But Korsgaard's persons are autonomous self-legislators: no delegation or representation occurs here. Accordingly, it is hard to see how anything becomes a law for them that they *must* obey. So Korsgaard can maintain the authority of the law over its subject legislator neither in Kant's way nor in the just hypothesized revisionist Hobbesian way.

Suppose I ask: *why* should I obey myself? Who am *I*, anyway, to issue a command to *me*?[13] Kant can answer that question. He can say that, although you *legislate* the law, the content of the law comes

---

[12] See her conclusion, 4.5.1. Korsgaard's claim that the solution to the problem of normativity *must* be imperativist puzzles me. She brings out, brilliantly, the difference between doing logic because of its merits as a subject and doing it because it is a required course (1.3.3, 3.3.4), but why isn't it good enough if our reason for being moral is as good as the one a person has for doing logic where that *isn't* a required course? This question relates to the point that morality is a choice within rationality, not a requirement of it: see section 5 below.

[13] Korsgaard rejects Pufendorfian voluntarism, remarking that 'the very notion of a legitimate authority is already a normative one and cannot be used to answer the normative question' (1.4.1). In her own answer to that question, *I* am the legislating will, so *I* must possess legitimate authority for my legislation to be valid. Does it follow, in a defeating way, that I cannot cite *my own* legitimate authority any more than Pufendorf can cite God's, by way of answer to the normative question? I *think* that Korsgaard's answer would be that I *must* have authority for me, in virtue of some or all of the argumentation that I discuss in section 7 below.

from reason, not from anything special about you, or *your* reason, or even *human* reason, but from reason as such. And, when that is so, then, perhaps, reflective endorsement of the law is inescapable. But if the content of the law reflects *my* nature, my engagements and commitments, then could I not *change* its content? Trafficking at the human level as she does, Korsgaard must say that my practical identity, with which the law is bound up, is inescapable, but one may doubt both that there is a special connection between morality and practical identity and that practical identity is inescapable. One may therefore doubt that Korsgaard can achieve her goal, which, so I read it, is to keep the 'must' that Kant put into morality while humanizing morality's source.[14]

I have said that, for Korsgaard, morality is rooted in human nature. But at one place Korsgaard says the somewhat different thing, that 'value is grounded in rational nature – in particular in the structure of reflective consciousness – and it is projected on to the world'.[15] But rational nature, if it means the nature of reason, is different from human nature, at least for Kant, and Korsgaard returns us to the fully human when she adds the gloss referring to the structure of reflective consciousness, for, as she will surely not deny, all manner of all-too-human peculiarities can gain strength in reflective consciousness. Kant can say that you must be moral on pain of irrationality. Korsgaard cannot say that.

3

What Korsgaard says, instead, is that you must be moral on pain of sacrificing your practical identity, which is to say, who you are from a practical point of view. You act morally because you could not live with yourself, 'it could be . . . worse than death', if you did not.[16]

But I find it very difficult to put together the motif of practical identity with the emphasis on law that Korsgaard takes from Hobbes and Pufendorf and, especially, Kant. *If* morality is to do with law, then the liaison between morality and practical identity is question-

---

[14] For further comment on Korsgaard's project, so conceived, see the final paragraph of the present article.   [15] 3.4.3.   [16] See 1.2.2.

able, since the commitments that form my practical identity need not be to things that have the *universality* characteristic of law. Practical identity is a matter of loyalty and identification, and whereas there is indeed such a thing as loyalty to general principles, there also exists loyalty to family, to group, to another individual; and no credible characterization of what practical identity is, in general terms, would yield a general priority for principled over particularistic identifications. Being Jewish plays a role in my practical identity, and so does being a Fellow of All Souls. But neither of those features signifies an attachment for me *because* I believe some principle that says: cleave to the ethnic group to which you belong, or to the College that was sufficiently gracious to receive you. As Bernard Williams famously said, if I save my wife not *just* because she is my wife, but because I believe that husbands in general have special obligations to their wives, then I act on 'one thought too many'.[17]

My sacrifice for a person need not come from a general belief about right and wrong, but from solidarity with that person, and not because of characteristics which she and I have and which are such that, where characteristics of that kind obtain, solidarity is always required. I might find it hard to live with myself if I gave nothing to Oxfam, which is for me a matter of principle, but I would find it harder still to live with myself if I gave to Oxfam instead of paying for the operation that my mother needs. It does not distinguish my moral from my other commitments[18] that if I resile on my principled ones I prejudice my practical identity.[19]

Korsgaard writes:

> The reflective structure of human consciousness requires that you identify yourself with some law or principle which will govern your choices. It requires you to be a law to yourself. And that is the source of normativity. So the argument shows just what Kant said that it did: that our autonomy is the source of obligation.[20]

---

[17] 'Persons, Character, and Morality', in *Moral Luck*, p. 18.

[18] And – see p. 177 below – it is not even true of all of my moral ones, any more than it is true of all of my non-moral ones.

[19] For a sensitive defence of the claim that one can act unselfishly for the sake of a collective to which one belongs, and other than for reasons of principle, see Andrew Oldenquist, 'Loyalties'. For an illuminating application of the point to Marx on proletarian solidarity, see the section on 'Morality' in Richard Miller's *Analyzing Marx*, especially pp. 63–76; see also, in the same connection, Frederick Whelan, 'Marx and Revolutionary Virtue', in J. R. Pennock and J. W. Chapman (eds.), *Marxism*, pp. 64–65.   [20] 3.3.3.

The reflective structure of human consciousness may require, as Korsgaard says, following Harry Frankfurt, that, on pain of reducing myself to the condition of a wanton, I endorse the first-order impulses on which I act, that, as we say, I *identify* myself with them. But it does not follow, and it is not true, that the structure of my consciousness requires that I identify myself with some law or principle. I do not do that when I identify myself with the impulse to save my own drowning child. What the reflective structure requires, if anything, is not that I be a law to myself, but that I be in command of myself. And sometimes the commands that I issue will be singular, not universal. If, as Korsgaard says, 'the necessity of acting in the light of reflection makes us authorities over ourselves', then we exercise that authority not only in making laws but also in issuing singular edicts that mean as much to us as general principles do.[21]

Using Richard Hare's terms, we can say that Korsgaard's solution is imperativist or prescriptive, but not universally prescriptive. And whether or not the moral *must* be law-like *if* it is prescriptive, Korsgaard says that it is law-like, yet it is just not true that every claim on me that survives reflection is, or, presupposes, a law.

Korsgaard remarks that, if she calls out my name, and I do not stop, then I am rebelling against her.[22] She then asks 'But why should you *have* to rebel against me?' Why should my failure to stop *count* as rebellion? Her answer is that 'It is because I am a law to you. By calling out your name, I have obligated you. I have given you a reason to stop.' Well, suppose we accept that, just by calling out my name, you've given me a reason to stop. I think that could be regarded as extravagant (maybe you've (also) given me a reason to speed up), but suppose we accept it. Then, even so, what you have given me is no law but just an order, a singular order lacking the universality of law.

Now whether or not morality is, as Korsgaard thinks, a matter of law, it is false that whatever I do for fear of compromising my practical identity counts as moral, and also false that whatever counts as

---

[21] Korsgaard's text continues (4.5.3): 'And in so far as we have authority over ourselves, we can make laws for ourselves and those laws will be normative.' Yes, we *can* makes laws in exercise of our authority, if, indeed, we have it. But, as I've just protested, we can do other relevant things too, in exercise of that (supposed) authority.   [22] 4.2.7.

moral is done for fear of compromising identity. It is a huge exaggeration to say, as Korsgaard does, that 'an obligation always takes the form of a reaction against a threat of a loss of identity'.[23] I could remain me, both in the evident banal sense and in every pertinent non-banal sense, if I gave nothing to help the distant dying who oppress my conscience. I just wouldn't *feel* very good about myself. And I might even say, in morose reflection: 'how typical of me, to be so bloody selfish'. And I might lose my grip on myself if I suddenly found myself being very philanthropic. So, this is not Korsgaard's point that my identity is solid enough to withstand a measure of wrongdoing that contradicts it.[24] This is the different point that plenty of what I do that I regard as wrong does not challenge my identity at all.

4

Korsgaard provides two (entirely compatible) characterizations of the problem of normativity, one general and unexceptionable, and the other more specific and of a sort which makes the problem so difficult that it seems impossible to solve. With the hard version of the problem in hand, she finds it easy to dismiss rival solutions to it. I shall argue that, if we press the problem in its harder form against her own solution, then it too fails. But I shall also hypothesize that the resources of Korsgaard's solution might be used to produce an interesting candidate for solving the normative problem if we characterize that problem differently, but not altogether differently, from the way she does.

Introducing the problem, Korsgaard says that what 'we want to understand' is 'the normative dimension', which is that 'ethical standards . . . make *claims* on us: they command, oblige recommend, or guide. Or at least, when we invoke them, we make claims on one another.'[25] The question is: 'Why should I be moral?' 'We are asking what *justifies* the claims that morality makes on us. This is what I am calling "the normative question".'[26]

Korsgaard lists three conditions which the answer to the normative question must meet. First, it must 'succeed in *addressing*'

---

[23] 3.3.2.   [24] 3.3.2, 4.3.14.   [25] I.I.I.   [26] *Ibid.*

someone who is in 'the first-person position of the agent who demands a justification of the claims which morality makes upon him'. Consequently, and this is the second condition, a successful normative theory must meet the condition of 'transparency': when I know what justifies my acting as required, I must 'believe that [my] actions are justified and make sense'. Third, 'the answer must appeal, in a deep way, to our sense of who we are, to our sense of our identity . . . [Moral claims] . . . must issue in a deep way from our sense of who we are.'[27]

I shall concentrate, in section 5, on the first condition, that the answer to the normative question must address the agent who asks it, for, as I shall argue, Korsgaard presents that agent as asking that question in so intransigent a spirit that I doubt that such an agent could be satisfied by any theory, Korsgaard's included. Here I remark that Korsgaard's third condition of adequacy on an answer is inappropriate in its assigned role. It is question-begging to say in *advance* that the answer must appeal to the agent's sense of her own identity, even if that should indeed turn out to be a feature of the right answer.

5

Korsgaard's answer to the normative question is that the reason why ethical standards make claims on me is that they represent commands that I give to myself, either *in virtue* of my practical identity or *in exercise* of my practical identity: I am not sure which of those is the right way to put her claim. On the first interpretation, the cost of violating ethical standards is loss of the practical identity that I would otherwise still have had; on the second, the cost is failure to have a practical identity, where I might never have had one anyway. I shall suppose that the first interpretation is correct – it fits more of what Korsgaard says.

Now, as I said, the further specification that Korsgaard attaches to the normative problem, the specification that fells the candidate

[27] 1.2.2. I cannot here forbear from the comment which restates, in a different way, points made in section 3, that who we are is not what we are. Who I am is a matter of my specified situation. And that takes us miles away not only from Kant, for whom only *what* we are enters the moral, but from the *specifically* moral, on *any* account of morality.

solutions to it which are rival to her own, makes the problem so hard that, so I believe, her own solution too is seen to fall if, as she did not, we forthrightly confront it with her tough specification of the problem.

Return to the general characterization of the problem. The problem is to answer the question 'Why should I be moral?' But consider two very different discursive contexts in which that question can occur. The first is the context of protest. 'Why should I be moral? If I behave morally here, I wreck my career, I lose friends, I become poor . . .' The second is the context of self-justification. 'Why should I be moral? Why should I act morally, like a decent human being? I'll tell you why I should act morally. Because I could not live with myself if I did not.' Now, Korsgaard has to fashion an answer which meets the question in its first, protestant, guise. But I doubt whether anything can be *guaranteed* to persuade *that* questioner, and I am certain that Korsgaard can do no better at persuading him than the rivals she criticizes do. Yet her answer does fit what the person figured above says when he addresses the question in its second, and milder, guise.

At various points in lecture 1 Korsgaard taxes moral realism in particular with incapacity to answer the normative question in its protestant form. We are told, first, that

when the normative question is raised, these are the exact points that are in contention – whether there is really *anything* I must do, and if so whether it is *this*. So it is a little hard to see how realism can help,[28]

since all that realism can say is: well, it's in the nature of things that this is what you must do. But, we have to ask, when so radical a stance of doubt is struck, how Korsgaard's own answer can be expected to help. Again:

If someone finds that the bare fact that something is his duty does not move him to action, and asks what possible motive he has for doing it, it does not help to tell him that the fact that it is his duty just is the motive. That fact isn't motivating him just now, and therein lies his problem. In a similar way, if someone falls into doubt about whether obligations really exist, it doesn't help to say 'ah, but indeed they do, they are *real*'. Just now he doesn't see it, and therein lies his problem.[29]

---

[28] 1.4.3.   [29] 1.4.5.

But when he is in such a state, a state in which he does not feel the force of reason or obligation, that can be because in such a state, and, indeed, if Korsgaard is right, that *must* be because in such a state he does not feel the force of, does not see what is involved in, his practical identity; and, echoing Korsgaard, we can say: therein lies his problem. He asks: why should I continue to dedicate myself like this? And then there is no point saying to him: because that is what you are committed to. Korsgaard says that 'the normative question arises when our confidence ['that we really do have obligations'] has been shaken whether by philosophy or by the exigencies of life',[30] and that someone's confident affirmation of the reality of obligation will then do nothing for us. But one thing which life's exigencies can shake is a person's practical identity, and, when that happens, then Korsgaard's answer will not help. Something shatters my sense of being and obligation in the world, consequently my confidence that obligation is real. It is then useless to tell me that it lies in my practical identity to be thus obliged. When I doubt that 'obligations really exist', or do not recognize that moral 'actions' are 'worth undertaking',[31] I am setting aside any relevant practical identity that the philosopher might have invoked.

In expressing scepticism about whether Korsgaard's – or anyone else's – theory could address and convert the radically disaffected, I am not comitting myself to scepticism about moral obligation. What I am sceptical of is the requirement that an answer to the normative question, in its general specification, has to sound good when addressed to the radically disaffected. If we scale down the difficulty of the question, we can, I think, find illumination in Korsgaard's answer to it.

'The normative question', says Korsgaard, 'is a first-person question that arises for the moral agent who must actually do what morality says . . . You . . . ask the philosopher: Must I really do this? Why must I do it? And his answer is his answer to the normative question.'[32] But, to repeat my objection, if his answer is that it belongs to my practical identity to do it, then why am I

---

[30] 1.4.5.
[31] 1.4.5 (quoted more fully in text to n. 29 above) and 3.3.1 (quoted more fully in text to n. 36 below).   [32] 1.2.1; see also 2.5.1.

asking the question in the alienated style on which Korsgaard insists?

If, on the other hand, we turn the thing around, we get something better. Suppose, again, that I am the moral agent, but this time not an alienated one, and *I* am faced by the sceptic who knows it will cost me to go on the march and who asks me why I bother. Then I can say a great deal that is persuasive about my practical identity. If I say, in radical disaffection: 'I do not know why I should march', then it is fatuous for you to reply: 'because your conscience compels you to'. But if *you* ask why *I* am going to do it, at substantial sacrifice of self-interest, it is not at all fatuous for me to reply, 'because my conscience compels me to'. 'Hier steh ich, ich kann nicht anders' makes sense. 'Dort stehst du, du kannst nicht anders' is manifestly false for the case of extreme disaffection which Korsgaard insists a moral theory must address.

If Korsgaard's defence of morality does not meet her own standard, which is that it should be capable of convincing the disaffected, then that could be because hers is the wrong standard, or hers is the wrong defence, or both. For my part, I am more clear that the standard is wrong than that the defence is. I do not think that we can show the intransigent why they should be moral. But I think that I can show the sincere inquirer why *I* must be moral. I have to be moral because, indeed, I could not otherwise live with myself, because I would find my life shabby if I were not moral. I can show that morality is *a* rational way, without being able to show that it is *the* (only) rational way.[33]

That morality is an option within rationality rather than a requirement of rationality necessitates the indicated first-person approach, in which the defender of morality is the moral agent herself. In the defence I sketch, the defender speaks in the first person, in Korsgaard's in the second person, to *me* as a sincere but disaffected inquirer. So I am not against the proposal that the issue

---

[33] I said earlier (see p. 177 above) that not all instances of failure to be moral compromise my practical identity. But to not be moral at all *would* wreck my practical identity, and that of all my fellow non-sociopaths. (I am conscious that this qualified rehabilitation of Korsgaard may achieve nothing more than a return to the Williams position that she wanted her own to supersede.)

be framed in I–thou terms, but I think that the roles of speaker and audience need to be reversed.

Korsgaard calls her solution 'the appeal to autonomy', and in one place she describes it as follows:

> the source of the normativity of moral claims must be found in the agent's own will, in particular in the fact that the laws of morality are the laws of the agent's own will and that its claims are ones she is prepared to make on herself. The capacity for self-conscious reflection about our actions confers on us a kind of authority over ourselves, and it is this authority which gives normativity to moral claims.[34]

I have asked some questions about our supposed authority over ourselves in section 2 above.[35] Right now I want to register that the rhetoric of the foregoing passage is more suited to how I would explain why I bother to be moral than to what someone else could say if *I* intransigently insist on being told why I *must* be moral.

Your practical identity is given by the

> description[s] under which you value yourself . . . description[s] under which you find your life to be worth living and your actions to be worth undertaking . . . these identities give rise to reasons and obligations. Your reasons express your identity, your nature; your obligations spring from what that identity forbids.[36]

I think all that is powerful stuff for me, the moral agent, to say to my interrogator, but it is entirely impotent when addressed to someone who, being disaffected, *ex hypothesi* finds no actions to be worth undertaking, or, more pertinently and more plausibly, no *moral* ones. It is powerful to say 'I couldn't live with myself if I did that',[37] but off the mark to say 'you couldn't live with yourself if you did that', to someone who is evidently managing to do so.[38]

---

[34] 1.2.3.

[35] Recall the Hobbesian conundrum with which I began, the problem of whether I have the authority to legislate over myself. If you say to me: but look, it is your law, your practical identity, then I might say: yes, but who am I to impose such a law on me? But when I say 'Hier steh ich', then it is odd for you to say: but who are you to issue such a command to yourself?   [36] 3.3.1.   [37] *Ibid.*

[38] 'A human being is an animal whose nature it is to construct a practical identity which is normative for her. She is a law to herself. When some way of acting is a threat to her practical identity and reflection reveals that fact, the person finds that she must reject that way of acting, and act in another way. In that case she is obligated' (4.3.7).

But you can't *get* me to construct a practical identity that will matter to *me*. And, if I do have one, then there is *my* answer to *you*.

The intransigent person who insists on a justification for being moral is close to saying: 'As far as my deep identity goes, I feel no force in morality's claims'. To that little can be said, so that, if we set Korsgaard's answer to the normative question against her own too demanding description of that question, then her answer to it does not work.

6

I have objected to Korsgaard's claim that 'An obligation always takes the form of a reaction against a threat of loss of identity.' It is an overstatement, whatever may be the truth that it overstates.[39] Not all obligations are like that. But, even if they were, it would remain true that, as I have also complained, not everything that *is* like that is an obligation of the sort for which, we can suppose, Korsgaard wants to supply foundations.

Consider an idealized Mafioso: I call him 'idealized' because an expert has told me that real Mafiosi don't have the heroic attitude that my Mafioso displays. This Mafioso does not believe in doing unto others as you would have them do unto you: in relieving suffering just because it is suffering, in keeping promises because they are promises, in telling the truth because it is the truth, and so on. Instead, he lives by a code of strength and honour that matters as much to him as some of the principles I said he disbelieves in matter to most of us. And when he has to do some hideous thing that goes against his inclinations, and he is tempted to fly, he steels himself and we can say of him as much as of us, with the same exaggeration or lack of it, that he steels himself on pain of risking a loss of identity.

What the mafioso takes to be his obligations can be made to fit Korsgaardian formulae about loss of identity as much as what most of us would regard as genuine obligations can be made to fit those formulae. So it looks as though what she has investigated is the experience or phenomenology of obligation, not its ground or authenticating source. Autonomy she says, 'is the source of obligation, and in particular of our ability to obligate ourselves',[40] but the

---

[39] See p. 177 above for the protest against it and n. 33 for the element of truth in it.
[40] 3.1.2.

Mafioso has that as much as anyone does, this capacity to transcend impulses through reflection and endorse or reject them.

Korsgaard realizes that she might be interpreted as I interpret her when I press the Mafioso example. Accordingly, she emphasizes that 'the bare *fact* of reflective endorsement ... is [not] enough to make an action right'.[41] It cannot be enough, she says, because, while there always is at least a minimal reflective endorsement of action, not all action is right. The argument has merit as far as it goes, but it is unreassuring, since it is consistent with the view that *more* than minimal reflective endorsement *does* always make an action right. It is unreassuring that the reason given for denying that reflective endorsement always makes an action right does not confront the reason we have for fearing that it might, reasons like this one: that the Mafioso is entirely capable of (more than minimal) reflective endorsement.

In section 3.4.4 Korsgaard seems to grant the present insistence, that the apparatus of reflective endorsement and practical identity is content-neutral: she thinks that it gains its different contents from the different social worlds that self-identifying subjects inhabit. But then we do not have what was demanded in the original characterization of the problem of normativity, which was an answer to the question why I must do the specifically *moral* thing. Unless, again, we turn the question around, and *you* are asking *me* why *I* undertake the labour of morality, as such. If I do undertake it, I can explain why. If I don't, Korsgaard supplies nothing sure to work that *you* can say to *me*, for morality might not be part of the practical identity that *my* social world has nourished. Or, worse, my social world might indeed be a morally constituted one, but the nourishment might have failed to take in my case.

7

An attempt to derive *specifically* moral obligation is prosecuted in lecture 3: see, in particular, sections 3.4.7–3.4.10 and the important summary in section 3.6.1. I shall here articulate the argument which I believe to be embodied in the cited sections, and which I

---

[41] 4.4.1.

find multiply questionable. I shall then pose some of the questions that I have in mind.

Here, then, is what I take to be Korsgaard's argument:

    1 Since we are reflective beings, we must act for reasons.

But 2 If we did not have a normative conception of our identities, we could have no reasons for actions.

So 3 We must have a normative conception of our identities (and our factual need for a normative identity is part of our normative identity).[42]

So 4 We must endorse ourselves as valuable.

So 5 We must treat (all) human beings as valuable.

So 6 We find human beings to be valuable.

So 7 Human beings *are* valuable.

So 8 Moral obligation is established: it is founded in the nature of human agency.

The above argument can be decomposed into four subarguments, on each of which I now invite focus: (1) from 1 to 3; (2) from 3 to 5; (3) from 5 to 7; and (4) from 7 to 8.

I

The passage from 1 (which I shall not question) to 3 rests on 2, but I do not see that 2 is true, except in the trivial sense that, if I treat something as a reason, then it follows that I regard myself as, identify myself as, the sort of person who is treating that item, here and now, as a reason. I do not see that I must consult an independent conception of my identity to determine whether a possible spring of action is to be endorsed or not, nor even that such endorsement must issue in such a conception, other than in the indicated trivial sense. When I am thirsty, and, at a reflective level, I do not reject my desire to drink, I have, or I think that I have, a reason for taking water, but not one that reflects, or commits me to, a (relevantly) normative conception of my identity. Merely acting on reasons carries no such commitment.

---

[42] See, in particular, 3.5.1.

2

The inference from 3 to 5 depends on the idea that, being, as we are, inescapably reflective, we must employ the normative conception of our identities (that we therefore necessarily have) to 'endorse or reject'[43] the impulses which present themselves to us as possible springs of action. But the very fact (supposing that it is one) that I must endorse *and* reject shows that I do not endorse a human impulse just *because* it is a human impulse. Human impulses are not, therefore, of value just because they are human. So, consistently with the structure of reflective consciousness, I can pass harsh judgment on my own, or on another's panoply of desires and bents, the more so if that other *is* disposed to endorse them. And if my endorsement of a given impulse means that I regard my humanity as *pro tanto* of positive value, then, by the same token, my rejection of another impulse must mean that I regard my humanity as *pro tanto* of negative value. No reason emerges for the conclusion that I must treat human beings, as such, as valuable, or for the requirement, which some might think a Kantian morality embodies, that I must treat them as equal in their value.

3

The inference from 5 to 7 might be thought to illustrate the fallacy of equivocation, for it seems to depend on an ambiguity in the expression 'to find',[44] which is sometimes a success-verb, where what is found to be thus and so must be so, and sometimes not. There is a sense of 'find' in which 6 follows from 5, and another one in which 7 follows from 6: but Korsgaard needs one sense, on pain of equivocation. Yet this comment of mine may reflect bone-headedness on my part about the character of transcendental arguments, for this is supposed to be one: maybe, in a transcendental argument, 'find' in its (normally) weaker sense is good enough to derive such a conclusion as 7. Accordingly, being uncertain whether there is any objection worth raising here, I pass on.

---

[43] 3.4.7.   [44] See 3.4.10.

4

My final comment concerns the passage from 7 to 8. My difficulty with it is that it appears to me that the mafioso can accept 7, in any sense in which what precedes it shows that it is true (I rely here on points made in comment 2 above), yet reject 8. For the mafioso can honour human beings the springs of whose actions are congruent with his *own* practical identity. So whatever endorsement of humanity as such comes out of this argument, it seems to me not to distinguish the mafioso ethic from morality, and therefore not to move us beyond the mere phenomenology of obligation to providing a foundation for specifically *moral* obligation.

The problem lies in our freedom at the level of endorsement, the old problem with which these remarks began: that the sovereign can change the law. To hammer that home a bit more, I want to look at Harry Frankfurt's concept of free personhood.

8

The debt that Korsgaard acknowledges to Frankfurt[45] is instructive in connection with my related claims that she has offered an option for the first person rather than a constraint that the second person must accept, and that what she has enabled the first person to provide is a defence of any set of commitments and not of specifically moral ones.

For Frankfurt, I am free when my will conforms to a higher order volition, when, that is, I act on a first-order volition that I wish to act on, when the spring of my action is one that I want to be moved by.

We should pause to modify this formula. We should add a restriction, a further condition for such conformity to betoken freedom, which has to do with the *direction* of the conformity. That is, the direction of conformity must be that my lower will conforms to my higher one, for, if it goes the other way, if my higher adjusts to my lower, then we have not freedom but second-order adaptive preference formation.[46] That category covers the addict who has

---

[45] See lecture 3, n. 8.
[46] *Second-order* adaptive preference formation because you adapt, here, not your first-order desire to the course of action that's available, but your second-order desire to the first-order desire that's available, or even unshakeable.

come to endorse his own pursuit of drugs: he now likes desiring drugs, and he likes acting on that desire. (I do not say that a willing addict's second-order volition could not be determinative: I am just using as an example the more plausible case in which it is not).

But there is no restriction either in Frankfurt's presentation or in fact on what the content of second-order volition can be, or, better, for this weaker claim will suffice here, no restriction sufficiently restrictive to yield moral obligation.[47] Thus, to return to my example, the ideal mafioso is entirely capable of Frankfurt freedom: he can prescribe the Mafia ethic to himself. Yet, to repeat my qualified defence of Korsgaard, *I* can defend *my* ethic even to him. I can explain why I strive not to succumb to some of my first-order desires, including some that move him.

Reference to Frankfurt also reinforces the point made earlier, that Korsgaard's legislator is too like the Hobbesian sovereign, as opposed to the Hobbesian citizen, to serve as the sort of model she requires. The Kantian reflective endorsement is inescapable, but Frankfurt's person, like Hobbes's sovereign, is at liberty to reassess his commitments.

So, I return to the thought that something transcending human will must figure in morality if it is to have an apodictic character. Kant was right that, if morality is merely human, then it is optional, as far as rationality is concerned. But it does not follow that morality cannot be merely human, since Kant may have been wrong to think that morality could not be optional. What does follow is that Korsgaard's goal is unachievable, because she wants to keep the 'must' that Kant put into morality while nevertheless humanizing morality's source.

---

[47] Frankfurt himself supports the stronger claim:

In speaking of the evaluation of his own desires and motives as being characteristic of a person, I do not mean to suggest that a person's second-order volitions necessarily manifest a *moral* stance on his part toward his first-order desires. It may not be from the point of view of morality that the person evaluates his first-order desires. Moreover, a person may be capricious and irresponsible in forming his second-order volitions and give no serious consideration to what is at stake. Second-order volitions express evaluations only in the sense that they are preferences. There is no essential restriction on the kind of basis, if any, upon which they are formed. ('Freedom of the Will and the Concept of a Person', in *The Importance of What We Care About*, p. 19, n. 6.)

LECTURE 6

Morality and identity

Raymond Geuss

In her third lecture Professor Korsgaard distinguishes between what she calls 'the categorical imperative' and 'the moral law' (3.2.4). The categorical imperative imposes a minimal condition on free choice: such choice must be guided by a principle we have given ourselves which has the form of a general rule or law (3.2.3). A free will must choose a maxim it can regard as a law. What Korsgaard calls 'the moral law', then, is a further specification of what this law which I give myself must be: it must be the kind of thing 'all rational beings could agree to act on together in a workable cooperative system' (3.2.4). As Professor Korsgaard quite rightly points out, Kant doesn't make this distinction and she suggests that awareness of the distinction will allow us to see a certain incompleteness in Kant's argument. He wants to show that any free will is bound by the moral law but he, in fact, establishes only the weaker claim that we are bound by the categorical imperative.

Korsgaard's argument, then, has two parts. First, she defends the bits of Kant where he got it right: normativity arises from the structure of the free will and the free will must stand under the categorical imperative. Second, she completes Kant's argument, showing that autonomous human agents stand not only under the categorical imperative but also under the moral law.

I'll start with the first part, the part that is supposed to parallel Kant's own discussion. As humans the form our freedom takes is that we are not forced to act on the desires we happen to find present in ourselves. We have the capacity to take a step back from them and decide whether or not we will endorse them as worthy grounds for action. Furthermore, we have no choice but to see ourselves and our whole lives under the aspect of a potentially continuous exercise of this capacity. We have no choice but to see ourselves as constantly endorsing, or failing to endorse, the various desires we encounter in ourselves. Note too that this rather odd way of speaking as if my desires were simply something I encounter in myself isn't just an unsympathetic way of putting it for the purposes of defaming the position, but rather it is something Kant's defenders emphasize. As Professor Korsgaard puts it: 'Anything outside of the will counts as an alien cause, including the desires and inclinations of the person' in question (3.2.3). There is of course a long tradition of criticizing Kant's ethics on this account – namely that as an ethical agent I see my own desires and inclinations as alien entities from which I must keep my distance – starting with Friedrich Schiller's well-known essay 'Über Anmut und Würde' (1793) and extending up to Professor Williams's paper here in Cambridge, in 1981.[1]

Standing back then from these alien entities that present themselves to me, my desires, I reflect on whether to endorse one or another of them as reasons for action. Since *all* of my desires are alien intruders I can't use any of them to decide which of my other desires to endorse. That is, it isn't open to me to say: I have a desire to listen to music, and now I'll endorse that desire because I like listening to music and I like the desire to listen to music. If I were to try this line I would have failed to reflect sufficiently, that is, I would not have sufficiently abstracted myself from my desires. But if I can't use my first- or second- or any higher-order desires, and don't want to admit that it could be an exercise of my freedom just to *pick* one existing desire for endorsement without following some antecedent principle of choice, then how do I come to endorse one of my desires as a reason for action? Kant's answer is that I must have a principle of choice which isn't derived from desire and which I give myself. But if such a principle of choice is not dependent on any desire, it can itself be nothing more than the principle: choose what you can will as a universal law. That, however, is, for Kant, just the formula of the categorical imperative (and for Kant, although not, it seems for Korsgaard, the formula of the moral law). For Korsgaard the situation is a bit more complicated because

---

[1] Published under the title 'Präsuppositionen der Moralität', in *Bedingungen der Möglichkeit*, pp. 251–261.

she seems to give two slightly different answers to the question. I assume that she thinks that these two answers amount finally to the same thing.

The first of Korsgaard's two replies is very much like Kant's: The principle of endorsement is that I endorse only such desires as are compatible with a maxim which I can will as a universal law. Actually Korsgaard gives this line of argument a particular twist, which allows her to connect it with the second of her two replies. For Korsgaard I don't just *use* a criterion of formal law-likeness as a principle of endorsement of desires as reasons for action, I '*identify*' with it. She writes: 'The reflective structure of human consciousness requires that you identify yourself with some law or principle which will govern your choices' (3.3.3) and of course this law will be the one prescribed in the categorical imperative. The question is whether 'using' a principle is quite the same as 'identifying' with it. Presumably Korsgaard holds that this is just a harmless linguistic variation of usage. After all, if in reflection I see all my desires as alien, then what else is there for me to identify with except the principle of endorsement (or rejection) I use?

I think it is striking, though, that Kant himself doesn't talk about 'identity' in ethical contexts, and notoriously Kant thinks that 'rational psychology', the metaphysical discipline purportedly studying the underlying bearer of personal identity, is a pseudo-science. Kant comes closest, I think, to discussing 'identity' in the sense in which Professor Korsgaard uses the term in his discussion of the 'interests of reason'. In his *Kritik der reinen Vernunft* he claims that the interest of reason is exhausted when one has given answers to the three questions: 'What can I know? What ought I to do? What may I hope?'[2] As Heidegger pointed out,[3] in the introduction to one of his unpublished lectures on logic Kant adds to these three the fourth question: 'What is the human being?' The question: 'Who am I?' doesn't appear, as if it were obvious that the correct answer is: 'A human being'; that is, as if the questions 'Who am I?' and 'What am I?' were philosophically not properly distinct.[4]

---

[2] Kant, *Kritik*, pp. 804–805.   [3] Heidegger (Frankfurt/m, 1929), p. 187.

[4] The failure to distinguish clearly between 'Who am I?' and 'What am I?', and thus to address the former question at all, is one of Heidegger's main criticisms of Kant, in his early works *Kant und das Problem der Metaphysik* and *Sein und Zeit*. Tom Baldwin has pointed

I make such heavy weather of this notion of 'identity' because Korsgaard's project of recentring Kantian ethics around notions of identity seems to me to push toward a position in which it will be difficult for the Kantian to reply to the line of argument developed by Friedrich Schlegel in the 1790s.

In Korsgaard's reconstruction, if I use my second-order desires as my principle for endorsing or failing to endorse a given first-order desire (as a reason for action) I have broken off reflection prematurely. I should continue until I reach the purely formal principle embodied in the moral law. In a similar way Schlegel claims that Kant broke off reflection prematurely: he stopped when he reached the point at which he saw that we have the capacity to prescribe to ourselves universal laws. But if what is at issue is my *identity* Kant should have realized that no universal law or mere formal principle can actually give me my identity. What 'I' am will always go beyond what can be given in *any* set of purely general laws, and to *identify* myself with any such law or set of laws or with the mere capacity to give myself such laws is to misunderstand and limit myself. What I am is something that essentially cannot be identical with a law or the capacity to give laws. If anything I am rather to be identified with a specifically human capacity that is higher and more complex than the mere capacity to prescribe universals laws, namely the capacity to give myself a freely chosen formal law and then consciously decide to violate it by making an exception of myself. Since I am not and cannot be identical with any general law or principle, my proper attitude toward any general law (even one I give myself) will be one of keeping it at a distance from me, i.e. at best treating it ironically, and precisely *not* identifying with it. What I should identify with is with my continuing ability to distance myself in thought and action from *any* general law. This is connected with an attempt on Schlegel's part to give a positive valuation of irony, frivolity, spontaneity, wilfulness

out to me that the place in his ethical writings where Kant comes closest to discussing something like my 'identity' is in his discussion of my '*Gesinnung*' (and of such related concepts as my '*Persönlichkeit*') in *Die Religion innerhalb der Grenzen der bloßen Vernunft* (Königsberg 1793, '*Erstes Stück*'). The *Religionschrift* was a favourite among the Romantics, but Kant's notion of '*Gesinnung*' seems to me still rather different from modern concepts of identity. For Kant it seems as if I could have only one of two possible '*Gesinnungen*': 'good' (if duty is a sufficient motive for me to act without the need of any further motive), or 'bad' (if I pervert the moral order and allow my inclinations to take precedence over the moral law).

(and also laziness).[5] My essential identity is a process of giving myself laws and consciously deciding to treat them ironically, act frivolously or wilfully, or consciously violate or change my self-given laws. Most people find this position unappealing. Hegel with uncharacteristic lack of charity cites Schlegel's views as the main instance of a category he calls 'Evil'.[6] The issue is not, however, whether or not we think Schlegel is wrong, but rather whether a Kantian position has the conceptual means to give us a reason to reject Schlegel. Hegel thinks he has grounds to reject Schlegel's position. The ideal Schlegelian life, after all, is a 'constant succession of self-creation and self-destruction'[7] and thus not a life devoted to the cultivation of continuing habits of socially responsible action. As Hegel points out, to keep frivolously making and unmaking laws or to treat given laws 'ironically' would be no way to run a state, but perhaps that just shows the difference between principles we might *use* in giving stability and decency to our social life and issues of our *identity*. The more the Kantian focuses on issues of identity the harder a time he or she is going to have in dealing with Schlegel.[8]

That then is the first of Korsgaard's two replies to the question how, in reflection, I can come to endorse some desires as reasons for action and reject others: I give myself a general rule, identify with this rule, and use it as a standard. Korsgaard's second reply to this question is the claim that 'the reflective structure of the mind' 'forces us to have a *conception* of ourselves' (3.3.1) and this conception functions as our standard. Such a conception gives me, she writes, 'A description under which you value yourself, a description under which you find your life to be worth living and your actions to be worth undertaking' (3.3.1). On this second view my identity (in this sense) gives rise to normativity both positively in that this identity allows me to turn desires into reasons and negatively in that 'obligations spring from what [my] identity forbids' (3.3.1).

This reconstruing of the Kantian project in terms of values seems to me to weaken the appeal of the position considerably. In

---

[5] Cf. Schlegel's *Lucinde* (1799). [6] Hegel (Berlin, 1821), section 140.
[7] Schlegel (1798), Fragment 51.
[8] Although Hegel thought Schlegel's position dangerously wrong, he also thought it the correct dialectical successor to Kantian ethics.

her lecture 3 Korsgaard considers the hair-raising claim that you might be able to obligate me to value what you value. It is a significant strength of the Kantian view that I stand under no obligation whatever to *value* what you empirically value – and a good thing that is, too, given that you might value rock music, sports cars, the ballet, geraniums, small porcelain figurines, or various other inherently worthless things. For Kant I am at best under certain obligations not to interfere in various ways with you in your misguided pursuit of worthless rubbish, not to value it myself.

Korsgaard seems to shift back and forth uneasily between a *very* strong sense of 'obligation' and an exceptionally weak one. Sometimes 'obligations' are unconditional demands I should die rather than violate, something the violation of which is a threat to my very identity. There might be such things, but what I normally call my 'obligations' aren't like this at all. I have, and acknowledge, an obligation to pay my legitimate debts and perhaps this is even an 'unconditional' obligation but one would have to have a pathologically fragile sense of self to feel one's identity threatened if one defaulted on a few debts. I would not even think of risking my life in order to be able to repay a small bank loan.

Failing to discharge minor debts doesn't threaten my identity, but I also don't think defaulting a desirable thing. I would prefer not to do it and will go to some lengths (although not to any length) to avoid it. But one could easily imagine cases in which doing something which was a violation of some of my obligations *did* form part of my identity, i.e. followed from my conception of what made my life worth living and my actions worth undertaking (3.3.1).

To use a very anachronistic example, Filipo Argenti is in the *Inferno* rather than in the *Purgatorio* not because he very frequently committed the sin of anger, but because anger formed a part of his identity. Part of what made him the person he was and wanted to be, of what made life worth living for him, was the angry 'violation of his obligations'.[9]

Korsgaard would presumably reply to this that although as a

[9] This example is anachronistic in at least two ways. First of all because I put it in terms of 'identity' rather than state of the soul, will, or form of 'love'. Second, a character trait such as 'anger' is something quite different from the violation of an 'obligation'. I hope the point can be seen through the smudge I have made of this.

matter of fact Argenti may have had a practical identity which gave undue prominence and inappropriately positive valuation to being angry, he *ought not* to have had this identity, and thus perhaps rightly ended up stewing in the dismal swamp he inhabits down there. He ought not to have identified himself as an essentially irate person but as a potential member of the party of universal humanity. So the issue then becomes in what sense it can be claimed that anyone 'ought' to acquire this particular identity (as a member of a Kingdom of Ends). I will come back to this later.

There is then in Korsgaard's lectures a very strong sense of 'obligation' which connects it with my very identity and with unconditional demands I should die rather than violate. Sometimes, however, the notion of an 'obligation' is so weak and thin that you can put me under an obligation just by calling my name. 'By calling out your name I have obligated you. I have given you a reason to stop' (4.2.7). I think it isn't just accidental that 'I have obligated you' and 'I have given you a reason' seem to be used interchangeably here.

I'm also somewhat unclear about the concept of 'reflection' Korsgaard uses. In lecture 3 she envisages two possible outcomes to a process of reflection:[10] Either I come to be able reflectively to endorse my initial set of desires (or a modified one that arises in the process of reflection), then I have 'reason' to act on them, or I reject them in reflection as incompatible with my identity. Then I have an obligation not to act on them (3.3.1). But it seems to me that earlier in her lectures Korsgaard countenanced a third possible outcome of reflection. She spoke there (for instance in the discussion of Hume) of the possibility that reflection might undermine the claims of certain considerations to be reasons for action. Reflection on morality might have a sceptical outcome, undermining the claims of morality. This would presumably not mean that we had an obligation to refrain from being moral, just that we saw we didn't have the kinds of reasons we once thought we had. I don't really know what to do with this observation about the concept of 'reflection' but I do think it important to dis-

---

[10] One possible outcome of reflection is that I am unable to decide whether to endorse certain desires or not, but let's leave that aside for the moment and consider just the case in which reflection does lead to a determinate decision.

tinguish carefully between reflective undermining of reasons and reflective generation of an obligation.

I said that the first part of Korsgaard's argument was a defence of the validity of the categorical imperative. I've now finished my discussion of that and would like to turn to the second part, the argument for the moral law in the version Korsgaard prefers. The conclusion is that my identity is really and essentially my relation to humanity as a whole or as an equal self-legislating member of the Kingdom of Ends, and thus reflection consists in endorsing those desires that are compatible with this identity and rejecting those incompatible with it.

I must confess that I don't understand the argument Korsgaard gives for this claim. Sometimes it seems as if for Korsgaard we just are able to see a real intrinsically moral fact: '. . . you are a human being and so if you believe my argument you can now see that that is *your* identity . . . And that is not merely a contingent conception of your identity, which you have constructed or chosen for yourself, or could conceivably reject. It is simply the truth' (3.4.9). So it is just a non-contingent *fact* about me that my essential identity is that of citizen of the Kingdom of Ends and that this identity trumps all my contingent identities (as a resident of a certain city, native speaker of a certain language, member of a certain association, etc.). If I just *see* that this is true of me, presumably we have a form of realism. Surprisingly, realism emerges at the end of the lectures as one of the positions that is 'also true'. This is rather puzzling given the vigorous criticism of realism in lecture 1. I assume that in lecture 1 Korsgaard was criticizing what she took to be a crude version of substantive realism, and that the realism which emerges as part of the winning team at the end is a more sophisticated version; indeed, in the passage just cited Korsgaard doesn't say we just *see* that we are essentially citizens of the Kingdom of Ends (and only contingently Muslims, atheists, Serbs, etc.) but rather that 'if you believe my argument' you will come to see this.

There should then be some kind of argument to the conclusion that I am essentially a member of the Kingdom of Ends (and only contingently an American). Or rather there need to be two arguments: one to convince me that *I* am necessarily a member of a Kingdom of Ends and then another to show the necessary universal extension for this Kingdom of Ends (for me) to *all* other humans.

Korsgaard's argument seems to run: if I reflect rightly I will see that no other feature of myself but only my mere humanity is the source of reasons and values for me. Thus I must see the mere humanity of *any* other human as equally a source of value and reason to act for me.

Korsgaard is well aware of the standard objection to this argument, namely I may well come to see *my* mere humanity as a source of value for *me*, your mere humanity as a source of value for *you*; how does it follow from that that *your* humanity must be a source of value for *me*? The Serbs have what I can see are quite good reasons *for them* to act as they do, reasons which (if you will) I can see as arising from their 'mere humanity', but it doesn't follow that these reasons have any standing *for me*; they aren't reasons for me to act the way they do or even to refrain from condemning their actions. It seems to me an elementary fact of life of the late twentieth century that we are constantly encountering people whose reasons for action we understand perfectly well and which we see are genuinely good reasons for them, without in the least endorsing these reasons or sharing their values.

I think it is a grave mistake to run together questions of the understanding of motives, reasons, and values and questions of endorsement. We understand perfectly well why certain groups of Muslims might want to kill Rushdie – he is a threat to their identity – and we can fully appreciate that the considerations that move them are quite good reasons *for them* without in the least thinking that they, or anything like them, are or would be reasons for us (and also without thinking that we stand under any obligation whatever to fail to try to protect Rushdie from their acting on their good reasons). We also assume, quite rightly I think, that the only way to change their minds would not be to present them with some new argument – they will have heard those that will occur to us and are not impressed – but to engage in some much more complicated process of restructuring their way of life.

Korsgaard's response to this, if I have it right (and I probably don't) is that the only reason you could have for denying that

you stood under an obligation to accept what you acknowledge
are good reasons *for them* as also good reasons *for you* would be
that you thought of reasons and reasoning as inherently private
entities and processes, but reasoning is public and we can sometimes share reasons. Not only *can* we share reasons, but we
usually in fact *do* exist in contexts of shared reasons. For me to
reject the project of obligatory common reasoning with you 'I
would have to hear your words as mere noise, not as intelligible
speech' (4.2.10) and that is impossible (if you are speaking a language I know).

Note the shift here from: 'We *can* share reasons (because they are
not in principle private entities)' and 'We usually *do* live in contexts
of shared reasons' to 'We *must* engage in common reasoning with
all other humans'. But from the fact that the sharing of reasons is
possible (or even, highly desirable) it only follows that I *could* get
together with you in a Kingdom of Ends (and that in many circumstances, when it is possible, it is also a very good idea), but not that I
must.

Equally I don't at all see why I should be thought to have the
choice *only* of hearing your words as mere noise, *or* being committed to joint citizenship with you in the Party of Humanity. I can
quite easily understand you perfectly well and ignore you and
what you say. That might not be very nice, but it is certainly possible, and why is it even immoral? Even if it were to turn out to be
immoral just to ignore people in some contexts, that would be the
result of bringing to bear further moral argumentation on *this*
situation; the fact that I ignore you is something to be evaluated
morally (perhaps), not itself an automatic origin of a moral claim.
I'm surely not required to listen to everyone's reasoning just
because he or she succeeds in producing some in my presence,
and I'm not even required to give any account of why I ignore
you unless there is some special reason for me to take you into
account.

Maybe it just is a Moral Fact (or a Divine Command) that we
stand under an obligation to take account of others in certain
ways. Even if it isn't a moral fact, it might be a good thing to do,
but that would be for further reasons which we would have to try
to specify and it isn't at all clear to me how one could get uni-

versal, strictly binding reasons to take account of everyone in all circumstances. What one would be left with would be a highly context-dependent, non-Kantian form of reflective endorsement.

Universality and the reflective self

Thomas Nagel

Christine Korsgaard has provided us with an illuminating analysis of the problem of the normativity of ethics. She observes that it is the reflective character of human consciousness that gives us the problem of the normative – the fact that unlike other animals, we can fix our attention on ourselves and become aware of our intentions, desires, beliefs, and attitudes, and of how they were formed. But it is not awareness alone that does it; a further aspect of our reflective consciousness is involved, which can appropriately be called freedom. Here is what she says:

> Our capacity to turn our attention on to our own mental activities is also a capacity to distance ourselves from them, and to call them into question . . . Shall I believe? Is this perception really a *reason* to believe? . . . Shall I act? Is this desire really a *reason* to act? (3.2.1)

The new data provided by reflection always face us, in other words, with a new decision.

The normative problem does not arise with regard to everything we observe about ourselves: we cannot decide whether or not to be mortal, for example (though we may have to decide how to feel about it). It is only beliefs, and acts, or intentions that face us with the problem of choice, and it is in our response to this problem that values and reasons reveal themselves.

Korsgaard's account of the normativity of ethics, and her criticisms of rival accounts, appear within the framework of this conception of the human mind and the human will. I should like to explore her view by considering how she would answer the following three questions, which the reflective conception naturally poses:

1　Why does the reflective self have to decide anything at all, either granting or withholding endorsement, instead of remaining a passive observer of the beliefs and actions of the non-reflective self?

2　Why, when it decides, must it try to do so on the basis of *reasons*, which imply generality, or something law-like?

3　How does it determine what those reasons are?

The third question of course comprehends all of moral theory and epistemology, but I plan to discuss only the general character of the answer.

Korsgaard's answer to the first question, with which I would agree, is that the reflective self cannot be a mere bystander because it is not someone else; it is the very person who may have begun with a certain unreflective perception, or desire, or intention, but who is now in possession of additional information of a special, self-conscious kind. Whatever that person now concludes, or chooses, or does, even if it is exactly what he was about to do anyway, will either have or lack the endorsement of the reflective view – even, as Korsgaard observes, if he behaves like a wanton and allows his first-order desires to move him without interference. Given that the person *can* either try to resist or not, and that he is now self-conscious, anything he does will imply endorsement, permission, or disapproval from the reflective standpoint.

The second question is more difficult. What is it about this reflective individual that leads him to make the new choices with which he is faced in a way that has universal implications – even when he merely endorses or refrains from interfering with his first-order beliefs or desires? As I understand her position, Korsgaard believes, in my view rightly, that we cannot avoid giving an answer which is in some way general. But why is this? Why isn't the reflective individual just someone with more information, who can therefore make choices which may be different but need be no less purely personal – or even temporally fragmented? How do reasons, law, and universality get a foothold here – one that cannot be dislodged? Presumably it has something to do with the difference between reflective and unreflective consciousness, but why should awareness of self bring with it this further regularizing effect?

Korsgaard's final answer will be one which attempts to transcend the opposition between the rational and the personal, and my doubts about it have to do with that ambition. But she begins by accepting an argument of Kant's that I have never understood: the argument from free will to the categorical imperative. The conclusion she draws from it is weaker, because she distinguishes between the categorical imperative and the moral law – meaning by the categorical imperative only the principle that we must act according to *some* law – but the form of the argument is the same. 'The free will must be entirely self-determining', she says, paraphrasing Kant. 'Yet, because the will is a causality, it must act according to some law or other' (3.2.3).

But why is the second sentence of this argument true? If the will is self-determining, why can't it determine itself in individual, disconnected choices as well as according to some consistent law or system of reasons? A neo-Humean regularity theory of causation seems an inappropriate model for free self-determination. If the idea makes sense at all, the free choice of actions which conform to a law is no more nor less a form of *causality* than the free choice of actions which do not. (And the same could be said of the free adoption of beliefs.) So far as I can see, choosing freely in a law-like pattern is merely a way of mimicking causality; if I always put on my left sock before my right, that does nothing to establish the causality of my will, so why does the categorical imperative do any better? There has to be something more compelling about the demand for universality than this.

I think the true explanation is quite different. We are drawn irresistibly to the search for general reasons and justifications in the endorsement of our actions and beliefs, not because of the requirements of causality but because of the externality of the reflective view. This does have something to do with freedom, but Kant's argument obscures the connection. The freedom in question is freedom from direct control by our impulses and perceptions. The capacity for self-consciousness changes the nature of the being who is making the choices – whether they are decisions to act or decisions to believe – by introducing irrevocably the distinction between appearance and reality, between how things seem from our personal point of view and how they really are – and facing us with the need and perhaps providing us with the capacity to arrive at an answer that can be seen to be right not just from our individual point of view but from the reflective standpoint that takes that view as its object.

The reflective self is in its nature more universal than the original, unreflective self, because it achieves its self-conscous awareness by detaching from the individual perspective. The reason we can no longer decide from the purely local perspective within which the original appearances or impulses are found, is that once we observe ourselves from outside, and achieve the distance of which Korsgaard speaks, our choice becomes not just what to believe or do, but what *this person* should believe or do. And that has to be a decision about what any person so situated should believe or do, since the external view does not give any consideration to the fact that the person is me – it describes me in terms which would be just as available to someone else sufficiently well informed about me.

Even before we reach this impersonal level, there is the perspective of one's life as a whole, which leads to the search for principles to govern choice which will apply at any time – not just, what shall I do now? but, what should I do in circumstances like this whenever they occur? Given the reflective perspective, every individual choice automatically becomes a general choice – even if it is the general choice not to strive for law-like consistency, and to act always on the impulse of the moment. (That is not easy, and its analogue for belief – staying with your impressions – is even harder.)

Suppose, then, that for whatever reason, it is granted that a reflective being will inevitably be led to seek general or law-like answers to the questions of belief and action which face him. The next question, and the largest, is the third on our list. What if anything will determine his reflective response when faced with the question what a person in his position should do or believe, in general?

Though she accepts the Kantian argument that freedom implies conformity to law, Korsgaard departs from Kant in holding that the content of the law depends on something else, namely our conception of our practical identity. This distinctly unKantian, rather existentialist idea is the heart of her position. It introduces a strong element of contingency and therefore of relativism, because depending on how we conceive of ourselves as reflective beings, the law may be egoistic, nationalistic, truly universal, or just plain wanton. In other words, occupation of the reflective standpoint, though it implies law-like determination, can yield different results for different individuals because each person has his own reflective point of view. The law selected by the categorical imperative will be the moral law only if that is the principle you regard as expressive of yourself, because you identify yourself as a member of the Kingdom of Ends – rather than just as someone with certain interests, for example. This is Korsgaard's answer to the third question. We give consent to the law by identifying with a certain self-conception, and that also explains the law's hold on us. Going against such a law flagrantly enough is like destroying yourself.

A natural question about this practical self-conception is, first, whether we are supposed to have some choice in the matter, and second, whether there is any right or wrong about it if we do have a choice. The way we think of ourselves seems in Korsgaard's conception to be an empirical matter of fact. Even if we could change our stripes, it would seem that there could be no reasons one way or the other for changing in a particular direction, since all reasons have to depend on a pre-existing self-conception. According to this picture, the final say goes to whatever determines our identity. She says:

The test for determining whether an impulse is a reason is whether *we* can will acting on that impulse as a law. So the test is a test of endorsement. (3.3.5).

But then:

When an impulse – say a desire – presents itself to us – we ask whether it could be a reason. We answer that question by seeing whether the maxim of acting on it can be willed as a law by a being with the identity in question. (3.3.7)

where 'the identity in question' is just whatever way I think of myself:

Different laws hold for wantons, and egoists, lovers, and citizens of the Kingdom of Ends. (3.3.7)

She discusses some of the pressures which push us toward wider and wider communities of identification, including those which derive from participation with other reflective beings in a public language. But at the end of the line, the explanation of the content of rationality that derives from these identifications is first-personal. It is a matter of who you think you are.

This is an anti-realist position in ethics, and I should like to connect my objections to it with what I think is the true issue about realism. In lecture 1 (1.4.4), Korsgaard introduces a false opposition between procedural moral realism, which she says is trivial, and substantive moral realism, by identifying substantive realism with a metaphysical belief in the existence of moral 'entities', 'facts', or 'truths' (though she turns Mackie's sceptical use of the term 'entities' against him to wonderful effect at the close of lecture 4). But a substantive realism need not (and in my view should not) have any metaphysical content whatever. It need only hold that there are answers to moral questions and that they are not reducible to anything else. Procedural realism, by contrast, is compatible with all kinds of reductionism. The issue is, what does the truth or falsity of statements about what we have reasons to do or believe, or what we *should* do or believe, depend on? Does it depend on what we think or what we choose, more or less, or not?

Korsgaard believes that in ethics, at least, it does. She does not say whether she believes the standards of reasoning with regard to theoretical and factual questions also derive from our self-conceptions. That too is a possible anti-realist view, but the two need not go together.

I think that giving the last word to the first person is a mistake in both domains. It is an example of the perennially tempting mistake of seeking to explain an entire domain of thought in terms of something outside that domain, which is simply less fundamental than what is inside. In the end, the explanation of why a belief or action is justified must be completable, if it is completable at all, within the domain of the relevant reasons themselves.

In deciding, for example, whether to accept a perceptual appearance or to substitute for it some other belief, the only thing to do, once one has adopted the reflective view, is to think about what the world probably has to be like, in order to explain why it appears as it does. In other words, you have to think about the world, of which you are a part, rather than about yourself and who you feel yourself to be.

Formally, it is the same with morality and other practical issues. To decide from the reflective standpoint what to do you have eventually to stop thinking about yourself and think instead about the question at issue – not in this case about what entities the world contains, but about whether what has made you want to do something is really a reason to do it. The answers to such questions may partly determine your identity, but they don't derive from it.

The temptation to offer an egoistic answer to egoism has been a weakness of ethical theory since the dawn of the subject. Korsgaard's grounding of morality in a self-conception which you would rather die than violate seems to me close to being an example of this strategy. But it is not the only possibility. Here is another one:

If someone accepts death rather than betraying a number of other people to the killers, it might be unappreciative to explain this in terms of the conception he had of himself. Of course if he cares about the survival of the others, and is unwilling to save his own life by betraying those others, then that *is* in fact an important aspect of his conception of himself. But to explain the grip on him of those reasons in terms of the self-conception would be to get things backwards, and incidentally to cheapen the motive. The explanation in its natural form can stop with the lives of the others versus his own – not with romantic thoughts of what it would annihilate his personality to do, however useful these may be in stiffening his resolve. Even if he can get motivational help from thinking that he couldn't live with himself if he saved his life by this method, that is not the final explanation – indeed it couldn't be. The real explanation is whatever would *make* it impossible for him to live with himself, and that is the non-first-personal reason against the betrayal. These remarks are not about what is on the conscious surface of the mind, but about the person's real reasons for acting.

This alternative story sounds rather high-minded, I realize, and to be frank, on the psychological level I have my doubts: perhaps only romantic egoists can make sacrifices of this extreme sort – on the model of religious martyrs who expect eternal bliss. It even helps to explain why some genuinely heroic personalities are so unbearable. But if that kind of answer is the only available solution to the problem of normativity, then morality is an illusion, in my opinion, and the sceptics are right.

I think moral truth requires another type of answer – one with the universal applicability that Kant sought. The reflective attitude abstracts from the present moment and the point of view of the particular individual, because it takes those perspectives as objects of its attention. Suppose it faces the choice between endorsing egoism or the moral law as the general principle of conduct for someone occupying such a perspective. Since the reflective attitude is being taken up by an ordinary human being, he is of course thinking about himself as well as everyone else. The issue is an evaluative one and it can only be addressed evaluatively.

I believe that the crucial question he has to answer is whether he is prepared to regard that individual, reflectively considered, as worthless. If so, then the reflective standpoint will offer no evaluative constraints to the carrying out of the individual's personal desires – will keep its hands off, so to speak. The reflective standpoint will bring no further reasons to bear on the individual's choices, in addition to those which appear from within his individual point of view, because it will then regard all reasons as existing only *for* individuals, in virtue of their aims or interests. This is itself a general attitude, but one which supports egoism (or wantonness, if even the egoistic value of present satisfactions is denied). Egoism as a general principle is equivalent to regarding myself as valueless from a reflective point of view, because it says that my interests, like those of every other person, provide others with no reason for action except in so far as they can be linked to the other person's prior motives.

If, on the other hand, from a reflective standpoint we do not regard ourselves as worthless, then we must accord a more general weight to at least some of our reasons for acting. And because of the character of the reflective attitude, this weight will automatically be accorded to similar reasons arising in the lives of others, and these will in turn constrain what we are justified in doing in the pursuit of our own lives. None of this can be explained in terms of our practical self-conception, though it might well be described as *determining* our practical identity.

I may be overestimating my disagreement with Korsgaard. She too believes that morality arises from the value we find it irresistible to grant ourselves as sources of reasons once we take up the reflective attitude towards our own actions. And she too wishes to identify her argument as a version of Kant's argument that, if we are to take our desires as providing reasons for action, we must on reflection regard ourselves, and hence humanity itself, as intrinsically valuable. The trouble is that she seems to hold that the kind of reflective value that comes out of this argument is consistent with egoism (4.2.1). But so far as I can see, the same kind of reflective judgment that yields reflective endorsement of rational self-interest can be carried further to yield reflective endorsement of values which obligate others. In each case, it is a matter of being faced with the alternatives, and having to decide which is more credible. We do not *make* these things true by taking some kind of leap, or even by taking a cautious collective step. The invocation of Wittgenstein doesn't help, because egoism doesn't violate publicity. I don't deny that some values are adopted or created, but morality, in its basic outlines, is not among them. Our practical identity is its product, not its source.

Because I don't know where else to put it, let me close with an unnconnected exegetical point. I think that in lecture 1, Korsgaard misinterprets Hobbes. He was not, in her sense, a voluntarist, because he did not believe the command of the sovereign was the source of obligation. Rather, the sovereign's commands, and his monopolistic capacity to enforce them, remove the excusing condition of insecurity which makes the laws of nature oblige only *in foro interno* when we are in the state of nature. Even the command of God is not the source of moral obligation. I read the passage from *Leviathan* she quotes in section 1.3.2 as a purely linguistic point – that we can't literally *call* these moral principles 'laws' except in so far as they are commanded – but they oblige us nonetheless, since they are rational dictates of self-preservation, which is our first aim.

Korsgaard has put before us a characteristically rich, ambitious, and original system of philosophical ideas developed to the highest intellectual standard. My comments, largely in opposition, constitute a very selective and inadequate response to the whole; her project is of the first importance.

History, morality, and the test of reflection

Bernard Williams

I THE NORMATIVE QUESTION

Korsgaard says that the normative question (which I shall label [N]) is necessarily formulable in different ways. It may be helpful to her argument to spell out more fully the relations between some of the formulations. For instance, there are significant differences between [N1] 'What justifies the claims that morality makes on us?' (1.4.3), and [N2] 'Is there anything we must do?' (1.1.1, 1.3). [N2] is at least broader than [N1], since there are non-moral forms of normativity. Korsgaard accepts this, and indeed uses the notion of means-end normativity to elucidate (via the idea of the will's relation to itself) the moral sort of normativity. But this does not seem to allow enough for non-moral forms of normativity (prudential, aesthetic, etc.) which, like the moral sort, can equally give trouble with inclination. It is not entirely clear to me whether Korsgaard thinks that there is a problem about the nature of normativity before we ever get to the specifics of morality. (Perhaps there is a Kantian preconception hovering here, in the idea that it is only the opposition of morality to inclination that *really* puts the nature of normativity on the line.)

I take it that the reflective question [R] 'Can morality survive reflection?' provides a way of approaching [N1] 'What justifies morality's claims on us?' But [N1] and [R] line up neatly with each other only if two things are granted. We have to assume (a) that the reflective question about morality is concerned overwhelmingly with its obligatory aspect, its 'claims on us': Aristotelians and others might be more impressed by morality's role as an enabling device for the agent's own life, or by other considerations distinct from those of obligation. The second assumption is (b) that the justification of morality is presented to the agent in the agent's own reflection. Morality might 'survive reflection' in the sense that we could recognize it as something that it is necessary to have around. Such reflection would show, in effect, why enough moral claims had to be recognized by enough people. I take it that on Korsgaard's view this kind of consideration would not in fact provide a positive answer to [R] in the sense in which it is meant. More needs to be said, then, to justify the requirements on [R] which Korsgaard assumes (a Socratic requirement, in fact) that the answer to [R] should be one that is given *to* each agent – or at least *for* each agent, as I put it in *Ethics and the Limits of Philosophy*.[1]

These questions are closely related to Korsgaard's idea that [N] and [R], as opposed to such issues as scepticism about the external world, are both very continuous with practice. I think that here, too, Korsgaard puts a lot of weight on the force of the conflicts with inclination: each agent, if minimally reflective (in a fairly uncontentious, not particularly philosophical, not culturally local, sense) *must* confront, in her terms, the status of the moral claim when it is so uncomfortably going against 'her heart's desire'. But can so much be taken for granted in getting the discussion started? Korsgaard is already confronting a motley crew of romantics, Nietzscheans, Lawrentians, and merely *Epicuri de grege porcos*, who will say that if the claim in question can and should have that much power against the heart's desire, it had better have a footing in the heart's desire. I come back to their concerns below, in sections 5 and 6.

2 REFLECTION AND EXPLANATION

The idea of morality's failing the reflective test is that the true explanation of why we have moral beliefs may not sustain those beliefs. But why should the explanation of morality have to sustain it in the sense of providing a normative reason for it? Why should morality not be sustained, rather, by *what is mentioned in* the explana-

---

[1] See pp. 39ff.

tion? We should consider here what Thomas Nagel in his remarks says about self-conceptions, and indeed these matters tie up with Nagel's much earlier work, about the absurd. Consider, for instance, the true explanation of (the other bits of) her heart's desire: what is revealed in psychological accounts of the origins of her passions may not normatively endorse them, but this does not mean that it renders them meaningless when they are considered 'from inside'.

How external to the agent's existing concerns is the explanation to be? If it is very external indeed (for example, very reductive), maybe all human interests will lose their significance under such explanation. If the explanation, on the other hand, uses much of the material of the agent's world, then it can make reflective sense of morality, and much else beside (such as her heart's desire). If the demand is that reflection should endorse morality in virtue of the way that it explains it, we need to be told the appropriate level or type of explanation, and what its materials are, for this to be a reasonable or even a determinate demand.

We can be misled in this respect by the case of factual knowledge. Here, not only are explanation and justification closely related to one another, but the *level* of explanation for which this holds is already understood in terms of the subject matter and (relatedly) in terms of what count as claims to knowledge in the area. Suppose I am disposed to believe that P. Then I can ask about the origin of this state: and I answer, Q, which is another belief of mine (about the origin of my belief that P). Moreover, Q is the kind of belief that could tend to falsify P, or, again, support it; or if it does not falsify P, it could falsify my claim to know that P. Granted this, it is desirable that the particular Q I come up with not be of either falsifying kind, and standardly it will be better if it actually supports P.

All this applies, however, just because of the relations between, and the origins of, factual beliefs, and because the explanations that we give of our own beliefs are of the kinds that can play a role in validating claims to knowledge. (Edward Craig's admirable discussion of the relations between knowledge and the origins of belief is relevant here: see his *Knowledge and the State of Nature*.) But the relation of a normative attitude to its explanation (which latter is a factual belief) surely could not, *ex hypothesi*, fit just this pattern, on anyone's view of the matter.

David Wiggins in some recent work ('Moral Cognitivism, Moral Relativism and Motivating Beliefs') has tried to apply a notion of 'justificatory (or vindicatory) explanation' to certain moral beliefs, in a way that is designed to parallel its application to some factual and simple arithmetical beliefs. It is significant in relation to Korsgaard's strategy that Wiggins takes such an argument to work only for very 'thick' ethical concepts. It is also significant that Wiggins's argument does not (in my view) actually work: basically, because it begs the question of the respondent's using the thick concept in question. This is just the reason, I take it, that Korsgaard would not want to follow Wiggins's path: she needs a thin concept, such as *ought*, that everyone must use.

3 A REMARK ABOUT MY OWN VIEW

Korsgaard perhaps suggests, at the end of lecture 2, that I think reflective questions are only of philosophical, not practical, interest. I do not think this.

I agree otherwise with her account of my views, except that – and this is only a matter of emphasis – she perhaps represents me as rather more neo-Aristotelian than I am. I am more sceptical than perhaps she suggests about the project of grounding the ethical life in something like psychic health or a state of flourishing. I have wanted to claim only that this project at least makes sense; that it operates, so to speak, in the right corner of the field. I agree with Korsgaard that the realist is in a weak position because he or she raises a question that he or she cannot answer. Korsgaard raises it and hopes to answer it. I myself think that if it is raised it cannot be answered, but I am less clear than she is about what counts as raising it, as comes out in my previous remarks about levels of explanation, and about the status of [N], 'the' normative question.

My basic doubt can be put like this: is there a question which at once

    1 is about ultimate justification,
    2 is rationally inescapable,
    3 is practically relevant,
and 4 the answer to which justifies by explaining?

4   A POINT ABOUT HUME

Hume did not think that there was a question that satisfied all these conditions, even leaving aside 4. It is not clear to me that Hume's method answers the same question as Korsgaard wants answered.

In any case, there is a problem. Korsgaard says that for Hume, the principles of the understanding fail the reflexivity test, but the moral sentiments pass it. This seemingly depends on the principle that if the understanding cannot justify itself, then it is not justified. (Though it is less than clear, of course, what this last claim would mean for Hume: the interpretation of his scepticism, its irrelevance to practical life, and so forth are relevant here.) But the operation of the moral sentiments requires the principles of the understanding, and the explanation of the moral sentiments invokes the principles of the understanding (as Hume remarked). So if '. . . cannot justify themselves' implies '. . . are not justified'; and if '. . . depends on what is not justified' implies '. . . is not justified'; then it looks as though the moral sentiments are not justified either.

5   FROM HUME TO BENTHAM

The lawyer in lecture 2, when she reflects, supposedly finds that her disapproval seems 'poorly grounded, and therefore in a sense irrational' (2.5.2); this can lead to utilitarianism, in parallel to an historical development from Hume to Bentham. But this brings us back once more to the level and type of explanation (which in this case is self-applied). Does the argument not underestimate the lawyer's normative resources – particularly her 'practical identity' as a lawyer, to use a phrase that occurs in lecture 3? The lawyer can, of course, have the thought: 'I just happen to have been brought up as a lawyer with these rules, etc . . .', and then this thought about her identity as a lawyer may go dead on her. But there is a real question of what resources do or can go dead on a given person, and of what this means (the question ties up with matters discussed earlier, in section 2).

Korsgaard's requirement seems indeed to be Kant's, that nothing will serve as an adequate normative resource in such reflections unless 'I just happen to . . .' *cannot even intelligibly* be applied to it (though, presumably, at a later stage we can go on to include considerations that can be legitimated by being based on considerations that pass this test). But is this a reasonable requirement? People say such things as 'I just happen to love him . . .', 'she just happens to be my daughter . . .', or 'I happen to be a vegetarian . . .' (It is interesting that such formulae as 'I happen to be a Catholic . . .' have an apologetic use in modern anti-dogmatic circles: no-one says 'I happen to be a Protestant . . .' in places where such things really matter, such as Belfast.) Indeed, might not someone say 'I happen to be someone who thinks in terms of principles'? And suppose nothing (relevant) passes the test? As Nietzsche was disposed to say, *what then?* Or rather (see next section): what now?

The immediate point, however, is that Korsgaard does not seem to me to have located Bentham's destructive (as I agree it to be) 'advance' from Hume securely in the process of reflection itself. I think that what is weak in Hume is his conception of self-interest and its relation to the moral sentiments, which themselves are constituted by various extensions, projections, and universalizations of 'self'-interest.

I come back to the historical dimension itself in section 7 below.

6 PRACTICAL IDENTITY: OTHER PEOPLE

I see a Platonic inheritance here, in Korsgaard's suggestion that the person who is not (sufficiently) open to the claims of morality is in some way cognitively defective in relation to others. Plato, using this line, can plausibly be charged with having ducked the full force of Callicles' challenge, by equating the bad with the addicted or brutal, whereas Callicles' suggestion (his first suggestion, at any rate) was that they did not need to be like *that*. *A fortiori*, they do not need to be like that if they are simply insufficiently open to the claims of morality. But let us exaggerate, and call the figure in question the 'amoralist'. One cannot, without further argument, claim that the amoralist has to be defective in these obvious, unlovely, and unenviable ways. One also cannot say, without further argument, that the amoralist regards other people as worthless; he may just regard them as others (for example, as enemies). (If the argument is going to turn on what is involved in the recognition of 'the Other', Korsgaard may want to consider someone who has tried to work out similar ideas in a different style, Levinas.)

My main question, however, is not whether there are answers to be found in this direction, but rather the following: even if there are, how do they help to answer the questions [N]? How, for instance, are these considerations supposed to work in the lawyer's reflection? What will they do to strengthen moral claims against an agent's heart's desire? If acknowledgment of others is implicit in one's practical identity, then it is already so – already, when the morally normative, and such things as her identity as a conscientious lawyer, supposedly go dead on her. Why is reflection on these considerations about other people going to make the required elements come alive again? If obligation is 'calling', it is already so: if others have the power to tell us what to do and make us do it (by telling us, by existing, by being there), then what happened when she did not hear them? (When I say that she did not hear them, I mean that she did not hear the supposedly morally compelling voice among them; her heart's desire, after all, may well have been listening to *some* one among them.)

I think that Korsgaard needs to provide some more argument on two things, which are in the end the same thing. (1) How are the considerations about others relevantly activated in reflection? (2) How do they mesh into 'practical identity' in such a way as to satisfy Kant's requirement that one speaks to oneself, and under an identity which one does not 'just happen' to have? (2) relates directly to what Korsgaard says about others telling us and making us do things. It relates, that is to say, to the Categorical Imperative (perhaps, in this way, it relates more directly to the idea of a Categorical Imperative of morality than Korsgaard suggests when she says that Kant's argument needs some supplementation to help in the direction of the Kingdom of Ends; but I am not sure about this). The idea that (some) people can make us do (some) things by telling us to do them is quite helpful, I think, in understanding how it is for the agent who *is* alive to obligation and its claims, but as of course Kant saw, it cannot explain the force of obligation from the ground up unless there is an account of how, from the ground up, the agent accepts the force of what other people say. This is the familiar point that 'Categorical' is not a grammatical category: unwanted, bullying, intrusive agents can make their imperatives to me as unconditional in form as they like, but it does not make their instructions Kantianly unconditional in the relevant dimension of my having a reason to obey them.

Hence (1) and (2) come to the same thing. To repeat: even if there is (which of course I doubt) a consideration linking practical identity in a sense that is inescapable with acknowledgment of others in a sense that is morally sufficient, how can this link be mobilized normatively in reflection, so as to answer Korsgaard's own very radical question?

7 HISTORICAL FOOTNOTE

Or, rather, a footnote about the very idea of the history. In comparing possible processes of individual rational reflection to historical developments from Hobbes to Hume, and from Hume to Bentham (or, better, from Hume to Kant), Korsgaard raises the question of how these historical developments are to be understood. There are several related questions. Does she accept a 'Whiggish' view to the effect that the historical emergence of universalistic morality is, so to speak, self-propelled (as might be implied, for instance, by certain remarks made in the discussion about the 'discovery of equality')? (I suspect that Nagel really does accept this, or at least is so uninterested in any further explanations that it comes to the same thing.)

If one accepts that historical and social developments were necessary to the emergence of universalistic morality – which is hard to deny – one is faced with some notorious Hegelian problems. First, does one accept that among the conditions of the emergence of universalistic morality were many historical activities that depended on the non-acceptance of universalistic morality? As Hegel himself (and of course in a nastier, less redemptive, sense, Nietzsche) asked, does the Kantian really wish that Kantian morality had prevailed?

Second, why should the history be supposed to stop at (roughly) Kant? After all, the history *in fact* went on from Kant to Friedrich Schlegel (as Geuss reminds us), and to Hegel (as Hegel reminds us), and might not as good a story be told about why it 'had to' develop in these later ways as can be told about the earlier developments? Indeed, cannot one also see why it should have gone on from Hegel to (some version of) Nietzsche?

This is not meant to imply, in the spirit of traditional historical materialism for instance, that we should be so impressed by the onward march of the historical process that we feel we must accept its latest stage. (That line of argument is anyway open to the unanswerable objection – a valid version of the 'naturalistic fallacy' argument – that if we have doubts about the 'latest stage', then it cannot be that stage, but rather our doubts, that constitute the latest stage.) The point is rather that if Korsgaard takes historical categories seriously (as she does, unlike many of her fellow Kantians) she has to explain why the Kantian moment in that history is privileged. She also, relatedly, has to take account of the fact that history having got to the present point, it is not only impossible to ignore that question, but it is also hard to take seriously most of the answers that have been given to it at earlier stages of that history, for instance in the Kantian moment itself.

Reply

Christine Korsgaard

My commentators have raised many important questions about, and made some very forceful objections to, what I have had to say in these lectures. I can only wish that I could give satisfactory responses to them all. In what follows, I address just a few of the points which they have raised. Specifically, in section 1 I address the question why we must will in accordance with a universal law. In section 2 I discuss some ways in which, according to my commentators, my account of obligation departs from Kant's, to its detriment, and I try to defend myself both against the claims of departure and of detriment. In section 3 I discuss the status of desire, both in Kant's account and in my own. In section 4 I take up the question whether my focus on the idea of identity makes my account of moral motivation unattractively egoistic. Finally in section 5 I consider some issues about the relationship between giving a psychological explanation of the sense of obligation, and giving a justification of obligation itself.

1 AN OLD QUESTION RAISED AGAIN: THE UNIVERSALIZABILITY REQUIREMENT

Near the beginning of lecture 3 (3.2.3), I cited the argument by which Kant undertakes to establish that we must submit our maxims to a test of universalizability. Kant argues: (1) that we must act 'under the idea' that we have free will, where a free will is one which is not determined in accordance with any law external to itself; (2) that a free will, if it is to be a *will* at all, must nevertheless be determined in accordance with some law or other; (3) that it must therefore be determined in accordance with its own law – that is, be autonomous; and (4) that this shows that the categorical imperative is the law of a free will. For by this point in the text (the opening of *Grundlegung*, chapter III), Kant has already shown that the categorical imperative is the law of autonomy. And indeed this is clear in any case, since the categorical imperative tells us to choose a maxim which has the form of a law, and that is what an autonomous will by its very nature must do – it must choose a law for itself. The categorical imperative, in fact, simply tells us to be autonomous. In so far as we must act autonomously, we must of course conform to it.

Confronted with this astonishingly simple argument, it is impossible not to feel that some sort of sleight of hand has taken place; and, accordingly, Kant's readers have protested at almost every point. Let me review the objections here.

The first objection is that Kant has not shown that a free will's dictates must be universal, even in a purely formal sense. Cohen, for instance, who agrees with me that the ability to reflect puts the will in a position of self-command, asks why the will cannot give itself singular commands, edicts, or orders, rather than deriving its reasons from general principles.[1] A yet more radical version of this objection emerges in Geuss's invocation of Schlegel, who thought that true freedom consists in violating one's laws, proving that one is something above and beyond any law.[2] Why, then, is what the will requires a *universal* law?

Assuming that this objection can be surmounted, we then get the series of related objections traditionally comprehended under the complaint 'empty formalism'. The first of these is the one I myself deployed in the lectures: that until we settle the domain over which the law universalizes, the requirement of universalizability does not yield any particular content. We must argue that the law ranges over human beings or rational beings in order to get what I called 'the moral law', and that, according to the objection, cannot be done. So universalizability does not get us to morality. Next comes the version of the objection made most familiar to us in a long tradition stretching from Hegel and his followers and John Stuart Mill down to the present day: that even once we get the

---

[1] Cohen, p. 176.   [2] Geuss, pp. 192.

domain specified as universalizing over human beings the requirement has no content: there are no maxims that cannot consistently
be willed as laws for all human beings or all rational beings. Again,
universalizability does not get us to morality. Finally, there are
those who argue that a universalizability requirement, even if it is
in a sense legitimate, cannot bridge the gap from what in lecture 4 I
called 'private reasons' (subjective, agent-relative, or egoistic
reasons) to what I called 'public reasons' (objective, agent-neutral,
or altruistic reasons). A universalizability requirement shows only
that if I think that it is rational for me to look out for my own interests then I must agree that is rational for you to look out for yours.
But it gives me no reason for giving normative weight to your interests: it only helps me to see what, if you are rational, I may reason-
ably predict you will do. Yet again, universalizability does not get us
to morality.

Universalization isn't necessary at all; universalization may be
necessary, but need not range over human beings as such; universalization may range over human beings, but even so does not yield
moral content, either because no proposed universal laws are in
fact contradictory, or because universal reasons do not therefore
cease to be private reasons, and so a universalizability requirement
cannot bridge the gap that divides your reasons from mine. For
some or all of these reasons, Kant's argument from free will to
morality has been regarded as a failure.

In making these remarks, I have tried to separate out different
lines of criticism of Kant's argument, but of course in actual
instances the criticisms tend to shade into one another. For
instance, the claim that no maxims really do turn out to be contradictory when universalized may be supported by the claim that the
reasons cited in the maxims remain ineluctably private; or, pressing
in the other direction, it may depend on the claim that we do not
need to universalize *qua* human beings or *qua* rational beings.
Nevertheless, I think that these are really different objections. And
in various places, I have tried to answer all of them except the first.
In the lectures, I granted the second objection – that Kant's argument does not show that universalization must range over human
beings as such – and I tried to supply the deficit by arguing that you
must treat your humanity as a normative identity, a source of laws

for you (3.4.1–3.4.10). In my paper 'Kant's Formula of Universal Law' I argued that the traditional 'no-content' objection popularized by Mill and the followers of Hegel may in some cases be met. There *are* maxims which cannot be willed universally without contradiction. But I also think that this objection has been overrated in importance. Kant's account of the foundation of morality requires that an agent will a maxim only if she can also will it to be a universal law. But it does not require that we use Kant's contradiction tests as a way of determining *which* maxims we can will as universal laws. It only requires that we have *some* determinate way of identifying those maxims which can or cannot be willed as universal laws.[3] Finally, both in my paper 'The Reasons We Can Share: an Attack on the Distinction Between Agent-Relative and Agent-Neutral Values' and in 4.2.1–4.2.12 of lecture 4, I have challenged the idea that a reason could be ineluctably private in its normative force and so disputed the claim that there *is* any gap between private reasons and public reasons that needs to be bridged.

Of course not everyone will think these arguments successful. But my critics here have pressed a question which, as I mentioned, I haven't taken up before, namely, why the dictates of the free will must be universal in any sense at all. So I want to begin my reply by addressing this question.

Nagel, who thinks that he has an answer, puts the objection helpfully:

Why isn't the reflective individual just someone with more information, who can therefore make choices which may be different but which need be no less purely personal – or even temporally fragmented? How do reasons, law, and universality get a foothold here – one that cannot be dislodged? Presumably it has something to do with the difference between reflective and unreflective consciousness, but why should awareness of self bring with it this further regularizing effect?[4]

Kant says that this happens because the will is a causality and a causality must operate in accordance with laws. But Nagel protests:

If the will is self-determining, why can't it determine itself in individual, disconnected choices as well as according to some consistent law or system of reasons? A neo-Humean regularity theory of causation seems

---

[3] See 3.2.4.   [4] Nagel, p. 201.

an inappropriate model for free self-determination. If the idea makes sense at all, the free choice of actions which conform to a law is no more nor less a form of *causality* than the free choice of actions which do not . . . So far as I can see, choosing freely in a law-like pattern is merely a way of mimicking causality; if I always put on my left sock before my right, that does nothing to establish the causality of my will, so why does the categorical imperative do any better?[5]

Instead, Nagel proposes his own way of establishing the need to universalize:

The reflective self is in its nature more universal than the original, unreflective self, because it achieves its self-conscious awareness by detaching from the individual perspective . . . once we observe ourselves from outside, and achieve the distance of which Korsgaard speaks, our choice becomes not just what to believe or do, but what *this person* should believe or do. And that has to be a decision about what any person so situated should believe or do, since the external view does not give any consideration to the fact that the person is me – it describes me in terms which would be just as available to someone else sufficiently well informed about me.[6]

Nagel, in other words, thinks that the answer lies in the fact that looking at oneself and one's impulses more reflectively *just amounts to* looking at oneself and one's impulses more objectively, as if from 'outside' of the personal point of view. If my impulse is indeed a normative consideration for me – if it is a reason for action – then it must be a normative consideration for the person who I am – and this fact must be perspicuous to anyone who takes up this objective view of my situation.

While I agree that our capacity to achieve reflective distance from our impulses and our capacity to view ourselves as persons are related, I think that Nagel brings in generality too quickly when he says that the self 'achieves its self-conscious awareness *by detaching from the individual perspective*' (my emphasis). I believe instead that an agent's capacity to view herself from outside – as 'a person' – is a *product* of her reflective distance from her impulses. And this means that the question *how* the achievement of reflective distance leads her to identify herself as 'a person' requires an answer. Furthermore, the agent will acknowledge that certain reasons pertain to

[5] Nagel, p. 202.　　[6] Nagel, pp. 203.

her in so far as she is 'a person' only if the conception of herself as 'a person' which is achieved in reflection is one that she finds to be normative. Together these facts imply that the route from the capacity for reflection to a normative conception of the self as 'a person' must be traced. This is part of what I tried to do in the lectures.

Let me see if I can clarify this response by putting it in a more polemical way. Nagel seems to agree with me that when you reflect, you ask whether your impulse (to believe or to act) is a reason. The business of reflection is to *arrive at* reasons.[7] But Nagel also thinks that 'reflection' *just amounts to* taking up a general view of yourself, viewing yourself from outside as 'a person'. The combination of these two ideas does yield the conclusion that reasons are general and apply to persons as such. But the way that it does so is by yielding the conclusion that your attempt to determine whether your impulse is a reason *just amounts to* an attempt to determine whether it is normative for you in so far as you regard yourself as 'a person'. In other words, Nagel assumes that practical reflection – the search for practical reasons – just is the search for considerations that are normative for you under some general description. But I don't see why we should accept this account of practical reflection unless we already suppose that practical reasons are general. Unless Nagel has some independent argument to show that reflection just amounts to viewing oneself as in general terms – or, better, unless he gives us independent reason for thinking that our ability to achieve reflective distance from our impulses is the *product* of our ability to conceive ourselves in general terms, Nagel is simply equating the activity of reflection with the search for a general answer. Notice that the point here doesn't depend on Nagel's specific claim that reflective distance is achieved by viewing yourself as 'a person'. The point would be the same if Nagel agreed that reflection might consist in viewing yourself as 'a teacher' or 'a mother' or under any other general description. In assuming that what you do when you ask whether your impulse is a reason is ask whether the impulse is normative for you when you view yourself under some general description, Nagel is assuming that reasons are

---

[7] 'Arrive at' here is meant to be neutral between realist and constructivist accounts.

general. But that was the point that we were supposed to be establishing. Nagel's answer therefore seems to me to be somewhat circular.

This is not to say that I cannot imagine an independent argument for thinking that reflective distance is the product of our ability to conceive ourselves in general terms. There are some murky issues involved here, concerning the relationship between linguistic capacity and self-consciousness: one might imagine someone arguing (very roughly) that: (1) linguistic capacity precedes and causes self-consciousness, and so is the source of our ability to achieve reflective distance from our impulses, (2) language is inherently general, and therefore (3) achieving reflective distance essentially involves conceiving oneself in general terms. I do not know whether Nagel has something along these lines in mind. I am not inclined to believe the first premiss of this argument, although I also admit I feel somewhat at a loss about how to sort such an issue.

In any case, I would like to propose another account of why we must will universally – one which, while it also appeals to the generality of language, does not assume that our ability to view ourselves in general terms is the source of our ability to achieve reflective distance from our impulses. Instead it tries to move *from* the fact that we have reflective distance from our impulses *to* the requirement that we conceive our reasons as universal, at least in a formal sense.

In advancing this account it will be useful to begin with a point Nagel makes in the course of the argument I've cited above. When he rejects Kant's claim that the will needs a law because it is a cause, Nagel remarks that 'a neo-Humean regularity theory of causation seems an inappropriate model for free self-determination'.[8] I don't think that this model is inappropriate. We may observe that a parallel problem seems to exist in two cases: the cases of 'is a reason for' and 'is a cause of'. Our ordinary notion of causality seems to combine two quite different ideas: the idea of *power* or (there is no non-redundant way to put this) of one thing *effecting* another or *making* another happen, and the idea of universality – that this occurs in a regular or law-like way.[9] Our ordinary

---

[8] Nagel, p. 202, quoted above. [9] See Hume, *A Treatise of Human Nature*, 1.3.

notion of a reason also seems to combine two quite different ideas: what in the lectures I have called the idea of *normativity* or (again there is no non-redundant way to put it) of *obligating* someone to do or believe something or *requiring* someone to do or believe something, and again the idea of universality – that the normativity must be captured in a regular or law-like formulation.[10] What the *normativity* of reasons and the *power* of causes seem to have in common is that they are forms of necessitation: a cause *makes* its effect happen, and so necessitates it (all else equal); a reason for action or belief necessitates that for which it is a reason in another way, namely, it necessitates a person to act or believe as it directs (again all else equal).[11] And in both cases we can raise the same question, namely, why the notion of necessitation – the power of causes, the normativity of reasons – must be combined with the notion of universality or regularity in order to make sense. Why can't these ideas of power and normativity stand alone?

A part of Hume's answer, accepted by Kant, was that we could never recognize cases of causality in the absence of regularity. Kant denied, of course, that regularity alone could have given us the idea of causality, but he accepted the negative part of Hume's account. Since we do not directly perceive power, we cannot perceive individual exercises of power. Even if there were such things

---

[10] As I said in 1.2.4, I use the term 'normativity' to refer to the ways in which reasons direct, guide, or obligate us to act, believe, or judge in certain ways: to what we might call their authoritative *force*. Now the term 'normativity' contains an etymological reference to law, and laws are usually thought of as universal. Since the connection between universality and authoritative force is exactly what has been challenged here, the use of the term 'normativity' is a little unfortunate in the present context, and Butler's 'authority' might have been a better choice. On the other hand, it is worth noticing that the same sort of point I am making about 'reason' and 'cause' can also be made about 'law': it seems to connect the idea of authoritative command with the idea of universality, and again we might wonder why these two ideas seem to belong together.

[11] The sense of 'necessitates' is different here, of course, since causal necessity makes its outcome inevitable, and rational necessity does not. Rational necessity is not the same as logical necessity either. In fact, it is easiest to bring out what it is by contrasting it with logical necessity. If all women are mortal, and I am a woman, then it necessarily follows that I am mortal. That is *logical* necessity. But if I *believe* that all women are mortal, and I *believe* that I am a woman, then I *ought* to conclude that I am mortal. The necessity embodied in that use of 'ought' is *rational* necessity. If I am *guided* by reason, then I will conclude that I am mortal. But of course it is not inevitable that I will do so; perhaps the horror of contemplating my own mortality will make me irrational. I discuss these ideas in 'The Normativity of Instrumental Reason'.

as single, anomalous instances of one thing *making* another happen, *we* would have no way of distinguishing those from mere temporal sequences of events. Causality is not mere temporal sequence, since it also involves necessitation. Without endorsing Hume's more reductive and sceptical conclusions, we can agree with him that we could never *identify* the element of necessitation and therefore distinguish cases of causal connection from cases of mere temporal sequence without regularity. And this is part of the story about why we need regularity or law for the idea of causality.

Now I have described the two cases – reason and cause – as parallel, but in Kant's argument the point about practical reasons is not only parallel to, but also depends upon, the point about causality. For to regard oneself as an agent is to regard oneself as a cause, as productive of certain actions and their effects. And given the connection between causality and regularity, to do that must be to regard oneself as productive of these actions and effects in some regular way. This is what Kant means when he says that since the will is a cause it must operate according to a law.

But this move might seem to be mere insistence in the face of an obvious, introspectively available fact. Of course I can decide right now to (say) act on a certain desire, and I can do it without committing myself to acting in the same way whenever I have this desire – much less committing myself to the principle that *everyone* should act the same way. I do not need to refer to past or future acts of my will in any way at all when I make the present decision. What on earth is to force me to do that? Surely not a conceptual argument about the conditions under which human beings can distinguish causal connections from mere temporal sequences! How could that have any force at all against the freedom which, as Kant is the first to admit, is inherent in the very standpoint of deliberative choice?

But I think that this objection has less force than it appears at first to have. For what it misses is that willing is *self-conscious* causality, causality that operates in the light of reflection. To will is not just to be a cause, or even to allow an impulse in me to operate as a cause, but, so to speak, to consciously pick up the reins, and make *myself* the cause of what I do. And if I am to constitute *myself* as the cause of an action, then I must be able to distinguish between *my* causing the action and some desire or impulse that is 'in me' causing my body to act. I must be able to see *myself* as something that is distinct from any of my particular, first-order, impulses and motives, as the reflective standpoint in any case requires. Minimally, then, I am not the mere location of a causally effective desire but rather am the *agent* who acts *on* the desire. It is because of this that if I endorse acting a certain way now, I must at the same time endorse acting the same way on every relevantly similar occasion. Let me try to explain why.

It would be tempting here, and not altogether wrong, to appeal to the generality that in any case must characterize all language and thought and so all reflective endorsement. When my will operates, that is, when I endorse acting on this desire, I must describe the desire and the action to myself in some way or other, if only as 'a desire' or perhaps 'satisfying a desire'. Thought traffics in the general – the human mind traffics in the general – and it is nonsense to think I could have some *wholly* particular way of conceiving what I am doing. This by itself, however, does not quite commit me to reaching the same conclusion about what it would be appropriate to do on all relevantly similar occasions as I reach now. Again, it would be tempting to say that it so commits me until I can find the resources for changing my mind. That's very nearly right. But I think the more accurate way to put the point is to say that it so commits me if there is to be such a thing as *my mind* to change. For if *all* of my decisions were particular and anomalous, there would be no identifiable difference between *my acting* and *an assortment of first-order impulses being causally effective in or through my body*. And then there would *be* no self – no mind – no me – who is the one who does the act.

The point I am making here is *exactly* analogous to the point about distinguishing causal connections from mere temporal sequences of events. Just as the special relation between cause and effect, the necessitation that makes their relation different from mere temporal sequence, cannot be established in the absence of law or regularity, so the special relation between agent and action, the necessitation that makes that relation different from an event's merely taking place in the agent's body, cannot be established in the absence of at least a claim to law or universality. So I need to

will universally in order to see my action as something which *I do*.
Nagel misses the point when he says that regularity does nothing to
establish the causality of my will. What it does is establish my own
ability to see myself as having a will, as having the kind of *self-conscious* causality that *is* a rational will.

Let me put this point another way. Hume argued not only that
we do not encounter the power of causes in experience, but also
that we do not encounter the active self in experience. We
encounter our thoughts and motives, but not the self who thinks
them or acts on them. Kant's reply to the first point was that the
mind in effect imposes the notion of causal law on certain temporal
sequences in its attempt to understand the empirically given world
as a single systematic whole organized in space and time. In a
similar way, we impose the form of universal volitional principle on
our decisions in our attempts to unify ourselves into agents or characters who persist through time – or rather – as I will explain below
– who are committed to making the same decision on *some* range of
possible occasions. In both cases, the function of the a priori principle is to impose the form of unity on what would otherwise be disparate phenomena. The function of the normative principles of
the will, in particular, is to bring integrity and therefore unity – and
therefore, really, existence – to the acting self.[12]

I am aware that there is an air of paradox in what I have just
said. Who, after all, is this apparently ephemeral self who has to
unify itself into an agent or character that can persist through a
series of relevantly similar occasions, and why, if it is indeed
ephemeral, does it have to do that?[13] The answer is that the
ephemeral self is the reflecting self, the one who looks at its impulse
from a reflective distance. And the reason that it has to unify itself
into an agent who can persist through a series of relevantly similar
occasions is *not* that it has some reason to want or anticipate that it
will persist into the *future*. It is not, for instance, that the ephemeral
reflective self already knows that it will be succeeded by a series of
future ephemeral reflective selves, who will all inhabit the same

---

[12] I say more about the idea that unity must be conferred on, or achieved by, the agent, and
the idea that this is something required by the agent's occupation of the deliberative (or
reflective) standpoint, in 'Personal Identity and the Unity of Agency: a Kantian Response
to Parfit'.   [13] I thank Arthur Kuflik for pressing me to be clearer on this point.

body, and with whom it must therefore coordinate its activities.[14] The reason is rather that the view of itself as active *now* essentially involves a projection of itself into other possible occasions.

To see this, consider first the simplest case: the hypothetical imperative. If I will an end, I ought to will the means to that end. This is not a mere description but rather a law, an imperative, expressed with an 'ought'. But who gives this law to whom, and when? It is a law that I give to myself, and its function is to bring unity to myself. And we can see this by considering when this law must be enforced. I have determined upon my end, but now I am reluctant to take the means. The imperative is conditional upon my willing the end, so if I just gave up the end, I could escape its force. Sometimes when we see what the achievement of an end will require of us, we give it up as not worth the bother, or consign it wistfully to the realm of mere wish. But I'm not talking about that kind of case; this end is one I *do* will, one I can't or won't give up. It is only that the means are difficult, or scary, or dull, and I am having trouble screwing myself to the task. That's when I am guided by the imperative – that's when I say to myself – 'since you will this end, you must take these means'. When I follow a hypothetical imperative, one part of me – say my will at one moment – governs another part of me – say at another moment – the part that is capable of being sidetracked or derailed by difficulty or dread or dullness. The reason I must follow hypothetical imperatives in general is that if I don't follow them, if I *always* allow myself to be derailed by difficulty or dread or dullness, then I never really *will* an end. The *desire* to pursue the end and the desires that draw me away from it each hold sway in their turn, but *my will* is never active. The distinction between my will and the operation of the desires and impulses in me does not exist, and that means that I, considered as an agent, do not exist.[15] It follows from this that when I will an end,

[14] In 'Personal Identity and the Unity of Agency: a Kantian Response to Parfit' I myself tentatively proposed an argument along these lines, but it was addressed to a somewhat different point. There I was arguing against the possibility of an ephemeral self-interested reason; here I am arguing for the universalizability requirement in general. I also argued, in that paper, that talk of cooperating with future selves is in a way misleading (pp. 112–114). In both that argument and this one, the real issue is not whether what I am here calling the ephemeral self has reason to desire or anticipate a special connection with some future selves, but rather whether the *active* self can coherently be conceived as ephemeral.

[15] These points are also discussed in 'The Normativity of Instrumental Reason'.

I must *ipso facto* will that even on another occasion, even when I am tempted not to, I will stay on the track of that end. Otherwise it's like promising your lover you'll be faithful until someone else catches your eye: no real action has been taken. So when you will an end, the form of the act of your will is general: you will a kind of law for yourself, a law that applies not only now, but on other possible occasions.

Now I need to clarify these remarks in one important way. In the above argument I appealed to the possibility of being tempted away from the end on another, temporally later occasion. But the argument does not really require the possibility of a temporally later occasion. It only requires that there be two parts of me, one that wills, and one that is capable of resisting my will. The possibility of resistance exists even now, on this occasion. When we act self-consciously, we act under the idea of freedom: we think that we could act otherwise on *this* occasion. But that means that 'this occasion' itself must be conceived in general terms: it cannot be an ineluctable particular. You cannot say of an ineluctable particular that *it* could be otherwise. Reflective distance brings the impulse into view: you then can say, 'that impulse, that desire – I can follow it or not'. And then you have thought of *it* in a general way, say as 'a desire'. To think that you could have done otherwise on this occasion, or in the face of this impulse, the occasion must be characterized in some way – which is to say, some general way. The importance of this will become clear in a moment.

The general requirement of universalizing our maxims has the same source as the general requirement of following hypothetical imperatives. I cannot regard myself as an active self, as *willing* an end, unless *what I will* is to pursue my end in spite of temptation. In the same way, I cannot regard myself as an active self, as willing a maxim, unless *what I will* is to follow my maxim in spite of temptation. Laws which cannot be violated cannot be followed either, so if I am to give myself a law it must be conceivable that I should break it. If I give myself a law, if I am not merely the place where an impulse is operating, then what I do essentially involves a reference to other occasions when I might do otherwise – or, to pick up the point in the previous paragraph – to *this* occasion, regarded as possibly other, and so regarded in general terms. And that means that if I am to regard *this* act, the one I do now, as the act of my *will*, I must at least make a claim to universality, a claim that the reason for which I act now will be valid on other occasions, or on occasions of this type – *including this one, conceived in a general way*. Again, the form of the act of the will is general. The claim to generality, to universality, is essential to an act's being an act of the will.[16]

A couple of paragraphs ago I put into the objector's mouth the claim that when I make a decision I need not refer to any past or future acts of my will. But now we see that this turns out to be false, for according to the above argument it is the claim to universality that *gives* me a will, that makes my will distinguishable from the operation of desires and impulses in me. If I change my mind and my will every time I have a new impulse, then I don't really have an active mind or a will at all – I am just a kind of location where these impulses are at play. And that means that to *make up my mind* even now – to give myself a reason – I must conceive my reason as an instance of some general type. Of course this is not to say that I cannot ever change my mind, but only to say that I must do it for a reason, and not at random. Geuss reports in his comments that Hegel characterized the Schlegelian life, in which laws are broken frivolously or for its own sake, as a 'constant succession of self-creation and self-destruction'.[17] This characterization seems to me to be perfectly apt. The active will is brought into existence by every moment of reflection, but without the claim to universality, it is no sooner born than dead. And that means that it does not really exist at all.

Williams is therefore *exactly* right when he says that he sees a Platonic inheritance in my view. For Plato too thinks that moral principles serve to hold the disparate parts of the human soul together, and in this way make the soul capable of unified and effective action. Moral principles, to put it in non-Platonic lan-

---

[16] I am not quite prepared to go so far as to propose that the generality of all thought *derives from* the freedom that is inherent in the achievement of reflective distance. I am not certain whether that makes any sense. More specifically, though, what I've said here raises a question about the source of the universality of theoretical reasons, reasons for belief. Although the view of belief as a voluntary act of the mind, paralleling choice, is controversial, it does look as if a parallel argument could be made about the (formal) universality of theoretical reasons, viz. that belief cannot be conceived as an act of the mind without a claim to the universality of the reason for which one believes. I will not pursue the ramifications of that possibility here, although they are obviously important.

[17] Geuss, p. 193.

guage, are what give the soul considered as a unified entity a *will*. The arguments first sketched in *Republic* I, to the effect that an unjust soul will fall into faction, and therefore will be incapable of acting effectively as a unit, say exactly this.[18] I do not agree with Williams, however, when he characterizes Plato as 'having ducked the full force of Callicles' challenge, by equating the bad with the addicted or brutal'.[19] I think that the work of the rest of the *Republic*, in particular, is to substantiate those early arguments by demonstrating and defending this equation, in particular, by showing that the democratic soul, in which each desire or impulse rules in its turn, is doomed to degenerate into the obsessive madness of the tyrannical soul, most enslaved of all human estates.[20] With Plato, I believe that neither human souls nor human communities can be held together, can be unified, and so can really *be*, unless they are (at least to some extent) Republics, submitting themselves to the rule of law. And that is why I think that freedom and autonomy require that we will in accordance with universal law.

It's important to remember that the argument of this section is intended only to show that reasons must be universal in a formal sense. The self-conception behind this requirement, the self-conception to which reflective distance first leads, is bare conception of oneself as an agent, as the subject of impulses which one may either follow or resist. To get all the way to Plato's conclusion – that what is required for our existence as unified agents is that we will in accordance with *moral* laws – two further points must be established: first, that the universal laws required by our conception of ourselves as agents must range over human beings as such; and second that the reasons that are derived from these laws are public. I have nothing new to say on those points now, so I leave the matter here.

---

[18] Plato, *Republic* I, 351b–352a. After filling out these initially unsatisfactory arguments in Books II–IV, Plato asserts that the just person binds together the three parts of his soul 'and any others there may be in between, and from having been many things he becomes entirely one, moderate and harmonious. Only then does he act' (443d–e).

[19] Williams, p. 215.   [20] Plato, *Republic* VIII–IX, 555b–579e.

2 APPARENT DEPARTURES FROM KANT

Cohen and Geuss think that my account of obligation departs from Kant's in some ways that are the worse for it; in this section, I will address these points, and in so doing try to clarify the sense in which I take my account to be Kantian.

Cohen begins his remarks by putting forth a problem about the very idea of grounding obligation in autonomy, which he raises in the form of a puzzle concerning Hobbes's theory. While an agent might on the one hand seem to be bound by a law she makes for herself, she also seems not to be bound, since she is free to unmake the law at will. According to what Cohen calls 'Hobbes's first argument' a citizen is bound by the sovereign's law because the sovereign is his representative and so the sovereign's laws are his own, while according to 'Hobbes's second argument', the sovereign himself is not bound by his law, since he makes the law himself and so can change the law at will. Being the legislator, it seems, both binds you to the law and makes you free from it. How is this consistent? Part of the answer lies in the fact that the citizens are represented: having granted their legislative power to the sovereign, they can change the law only by changing the sovereign's mind about what the law should be. And as Cohen himself points out, another part of the answer lies in what the second argument ignores: that even if I can change the law that I make for myself, I remain bound by it until I change it.[21] The argument that I gave in the previous section backs Cohen up on this point: if I am to be an agent, I cannot change my law without changing my mind, and I cannot change my mind without a reason. But it follows that the sovereign himself cannot change his own law without changing his mind, and this makes escape from the authority of the law less easy than Hobbes's second argument would have it, for we cannot change our minds about just anything. Now Cohen thinks that this answer is available to Kant, but not to me. And this is because Cohen thinks that according to Kant there is a standard the human will must meet when it legislates, namely the standard of universalizability, which is not itself the product of human legislation, but rather is imposed on that legislation by reason. Whereas on my

[21] Cohen, p. 170.

version of the view, the 'subject is unequivocally the author of the law that binds it'.[22] With no standard to constrain the agent's law-making, the agent can make and unmake laws at will, and so is not in any very interesting sense bound by them. And so my view falls prey to Hobbes's second argument.

My answer to this objection depends in part on what I said in section 1. Cohen makes it sound as if autonomous lawmaking were one thing, and universal autonomous lawmaking another, and this in turn makes it sound as if universalizability is a rational constraint which is imposed on what would otherwise be the arbitrary or unconstrained activity of autonomous lawmaking. But I think that Kant himself means something else, namely autonomous lawmaking just *isn't* autonomous lawmaking unless it is done universally. The requirement of universalization is not imposed on the activity of autonomous lawmaking by reason from outside, but is constitutive of the activity itself.

More generally, if we contrast activities which are totally unconstrained with activities which are constrained in an external way by certain rules or principles, we may leave an important option out, and at the same time make too much of a mystery of the question why we have to conform to those rules and principles. The option is that the rules and principles are constitutive of, and therefore internal to, the activities themselves, so that we have to conform to those principles if we are really to engage in those activities at all. If I am to walk, I must put one foot in front of the other: this is not a rule that externally constrains my walking, or boxes me in like the walls of a labyrinth, or that I can with much coherence rebel against. In the same spirit one might argue that if I am going to think I must think in accordance with the principle of non-contradiction, or that if I am going to will an end, I must also will the means to that end, or that if I am going to will at all I must do so universally. I am not saying that it is *obvious* that these rules are constitutive of these activities and that no argument needs to be made. I am making a point about what such arguments, when they are made, aim to achieve. If the argument of the previous section works, then the requirement of universality is in this way constitutive of willing. Of

---

[22] Cohen, p. 170.

course it is a separate question why I must walk, or think, or will an end or will at all. But once I am engaged in these activities it should not be a mystery why I have to conform to principles that in a sense simply constitute the carrying on of the activities themselves.[23]

Now this in turn is related to the way in which I understand the Kantian enterprise more generally. There are in our tradition two things which philosophers have meant by 'reason'. 'Reason' refers to the active as opposed to the passive capacities of the human mind, and 'reason' also refers to certain sets of principles – logical principles, moral and other practical principles, and the principles that Kant associates with the pure concepts of the understanding. What Kant did, as I see it, was to try to bring these two conceptions of reason together: to explain the normative force of the principles by showing that they are constitutive of reflective mental activity itself.[24] To choose *is* to follow the hypothetical and categorical imperatives; to understand *is* to employ the concepts and principles of the understanding, and so on. And in the same way, my own aim is to portray moral principles as constitutive of, and so as essential to, making human choices, and leading a human life.

So when Cohen portrays Kant as thinking that reason imposes a constraint on lawmaking, and concludes that in Kant's theory the subject is not unequivocally the author of the law, I think he creates a false opposition between my version of the view and Kant's. In both Kant's version and in mine the subject is unequivocally the author of the law, but autonomous lawmaking is not something

---

[23] I don't mean to suggest that these principles are descriptive rather than normative; nor do I mean to suggest *either* that we always follow them automatically, *or* that we are always conscious of being guided by them, when we engage in these activities. It is the nature of activities, as opposed to mechanical processes, that one who engages in them is self-guided (in an extensive sense, therefore, autonomous). The rules constitute the activities in the sense that what it means to be engaged in them is to guide yourself in accordance with these rules. For an activity to be self-guided, it must be one that you perform consciously, but you need not be conscious *that* you are doing it, or that you are guiding yourself by these rules. The difference here is between doing something that essentially involves consciousness and being conscious *that* you are doing it. An animal may walk consciously, but it need not be conscious that it is walking. The thinker swerves away from self-contradiction without thinking *about* it when the contradiction is obvious and the option not particularly tempting.

[24] This point is independent of Kant's own distinction between regulative and constitutive principles, which has to do with the relation of the principles to the objects to which they are applied, not with their relation to the agents who follow them.

you can do any way you like, any more than thinking is. It must be done universally.

To get the conclusion that the laws in question must be *moral* laws, however, I think we need another argument, and I tried to provide it by arguing that we must identify ourselves, normatively, as human beings as such. But Geuss argues that this further move is unKantian in another way. It depends on the idea of 'identifying' with a principle of choice (rather than merely 'using' it), whereas Kant does not invoke such a notion.[25] Nagel also makes this point, characterizing my appeal to identity as 'rather existentialist' (I think correctly) and also as therefore unKantian (I think incorrectly). Geuss suggests that the closest Kant comes to making an appeal to identity is in *Religion Within the Limits of Reason Alone*, where Kant associates one's most fundamental principles with one's 'intelligible character'. But intelligible character, Geuss points out, isn't quite the same thing as identity in the modern sense, since there are only two intelligible characters you can have, good or bad.

But although Kant doesn't use the term, it seems to me that he appeals quite straightforwardly to notions of identification in *Grundlegung*, chapter III, when providing his 'deduction' of the moral law. Kant first establishes that in so far as a person is active – 'in respect to that which may be pure activity in himself' – he regards himself as a member of the intelligible world. The moral law is the law of the intelligible world, and Kant argues that it binds the person because 'it is only as intelligence that he is his proper self'. In contrast, because the person is passive in the face of his desires, and regards them as the result of the operation of natural forces on him, 'He does not even hold himself responsible for these inclinations and impulses or attribute them to his proper self'.[26] According to this argument, our identification with the active side of our nature is what binds us to the moral law. That the moral self is a self normatively conceived, what I call a practical identity, emerges nicely when Kant says that 'even the most malicious villain (provided he is otherwise accustomed to using his reason)' – that is, provided he is reflective – 'imagines himself to be this better

[25] Geuss, p. 191.
[26] *Foundations of the Metaphysics of Morals*, pp. 457–458, in Beck's translation, p. 77.

person when he transfers himself to the standpoint of a member of the intelligible world'.[27] The 'better person' here functions at once as an object of aspiration and identification. The idea of identifying normatively with a certain conception of one's nature – the conception of oneself as active and rational – therefore plays a central role in Kant's view, just as the idea of identifying normatively with the conception of oneself as human does in mine.

3   THE STATUS OF DESIRE

The Kantian argument I just discussed, however, is the source of another of Geuss's criticisms, this time both of Kant and of me. Doesn't Kant portray the moral agent as regarding her desires and inclinations as 'alien intruders' or at least as 'alien entities from which I must keep my distance'?[28] And in speaking of our first-order impulses as things that we are confronted with, and must either endorse or reject, am I not doing the same thing? Why wouldn't it be enough to endorse or reject some of our desires in the name of, or from a point of view provided by, our other desires, rather than appealing to abstract principle? Perhaps we should identify with our desires, rather than regarding them as alien. Williams, whom Geuss cites, makes a similar point when he argues that perhaps we should not regard our moral motives as alien from our desires. In response to my remarks in section 1.1.1, about the possibility that we may have to sacrifice our heart's desire for moral reasons, Williams remarks that I am going to have to face 'a motley crew of romantics, Nietzscheans, Lawrentians, and merely *Epicuri de grege porcos* . . . say[ing] that if the [moral] claim . . . can and should have that much power against the heart's desire, it had better have a footing in the heart's desire'.[29]

A first point, as always, is that the picture of Kant invoked here is somewhat exaggerated. Kant did not think that all of our desires simply spring up in us, like mushrooms in the back yard, to be approached with caution. As his essay 'Conjectures on the Beginnings of Human History' brings out most clearly, Kant

---

[27] *Foundations of the Metaphysics of Morals*, pp. 454–455, in Beck's translation, pp. 73–74.
[28] Geuss, p. 190.   [29] Williams, p. 211.

believed it is an important fact about human beings that our first-order desires and impulses do not all derive immediately from instinct, like those of the other animals, but rather arise from a complex interplay of instinct and reason. Certain powers associated with reason, such as the capacities for comparison and foresight, operate on the materials provided by instinct, leading to a vast proliferation of the objects which human beings are capable of finding desirable, interesting, arousing, compelling, and so forth. The result is a set of specifically human interests that do not have a simple instinctual basis, such as the concern for long-term happiness, the capacity for romantic love, and the sense of the beautiful. All of the interests that we associate with the specifically human phenomenon of 'culture' are the result of reason's reworking, so to speak, of materials supplied by instinct. Specifically human interests *are* in a sense the products of our own activity.

Yet it cannot be denied that Kant seems to have made little use of this point in his moral philosophy, and it does raise some questions: if we identify with the active dimension of our minds, and if we play an active role in generating these impulses, why shouldn't these impulses seem to be more deeply our own – why shouldn't we, at least to some extent, identify with them? I don't know why exactly Kant didn't take up this question. But whatever the reason, my own employment of the notion of practical identity is in part intended to rectify the problem.

Our contingent practical identities are, to some extent, given to us – by our cultures, by our societies and their role structures, by the accidents of birth, and by our natural abilities – but it is also clear that we enter into their construction. And this means that the desires and impulses associated with them do not just *arise* in us. When we adopt (or come to wholeheartedly inhabit) a conception of practical identity, we also adopt a way of life and a set of projects, and the new desires which this brings in its wake. In some cases our conception of a contingent practical identity will give rise to new motives in a way that parallels the generation of the motive of duty by the thought of the categorical imperative. You may be tempted to do something but find that it is inconsistent with your identity as a teacher or a mother or a friend, and the thought that it is inconsistent may give rise to a new incentive, an incentive not to do this thing. As Luther's 'here I stand, I cannot do otherwise' reminds us, the human heart, being human, discovers itself not only in spontaneous desire, but in imperatives.[30] The motives and desires that spring from our contingent practical identities are therefore like the cultural desires Kant discussed in his historical essays. They are in part the result of our own activity, and, as such, we may identify with them in a deep way. And if a person also identifies deeply with the conception of herself as a Citizen of the Kingdom of Ends, she is not going to experience moral obligation as something alien to her inmost self or to her heart's desire either. Part of my intention in invoking the concept of practical identity is to break down Kant's overly harsh, and even in his own terms oversimplified, division between natural impulses that do not belong to my proper self and rational impulses that do.

Having said that, however, I want to return to, and emphasize, what is right about Kant's view that we should identify with our principles of choice rather than with our desires and impulses. Geuss seems to think that it is because of the supposed alienness or intrusiveness of desire that Kant thinks one must *use*, and I think that one must *identify with*, the categorical imperative. He writes:

Since *all* of my desires are alien intruders I can't use any of them to decide which of my other desires to endorse.[31]

And later:

After all, if in reflection I see all my desires as alien, then what else is there for me to identify with except the principle of endorsement (or rejection) I use?[32]

But that isn't the reason why one must ultimately identify with one's principle of choice or endorsement rather than one's first-order desires and impulses. It is rather that when I act I must see myself as an *agent* and to do that I must identify, as Kant says in the *Grundlegung*, with 'that which may be pure activity in [myself]'.[33] Although I have just been suggesting that we do make an active contribution to our practical identities and the impulses

---

[30] As Williams himself points out in 'Practical Necessity', p. 130.
[31] Geuss, p. 190.   [32] Geuss, p. 191.
[33] *Foundations of the Metaphysics of Morals*, p. 451; in Beck's translation, p. 70.

that arise from them, it remains true that at the moment of action these impulses are the incentives, the passively confronted material upon which the active will operates, and not the agent or active will itself. This is clear in Geuss's own formulation 'I can't use any of them to decide which of my other desires to endorse'. Who is the 'I' who decides to 'use' these desires, and how does it decide? The reason I must identify with my principle of choice when I act really has nothing to do with whether my first-order impulses seem totally alien to me or I regard them as my own productions. It is rather that at the moment of action I must identify with my principle of choice if I am to regard myself as the *agent* of the action at all.

Let me now turn to a related issue. A moment ago I responded to the objection that Kant doesn't allow us to identify with our desires by pointing out that in a Kantian theory one may play an active role in the formation of one's desires, and may therefore identify with them. But one might think that this close association between what we can identify with and our own agency is objectionable in itself. Williams, in his comments, complains that in a Kantian account, nothing will serve to justify action unless 'I just happen to. . .' cannot be applied to it. Williams thinks that a Kantian could not justify action by saying, for instance, 'I just happen to love him' or 'she just happens to be my daughter'.[34] And the Kantian association between identification and activity might be thought to support this claim, for to say that one *just happens to* does seem to suggest a kind of passivity, that this is a concern one has stumbled into rather than actively formed. Must a Kantian regard concerns one 'just happens' to have as 'alien entities from which I must keep my distance'?[35] I agree with Williams that this would be an unattractive result, because we surely *do* stumble into some of our deepest concerns, perhaps most obviously the ties associated with family, ethnicity, and nationality, but also sometimes and to some extent our religions, friendships, and careers. And it is the mark of a kind of immaturity not to accept the deep role of contingency in human life associated with this fact. We think that the person who keeps searching for the perfect career or the perfect mate rather

---

[34] Williams, pp. 214–215.   [35] Geuss, p. 190.

than finally *giving* his heart to some one of the projects or lovers that life has brought his way has failed to grow up.

But I think that it is essential, if we are to get this right, to distinguish our attitudes towards *contingency* from our attitudes towards *passivity*. For contingency itself is something that may either be actively embraced or passively endured, and this makes all the difference: the mature attitude is the one that actively embraces it, not the one that passively endures it. Kant's theory of value, in marked contrast to realist theories, embodies an advocacy of this attitude. For Kant urges us to take things to be important *because they are important to us*. And this means that we must do so in full acceptance of the fact that what specifically is important to us is at bottom contingent and conditional, determined by biological, psychological, and historical conditions that themselves are neither justified nor unjustified, but simply there. In a deep way, all of our particular values are ones we *just happen* to hold. But the transition from contingency to necessity is sometimes our own work. True lovers learn how to be made for each other. Kantian agents transform contingent values into necessary ones by valuing the humanity that is their source.

4 SELF-CONCEPTION AND THE PROBLEM OF EGOISM

Nagel argues that my view is unattractively egoistic. He says:

> If someone accepts death rather than betraying a number of other people to the killers, it might be unappreciative to explain this in terms of the conception he had of himself . . . to explain the grip on him of those reasons in terms of the self-conception would be to get things backwards, and incidentally to cheapen the motive.[36]

A great deal depends on what Nagel means by 'explain[ing] the grip on him of those reasons'. In approaching this question it will help to have some background points in place.

In a Kantian conception of moral psychology there is an important distinction between the first-order impulse or 'incentive' to the performance of an action and the principle of volition under which one chooses to act on that incentive. An agent is confronted

---

[36] Nagel, p. 206.

with an incentive – a desire or other impulse that presents a certain action as worth doing – and, in response to the presentation, then decides, in accordance with a principle of choice or volition, whether to do the action or not. I like to think of this as a 'double-aspect' theory of motivation, since we need not imagine that there is always something like a deliberate two-step process, in which the agent *first* notices the incentive and *then* decides whether to act on it by consciously applying the principle of choice. It is rather that the motive of a chosen action has two aspects: the aspect under which the action is presented to the agent as something she might do and the aspect under which she actually chooses to do it. Kant thinks that there are two principles of choice that may govern our actions: the principle of self-love, which is roughly that of choosing to do an action because you want to do it; and the moral principle, which adds a governing requirement that we should be aware that the maxim of doing the action is fit to be a universal law. Neither the incentive nor the principle of choice is, by itself 'the reason' for the action; rather, the reason is the incentive as seen from the perspective of the principle of choice. That you desire something is a reason for doing it from the perspective of the principle of self-love. From the perspective of the moral principle, however, it is only a reason for doing it if the maxim of doing it passes the categorical imperative test. In my own account, the principle of self-love is replaced by the various principles associated with our contingent practical identities. That Susan is in trouble is a reason for action from the perspective of Susan's friend; that the law requires it is a reason for action from the perspective of a citizen, and so forth.

Now there are certain familiar errors people make about this psychological model, which involve the idea that the operation of a principle of choice must somehow infect the original incentive, or change its content, or replace it.[37] Consider for instance a standard reaction to Kant's criticism of the naturally sympathetic person in the famous example of *Grundlegung*, chapter 1, When Kant suggests that the sympathetic person's action is on a footing with action prompted by other inclinations, meaning that it is chosen under the principle of self-love, readers often suppose Kant *must* be implying

---

[37] In thinking about this issue I have benefited from discussions with Scott Kim.

that the sympathetic impulse is not after all disinterested. But Kant is perfectly clear that he does not think that, for he characterizes such people as being 'without any motive of vanity or selfishness'.[38] The content of one's desires and impulses is not somehow changed by the principle of volition under which one chooses to act on them. Kant's complaint about the naturally sympathetic person is not that he *wants* to help others only because it *pleases* him to do so. It is rather that he *chooses* to help others only because he *wants* to. This is indeed a reason to help others, if an incomplete one, but there is a better one available, which the sympathetic person would have encountered, if he had only taken thought about whether he could universalize his maxims. Kant condemns the naturally sympathetic person not for the content of his incentive, but rather for making an insufficiently reflective choice.[39]

A closely related confusion involves the idea that the principle of choice somehow *replaces* the original incentive as '*the reason*' for the action, as if the two were in competition for this role. People are tempted to say that in Kant's view the moral person chooses to help another 'because it is his duty', and the sympathetic person chooses to help another 'because he enjoys doing so', and that this means that neither of them can be helping the other 'because the other is in need'. I think instead that for both of these characters the very fact that someone is in need is an incentive and to that extent is a reason to help. But it is a different sort of reason for one who sees the needs of another as the source of a claim on him, as the source of a duty, than it is for one who sees helping another merely as something he would like to do.

I have described the two views above as confusions, which I think is what they usually are when offered as hostile interpretations of what Kant must mean. But of course there are versions of both of them that do not spring from mere confusion, but from anti-Kantian philosophical outlooks. A traditional empiricist would deny the radical distinction between choice and desire on which my response to the first one depends. And a realist would

---

[38] *Foundations of the Metaphysics of Morals*, p. 398; in Beck's translation, p. 14.
[39] For a more extensive analysis of this example and the light it throws on Kant's conception of moral psychology, see my 'From Duty and for the Sake of the Noble: Kant and Aristotle on Morally Good Action'.

deny the perspective-dependence of reasons on which my answer to the second depends. Nagel says, of his exemplar:

> Even if he can get motivational help from thinking that he couldn't live with himself if he saved his life by this method, that is not the final explanation – indeed it couldn't be. The real explanation is whatever would *make* it impossible for him to live with himself, and that is the non-first-personal reason against the betrayal.[40]

What I would say is that the fact that the others would die if he got out of his difficulty by betraying them is a reason not to do so *from the perspective* of someone who regards himself as a Citizen of the Kingdom of Ends. Nagel's disagreement with that aspect of my view, as well as his commitment to what I have called 'substantive realism', are both signalled by his use of the phrase 'non-first-personal' here. There is certainly a sense in which Nagel thinks that reasons depend for their existence on perspective, for he asserts that the objective point of view is itself a perspective, and that no reasons would exist in a world devoid of creatures who can take that perspective up.[41] But he also thinks that reasons are not constructed from, but rather discovered in, the objective point of view, and that choice should be a *response* to them. That's why he thinks I get it 'backwards'.

Nagel's view about this, I think, is the result of his view, which I discussed in section 1, that reflection just amounts to viewing things more objectively or impersonally, where 'objectivity' is understood in a 'realist' way: to seek an objective understanding is to try to see what is really there, or, in the case of practical reasons, what you should really do, in a way that is uninfected by the particularities of the perspective from which you see it. The ideal of objectivity is to approach as closely as possible to seeing the world from no particular perspective at all – in Nagel's famous phrase, *From Nowhere*. In a more 'constructivist' view like mine, by contrast, that ideal is regarded as incoherent: the fact that we can never escape viewing the world *from somewhere* is not a regrettable limitation, since there is *nothing* that the world is like *from nowhere*. There may be, however, something that the world is like for knowers as such or for rational agents as such, and the quest for 'objectivity' – that is, the sur-

---

[40] Nagel, p. 206.   [41] See *The View From Nowhere*, p. 150.

mounting of more local and contingent perspectives – is understood as the quest to view the world from these more necessary and inescapable points of view. Practical reasons that can only be found in the perspective of rational agents as such or human beings as such are 'objective' if we have no choice but to occupy those perspectives.[42]

Since my disagreement with Nagel depends in part on these much larger issues between realists and constructivists there are a number of different ways we might prosecute it. The specific one that concerns me here is the one about whether my view renders the agent's motivation unattractively egoistic. In my view a reason derives its normative force for an agent from a perspective provided by her identification with a principle of choice. For instance another's need might be a reason for her from the perspective of her self-identification as a Citizen of the Kingdom of Ends. Does this cheapen her motive? An initial point is that it would be a mistake to suppose that the self-conception in question is a view of herself *rather than* of others. To conceive oneself as a Citizen of the Kingdom of Ends is to conceive oneself as related to others in a certain way – it is not a private ideal. But of course it is still a conception in which the self appears – it is not just a thought about the others, say about their needs or their rights, as Nagel apparently thinks it should be. Nagel acknowledges that appeals to self-conception may serve a psychological function, in stiffening the agent's resolve, and even concedes that they may be psychologically necessary if one is to perform actions of the sort under discussion: 'perhaps only romantic egoists can make sacrifices of this extreme sort – on the model of religious martyrs who expect eternal bliss'.[43] I have to protest the part about the expectation of eternal bliss,

---

[42] Of course, in my view there is one sense in which we *do* have a choice about whether to occupy the perspective of a Citizen of the Kingdom of Ends (or a valuer of humanity) – we can take refuge in complete normative scepticism (see 4.4.2). One might think that this limits the sense in which what I've provided here is an adequate substitute for the 'realist' conception of objectivity. But Nagel argues that the realist conception of objectivity itself must leave a sceptical possibility permanently open: since we cannot literally view the world from nowhere, it is always possible that any conception of the world we form is distorted by the point of view from which we form it. (See *The View From Nowhere*, especially pp. 67–71.) Both of these conceptions of 'objectivity', therefore, must leave the door open for scepticism, but we conceive the threat of scepticism in very different ways.

[43] Nagel pp. 206–207.

since the 'egoism' that my view involves is a matter of being concerned with what you *are*, not a matter of being concerned with what you *get*, and no question of being rewarded is at issue.[44] Yet I certainly grant that my view implies that self-conceptions are essential to the normativity of reasons. I have suggested that an agent could not bring herself to make extreme sacrifices unless not making them seemed to her to be worse than death, and I do mean worse for the agent herself. Nagel clearly thinks that if I am right about this then we are not as good as we should be.[45] I on the other hand take it to throw important light on the grounds of moral obligation.

There are various ways in which one might suppose that the need for identification with a principle of choice cheapened one's motive. First, one might suppose that no principle of choice should operate at all, that our natural impulse of love for these others (say) should propel us into making the sacrifice without the

---

[44] Nagel says 'The temptation to offer an egoistic answer to egoism has been a weakness of ethical theory since the dawn of the subject' (p. 206). But I think that the 'egoism' of which people sometimes accuse Plato and Aristotle is, in the first instance, a concern with what you *are*, not a concern with what you *get* (including, now, experiences of a certain kind as part of what you get). This can be hard to see because both of them were deeply convinced that the achievement of εὐδαιμονία depends above all on what you *are*, and they were both prepared to defend the virtuous life on these grounds. I am not saying that they were wrong, but merely that the strategy can be misleading, especially for a modern audience predisposed to think of εὐδαιμονία (or happiness) *itself* as primarily a matter of having certain experiences, of getting things.

[45] Nagel says that if the normative force of reasons depends on self-conception in the way that I suggest, then 'morality is an illusion . . . the sceptics are right' (p. 207). But he also asserts that morality depends on whether, in reflection (by which he means, when we view ourselves objectively), we are 'prepared to regard' *ourselves* as worthless (p. 207). As Arthur Kuflik reminded me, Nagel himself, in *The Possibility of Altruism*, tied morality to the conception of oneself as 'one among others equally real', and based his argument on the cost of giving up that conception. As Nagel argued there and reasserts here, 'if . . . from the reflective standpoint we do not regard ourselves as worthless, then we must accord a more general weight to . . . our reasons for acting. And . . . this weight will automatically be accorded to similar reasons arising in the lives of others' (p. 207). This sounds a lot like what I think. But it turns out that when Nagel talks about how we 'are prepared to' regard ourselves on reflection, he actually means what we find to be true about ourselves when we reflect; and when he says that we 'accord' weight to various reasons he actually means that we discover that they have this weight: '. . . it is a matter of being faced with the alternatives, and having to decide which is more credible. We do not *make* these things true . . .' (p. 208); '. . . you have to think about the world . . . rather than about yourself and who you feel yourself to be' (p. 206). In section II of 'The Reasons We Can Share: an Attack on the Distinction Between Agent-Relative and Agent-Neutral Values', I suggested that Nagel sometimes evinces a certain ambivalence about his realism. I see that ambivalence emerging again in some of the language, to my ears constructivist, which he uses here.

operation of any self-conscious volition. Here is romance of another kind, by which I think moral philosophers in the sentimentalist tradition have sometimes been tempted. A mother animal rushes to the salvation of her cubs in this spirit; it is in its way deeply impressive and lovely that she should do so, but it is not morality, nor do I think there is anything to regret in that fact. Human actions are for the most part chosen, not merely impelled: this is why they are subject to a moral standard, a standard that governs the way in which they are chosen. In my view, that is why there is such a thing as morality at all. It is pointless to protest that there should not have been any act of choice: if there had not been, the action would not have been subject to moral evaluation.[46]

Second, one might suppose that the specific *content* of the principle of choice cheapens the motive. This certainly can be true. It is true in one of Nagel's descriptions of the case, the one in which the agent chooses those actions which he thinks will bring him eternal bliss. But unless you accept the romantic view I rejected above, it does not have to be true. And in any case, the content of the principle of choice here is just that of the Kantian moral law, the law of acting as a Citizen of the Kingdom of Ends. Surely there is nothing cheap about that.

The third possibility, and the one I believe is bothering Nagel, is that what supposedly cheapens the motive is neither the fact of choice, nor the content of the principle of choice, but rather the fact that the principle of choice derives its ability to confer normativity on the incentive from the way that the agent identifies herself. This is what I think Nagel means when he talks about 'explaining how the reason gets its grip' on the agent. Now it is worth pointing out that even on my view of the situation *explicit* thoughts about one's identification with the principle of choice need come into play only when the agent must stiffen her resolve, when she is tempted not to do what she ought. Perhaps someone might think that it is bad that she is so tempted, but I think this would involve, at a higher level, the same romantic error as the view that incentives

[46] I set forward this view about the relationship between choice and morality in 'From Duty and for the Sake of the Noble: Kant and Aristotle on Morally Good Action'.

of love should move us in a way that bypasses choice altogether. It suggests that we ought not to raise what I have called 'the normative question'. But I think that it befits an adult rational being to question the necessity of extreme sacrifice, and it is to be hoped that if she does not it is because she already has a grip on the answer. But the answer certainly is, in my view, that the she is unprepared to give up a certain way she looks at herself, a description under which she finds her life worth living and her actions worth undertaking. And this is what bothers Nagel – the idea that, in this way, normativity derives from our self-conceptions. And I do think this.

I can best explain my view on this matter by comparing it to the very similar one which Kant held. Kant supposed that we have a natural tendency to treat our own desires as reasons – or, as he puts it, 'to make the subjective determining grounds of one's choice into an objective determining ground of the will in general'.[47] This tendency, which Kant says is 'natural and active in us even prior to the moral law' seems to be based on a natural and extremely primitive tendency we have to value ourselves.[48] Kant does not attempt to trace the source of this primitive tendency, but in these lectures I have suggested that it results from the combination of our reflective consciousness with our animal nature, since every animal is so constructed as to value itself (4.3.6–4.3.9). Kant thinks that this primitive tendency to value ourselves is the basis of our capacity for *both* good and evil. Guided by reflection, we may be led to see that our tendency to regard our desires as reasons implies that we set a value on our own humanity and so on humanity in general.[49] This realization leads us to the principle of morality. In the absence of such reflection, the tendency to treat our desires as reasons remains the insufficiently reflective principle of self-love on which, for instance, the sympathetic person in *Grundlegung*, chapter 1, acts.[50] Finally, if an agent consciously and reflectively *decided* to treat his desires as reasons merely because they were his *own* desires, either ignoring the claims of morality altogether or deliberately subordinating

[47] Kant, *Critique of Practical Reason*, p. 74; in Beck's translation, p. 77.
[48] I am indebted here to discussions and correspondence with Allen Wood.
[49] See the account of Kant's argument in 3.4.8.
[50] Kant, *Foundations of the Metaphysics of Morals*, pp. 398–399, in Beck's translation, pp. 14–15.

morality's claims to the claims of his own self-interest, then he would be evil.[51]

I believe something very similar to this, but in place of the principle of self-love, I put the fact of normative self-conception, the fact that we naturally form conceptions of our identities which we are inclined to treat as normative. Apart from that difference the view is supposed to work just like Kant's does. Guided by reflection, we may be led to see that our tendency to treat our contingent practical identities as the sources of reasons implies that we set a value on our own humanity and so on humanity in general. This realization leads us to the moral principle of valuing humanity as an end in itself. In the absence of such reflection, the tendency to treat our contingent practical identities as the sources of reasons may be condemned as insufficiently reflective, just as the principle of self-love on which the sympathetic person in *Grundlegung*, chapter 1, acts may be condemned as insufficiently reflective. For example, although someone's being a family member or a member of your ethnic group may provide very good reasons for, say, helping him, such identifications do fail to capture one important reason that also exists: namely, the claims of his humanity, which make helping him a *moral* duty. Finally, if an agent consciously and reflectively *decided* to treat a contingent practical identity as giving him a reason that is ungrounded in moral or human identity, either ignoring the claims of morality altogether, or deliberately subordinating morality's claims to the claims of this practical identity, then he would be evil. To take some salient examples, someone who deliberately decided or anyway consciously thought that being Aryan or white or male mattered *more* than being human or *rather* than being human would be evil.

I think that Kant was mistaken in focusing exclusively on the principle of self-love, if that is taken simply to be a will to satisfy one's desires. Evil *may* take the form of ungoverned self-interest or selfishness, but it takes many other forms as well. In fact I think that the kind of pure grasping self-interest which the British empiricists and their heirs tend to identify as the primary enemy of morality is rather rare. People who care only for what they get and not at all for

[51] Kant, *Religion Within the Limits of Reason Alone*, p. 36, in Greene and Hudson's translation, pp. 31–32.

what they *are* are surely uncommon. Even the worst of us seem to want others to like and admire us (if not morally then in other ways) and wither in the face of contempt. It isn't enough to say that this is because praise and admiration are pleasant things, and the thought that you are disliked is nasty. Why should the opinions of others be sources of pleasure and pain to us in the first place? We live in the eyes of others because we must live in our own.[52] And I think that this is because the distinctive fact about being human – the thing that makes us different from the other animals – is self-conception. Self-conception is the source some of our sweetest pleasures – knowing ourselves to be loved or to have done well; and our greatest (and often self-inflicted) torments – believing ourselves to be worthless, unlovely, or unlovable. A sure sense of self-worth, based on the wholehearted endorsement of our practical identities, is enough in most circumstances to make life worth living. A sense of personal worthlessness, on the other hand, can be the motive for suicide or – as Nietzsche argued – the germ from which nihilism and the rejection of all value spreads. And I believe that self-conception is, and relatedly, the source of our capacity for everyday decency as well as of heroic virtue; and of our capacity for trivial pettinesses as well as for great crimes. I think that self-conception is, in short, the root of both moral good and evil.

5 EXPLANATION AND JUSTIFICATION

Williams raises some questions about the relationship between explanation and justification in my account, and in this section I wish, at least in a tentative way, to explore this relationship. Williams thinks that my aim is to produce an answer to the normative question which justifies the normativity of obligation by explaining it. A model for this sort of justificatory structure is provided by Williams's own realist account of scientific knowledge. Williams believes that scientific explanations of, say, *how* vision represents features of the real world to us can sustain the claim that vision really is a form of perception. I have already raised some

---

[52] Hume's discussion of the effects of sympathy on self-conception, which I describe in 2.2.3, is one of the best accounts of this matter. See especially *Enquiry Concerning the Principles of Morals*, p. 276.

doubts, in 2.3.3, about that account, so I won't say any more about it here. In any case, Williams thinks that it is an inappropriate model for the justification of morality. He asks:

But why should the explanation of morality have to sustain it in the sense of providing a normative reason for it? Why should morality not be sustained, rather, by *what is mentioned in* the explanation? . . . Consider, for instance, the true explanation of (the other bits of) her heart's desire: what is revealed in psychological accounts of the origins of her passions may not normatively endorse them, but this does not mean that it renders them meaningless when they are considered 'from inside'.[53]

Now I did not intend to suggest that an explanation of obligation by itself could provide a normative reason for it. Normative reasons, in my view, always come from reflective endorsement. The explanation provides the material with which reflection works in endorsing or rejecting an obligation, but it does not do the work itself. The question that is bothering Williams is, I think, the question in what sense it 'provides the material'. Is it that the explanation provides a reason for endorsing the impulse to act or believe? Or is it that it causes the agent to endorse or reject the impulse to act or believe? Or what? For instance when I say, of the knavish lawyer in 2.5.2, that 'her disapproval seems poorly grounded, and therefore in a sense irrational' what exactly do I mean? Hume does not believe that our passions are things that we have reasons for having; nor does he ever suggest that the disutility of injustice is the reason for disapproving it. His theory, rather, is that the general disutility of injustice *causes* us to disapprove it and that our disapproval causes us to deem it immoral, with all that that involves. How exactly is this causal story supposed to be unseated by the lawyer's discovery that the unjust action in question is useful?

Now while I agree that our passions are not, or anyway not always, based on reasons, I think, contrary to Hume, that we must act for reasons. This is, so far, not a substantive claim about having to act according to particular rules or principles. It is rather a formal claim based on the psychological structure of human action: the reflective structure of human consciousness forces us to act for reasons, so that we cannot act on a passion without, formally, taking it to be a reason. Then we might ask: but when can we take a passion to be a reason? If our passions are caused in us, rather than being based on reasons, then the answer cannot be that we can take a passion to be a reason when we think we have a good reason for having it. So it may seem a little off the mark to say of the knavish lawyer that her passion seems to her to be 'irrational'.

It is at this point that Williams raised the criticism I discussed in section 3 above, that in a Kantian view you cannot ever justify action simply by saying that you just happen to have a certain passion or commitment. I have already addressed that point, but I must now qualify my answer in an important way. Suppose the knavish lawyer proposes that she just happens to have a moral sense constructed in such-and-such a way, that this is just the way she naturally is, and so that her moral distaste for the unjust but useful action needs no further justification. The answer is that accepting the role of nature in the construction of our values, and so accepting the element of arbitrariness and contingency that lies at their basis, does not commit us to accepting everything that nature provides, or to being unable to distinguish the sick from the healthy. Williams's own comparison between investigating the etiology of values (or, in this case, of moral sentiments) and investigating the etiology of passions is perfectly apt here. In both cases, we sometimes find that there is in the end nothing more to say than that this is how it is, this is what nature and history have made of us. The human delight in certain effects of light, colour, and sound; our curiosity about the way things work; our fascination with the development and exploration of our physical and mental powers – these may not admit of further justification; it is just how we are. And it is also true on the individual level that certain interests and concerns and loves are just the ones we have. I suggested, in section 3, that Kant's theory of value invites us to accept and even celebrate these facts.

But the investigation of the etiology of passions and values doesn't always end so simply. Sometimes they are revealed to be neurotic or phobic or fetishistic or self-contradictory. If they are more local concerns this means that a person who sets a value on herself may try to be rid of them, or at least to avoid allowing her actions to be governed by them. If they are large and self-constituting concerns, the very possibility of valuing oneself or one's humanity may be called into question. This is the result that Freud and Nietzsche and in a way Hume feared from an investigation of the etiology of moral values; and this is what I claim happens to the knavish lawyer at the end of lecture 2. Perhaps what I ought to have said is not that her disapproval will seem to her to be irrational, but simply that it will tear itself apart, or rather it will tear her apart. For it is the very same disinterested sympathy directed to the same object, the public good, that makes her both hate and love the unjust but useful action. And as Plato has taught us, this kind of conflict cannot subsist without breaking the soul into disparate parts.[54] The way it works in this case, then, is that the explanation prevents endorsement by revealing a kind of incoherence in *the point of view from which* the lawyer is supposed to endorse acting on her moral sentiments. Her moral distaste for the unjust action is after all irrational, in the sense that it cannot be reflectively endorsed as a reason to act.[55]

In cases where endorsement is possible, however, there may still seem to be a question about what is doing the justificatory work: the endorsement or the explanation that makes it possible. If we recast my own project in these terms, then I have offered an explanation of the existence of moral obligations which, I claim, should lead you to endorse those obligations, unless you are prepared to be a complete sceptic about reasons and values. But (assuming that the argument is successful) what does the work here, your reflective endorsement or the explanation itself? Now as the caveat about avoiding scepticism shows, I must say that it is the endorsement that does the work, since I am prepared to agree that if human beings decided that human life was worthless then it *would be* worthless. And in any case, I want to say that it is the endorsement that does the work, for I think that this is what a theory that grounds normativity in autonomy must say. But this claim will subject me to another criticism, which Cohen puts forward in a strong form.

Cohen places before us an idealized Mafioso, who has a code of

---

[54] See *Republic* IV, 436ff.
[55] Perhaps it's worth a reminder that I don't mean to suggest that she should *do* the unjust act. I just mean that she must now think more about why she should or shouldn't do it.

strength and honour, and who would feel threatened by a loss of identity should he violate it. This person's psychological structure fits the pattern I have described as giving rise to obligation, yet surely we don't want to say that he has a 'genuine obligation' – or so Cohen suggests. Doesn't this show that all I have done is describe the 'experience or phenomenology of obligation, not its ground or authenticating source?'[56]

Let me recall a point I made at the beginning of lecture 3: that I do not believe that all obligations are moral or that obligations can never conflict. That said, the similarity between the idealized Mafioso and the morally obligated person is one that I welcome. If we are to successfully address the question of the ground of moral obligation, we must ask the question in the right way, and that means that we must be aware of the way in which it emerges as a problem in the context of actual human life. Many philosophers (I don't mean Cohen) address the problem as if it arose in this way: people go through life doing what they please, acting on their desires, either in a spirit of wantonness or prudence, and once in a while moral obligation strides in, like a teacher striding on to the playground, to crush desire and spoil the fun. Why should we put up with it? But this isn't a picture of how the problem of moral obligation arises, because it isn't a recognizable picture of human life. We do not go through our days doing what we please, following the beckoning of desire. Human life, or anyway, adult human life, is pervaded through and through with obligation. It consists of things like doing our jobs, helping our friends, and living up to our roles as teachers, citizens, neighbours, parents, and so forth. And being obligated – having to keep ourselves on the track determined by our roles and projects in spite of temptations to laziness or self-ishness or cowardice – is part of our everyday business. For human beings, obligation is as normal as desire, something we experience every morning when the alarm goes off. So far, obligation is simply a psychological reality and as such it does not need a justification, only an explanation: one that I meant to be giving in my story about the structure of reflective consciousness and the need for practical identity that it generates.

[56] Cohen, p. 183.

Moral obligation, however special it may be, is a form of obligation, and that means its psychological structure *should* turn out to be similar to the psychological structure of these more mundane obligations. Our *capacity* for obligation in general, and our *capacity* for moral obligation, should be explained in the same way. What makes actual moral obligation different from other kinds is supposed to be its applicability to everyone and its rational inescapability. It is these features that seem to give rise to special issues about justification.

Yet any obligation can, when it presses, give rise to the demand for a justification, and what I have tried to do in my story is relate this fact to the special status of morality. When we question the importance of living up to the demands of our contingent practical identities, what we discover is not (or not always) the necessity of living up to demands of this or that role, but rather the necessity of living up to some of our roles, of maintaining some sort of integrity as human beings.[57] It is the value we place on our humanity that stands behind our other roles and imparts normativity to them. And if my other arguments work, that means we are committed to valuing the humanity of others as well.

But this conclusion only emerges from a course of reflection, a course which may never be undertaken, or may only be partially carried out, and this does give rise to a problem. What I would like to claim about a person's relation to an immoral form of self-identification parallels what I claimed about the knavish lawyer's relation to her moral objection to the useful but unjust act – that there is no coherent point of view *from which* it can be endorsed in the full light of reflection. If Cohen's Mafioso attempted to answer the question why it matters that he should be strong and in his sense honour-bound even when he was tempted not to, he would find that its mattering depends on the value of his humanity, and if my other arguments go through, he would find that that commits him to the value of humanity in general, and so to giving up his role as a Mafioso. But suppose – as is likely enough! – that he never does work all this out? Where does that leave him?

---

[57] Of course *sometimes* we will have to live up to the demands of a particular role, namely when we cannot abandon it without moral wrongdoing. Consider the difference between deciding not to be a parent and deciding not to be a parent any more.

It would be intellectually tidy, and no doubt spare me trouble from critics, if I now said that only those obligations consistent with morality are 'real' or in Cohen's phrase 'genuine'. Then I could say that it seems to the Mafioso as if he had an obligation to be strong and in his sense honour-bound, but actually he does not. I could say that there's no obligation here, only the sense of obligation: no normativity, only the psychic appearance of it. And one of my characterizations of normativity – that it is the ability to survive reflection – might seem to entitle me to that conclusion, at least if I am right that reflection leads us to morality and so should lead the Mafioso to abandon his immoral role. But I am not comfortable with this easy way out, for a reason related to one of Cohen's own points – that there is a real sense in which you are bound by a law you make for yourself until you make another.[58] I want to say of the Mafioso what I said of the Knight in 2.3.5, who felt himself to be obligated to fight a duel. There is a sense in which these obligations are real – not just psychologically but normatively. And this is because it is the endorsement, not the explanations and arguments that provide the material for the endorsement, that does the normative work.

I know that this conclusion will seem outrageous to some readers. I can only repeat again that I don't think all obligations are moral, or that obligations can never conflict. I am certainly not suggesting that the *rest of us* should encourage the Mafioso to stick to his code of strength and honour and manfully resist any wanton urges to tenderness or forgiveness that threaten to trip him up. The rest of us should be trying to get him to the place where he can see that he can't see his way to this kind of life anymore. The point is just this: if one holds the view, as I do, that obligations exist in the first-person perspective, then in one sense the obligatory is like the visible: it depends on how much of the light of reflection is on.

But I don't mean to suggest that the Mafioso's obligation to give up his immoral role is something that exists only in the perspective of the rest of us, and not in his own. For he *is* a human being, who arrives at his reasons through reflection. And the activity of reflection has rules of its own, rules which, in the way I described in

[58] Cohen, p. 170, and the discussion in section 2 above.

section 2, are constitutive of it. And one of them, perhaps the most essential, is the rule that we should never stop reflecting until we have reached a satisfactory answer, one that admits of no further questioning. It is the rule, in Kant's language, that we should seek the unconditioned. If the argument of the lectures is correct, following that rule would have led the Mafioso to morality, and, since he was reflecting, he ought to have followed it, and therefore he ought to have arrived there. His obligation to be a good person is therefore *deeper* than his obligation to stick to his code.[59]

Since I must end here, I would like once again to thank my commentators for presenting me with such difficult questions and acute criticisms. Their comments have certainly helped *me* to keep reflecting, and for that I am very grateful. [60]

[59] See 3.3.2
[60] I am also grateful to Charlotte Brown, Peter Hylton, and Arthur Kuflik for extensive comments on drafts of this reply.

Bibliography*

Aristotle. *The Complete Works of Aristotle.* Edited by Jonathan Barnes. Princeton: Princeton University Press, 1984.

Balguy, John. *The Foundation of Moral Goodness* (1728–1729). Facsimile of the original edition published in New York: Garland Publishing Company, 1976. Some selections from Balguy, although not the passage I have quoted, can be found in D. D. Raphael, *British Moralists 1650–1800.*

Bentham, Jeremy. *A Fragment on Government; with An Introduction to the Principles of Morals and Legislation* (1776; 1789). Edited by Wilfrid Harrison. Oxford: Basil Blackwell, 1948.

Brink, David O. *Moral Realism and the Foundation of Ethics.* Cambridge: Cambridge University Press, 1989.

Brown, Charlotte. 'Hume Against the Selfish Schools and the Monkish Virtues'. Delivered at the meetings of the Hume Society, 1989.

Butler, Joseph. *Fifteen Sermons Preached at the Rolls Chapel* (1726). The most influential of these are collected in Butler, *Five Sermons Preached at the Rolls Chapel and A Dissertation Upon the Nature of Virtue.* Edited by Stephen Darwall. Indianapolis: Hackett Publishing Company, 1983.

Clarke, Samuel. *A Discourse Concerning the Unchangeable Obligations of Natural Religion, and the Truth and Certainty of the Christian Revelation: the Boyle Lectures 1705.* I have quoted from both J. B. Schneewind, *Moral Philosophy from Montaigne to Kant,* and D. D. Raphael, *British Moralists 1650–1800.*

Craig, Edward. *Knowledge and the State of Nature.* Oxford: Clarendon Press, 1990.

Cumberland, Richard. *De legibus naturæ* (*Treatise of the Laws of Nature,* 1672). Translated by John Maxwell, London, 1727. There is no modern edition; I have quoted from J. B. Schneewind, *Moral Philosophy from Montaigne to Kant.*

* When 'I' is used in this bibliography the speaker is Christine M. Korsgaard.

Foot, Philippa. 'Moral Arguments' (*Mind* 67 (1958)). Reprinted in Foot, *Virtues and Vices and Other Essays in Moral Philosophy.* Berkeley: University of California Press, 1978.

Frankfurt, Harry G. 'Freedom of the Will and the Concept of a Person'. *Journal of Philosophy* 68 (January 1971): 5–20. Reprinted in Frankfurt, *The Importance of What We Care About.* Cambridge: Cambridge University Press, 1988: pp. 11–25.

Freud, Sigmund. *Das Unbehagen in der Kultur* (*Civilization and Its Discontents,* 1930). Translated and edited by James Strachey. New York: W. W. Norton & Co., 1961.

Gauthier, David. *Morals by Agreement.* Oxford: Oxford University Press, 1986.

Gewirth, Alan. *Reason and Morality.* Chicago: The University of Chicago Press, 1978.

Grotius, Hugo. *De juri belli ac pacis* (*On the Law of War and Peace,* 1625). Translated by Francis W. Kelsey. Oxford: Oxford University Press, 1925. I have quoted from J. B. Schneewind, *Moral Philosophy from Montaigne to Kant.*

Harman, Gilbert. *The Nature of Morality: an Introduction to Ethics.* New York: Oxford University Press, 1977.

Hegel, G. W. F. *Grundlinien der Philosophie des Rechts* (1821). Frankfurt: Suhrkamp Verlag, 1970. (Band 7.)

Heidegger, Martin. *Sein und Zeit.* Tübingen: Niemeyer Verlag, 1927.

Hobbes, Thomas. *De Cive or The Citizen.* Edited by Sterling P. Lamprecht. New York: Appleton-Century-Crafts, 1949.

Leviathan (1651). Edited by Richard Tuck. Cambridge: Cambridge University Press, 1991.

Hume, David. *A Treatise of Human Nature* (1739–1740). 2nd edition edited by L. A. Selby-Bigge and P. H. Nidditch. Oxford: Oxford University Press, 1978.

Enquiry Concerning Human Understanding (1748), in *David Hume: Enquiries Concerning Human Understanding and Concerning the Principles of Morals.* 3rd edition edited by L. A. Selby-Bigge and P. H. Nidditch. Oxford: Clarendon Press, 1975.

Enquiry Concerning the Principles of Morals (1751), in *David Hume: Enquiries Concerning Human Understanding and Concerning the Principles of Morals.* 3rd edition edited by L. A. Selby-Bigge and P. H. Nidditch. Oxford: Clarendon Press, 1975.

Dialogues Concerning Natural Religion (1779). Edited by Norman Kemp Smith, New York: Macmillan Library of Liberal Arts, 1947.

The Letters of David Hume. Edited by J. Y. T. Greig. Oxford: Clarendon Press, 1932.

Hutcheson, Francis. *Illustrations on the Moral Sense.* (Part II of *An Essay on the*

Nature and Conduct of the Passions and Affections with Illustrations on the Moral Sense (1728).) Edited by Bernard Peach. Cambridge, Massachusetts: Harvard University Press, 1971.

Inquiry Concerning the Original of our Ideas of Beauty and Virtue (1725). I have quoted from D. D. Raphael, *British Moralists 1650–1800*; except on one occasion when I have quoted a passage not in Raphael from L. A. Selby-Bigge, *The British Moralists*. Oxford: Clarendon Press, 1897; printed by The Library of Liberal Arts, 1964.

Kant, Immanuel. *Die Religion innerhalb der Grenzen der blossen Vernunft (Religion Within the Limits of Reason Alone*, 1793). Translated by Theodore M. Greene and Hoyt H. Hudson. New York: Harper & Row, 1960.

Eine Vorlesung Kant's über Ethik im Auftrage der Kantgesellschaft (Lectures on Ethics, 1775–1780). Drawn from the lecture notes of Theodor Friedrich Brauer, Gottlieb Kutzner, and Christian Mrongovious by Paul Menzer in 1924. Translated by Louis Infeld. London: Methuen, 1930; reprinted Indianapolis: Hackett Publishing Company, 1980.

Grundlegung zur Metaphysick der Sitten (Foundations of the Metaphysics of Morals, 1785). Translated by Lewis White Beck. New York: Macmillan Library of Liberals Arts, 1959.

Kants gesammelte Schriften, The Prussian Academy Edition. Twenty-eight volumes. Berlin: Walter de Gruyter & Company, 1902–. The page numbers found in the margins of most translations refer to this edition. When I have cited Kant, I have therefore referred to these page numbers. The English translations quoted or cited are listed in separate bibliographical entries for the works in question.

Kritik der praktischen Vernunft (Critique of Practical Reason, 1788). Translated by Lewis White Beck. New York: Macmillan Library of Liberal Arts, 1956.

Metaphysik der Sitten (The Metaphysics of Morals, 1797). Translated by Mary Gregor. Cambridge: Cambridge University Press, 1991.

Kim, Scott. *Morality, Identity, and Happiness: an Essay on the Kantian Moral Life*. Unpublished dissertation, University of Chicago, 1993.

Korsgaard, Christine M. 'Creating the Kingdom of Ends: Reciprocity and Responsibility in Personal Relations'. *Philosophical Perspectives 6: Ethics*. Edited by James Tomberlin. Atascadero, California: The Ridgeview Publishing Company, 1992. Forthcoming in Korsgaard, *Creating the Kingdom of Ends*, chapter 7. New York: Cambridge University Press, 1995.

'From Duty and for the Sake of the Noble: Kant and Aristotle on Morally Good Action', in Stephen Engstrom and Jennifer Whiting, editors, *Aristotle, Kant, and the Stoics: Rethinking Happiness and Duty*. Forthcoming from New York: Cambridge University Press.

'Kant's Analysis of Obligation: The Argument of *Foundations I*'. The

Monist 72 (July 1989): 311–340. Forthcoming in Korsgaard, *Creating the Kingdom of Ends*, chapter 2. New York: Cambridge University Press, 1995.

'Kant's Formula of Humanity'. *Kant-Studien* 77 (April 1986): 183–202. Forthcoming in Korsgaard, *Creating the Kingdom of Ends*, chapter 4. New York: Cambridge University Press, 1995.

'Kant's Formula of Universal Law'. *Pacific Philosophical Quarterly* 66 (January/April 1985): 24–47. Forthcoming in Korsgaard, *Creating the Kingdom of Ends*, chapter 3. New York: Cambridge University Press, 1995.

'Morality as Freedom', in *Kant's Practical Philosophy Reconsidered*. Edited by Yirmiyahu Yovel. Dordrecht: Kluwer Academic Publishers, 1989: pp. 23–48. Forthcoming in Korsgaard, *Creating the Kingdom of Ends*, chapter 6. New York: Cambridge University Press, 1995.

'Normativity as Reflexivity: Hume's Practical Justification of Morality'. Delivered at the meetings of the Hume Society, 1989.

'Personal Identity and the Unity of Agency: a Kantian Response to Parfit'. *Philosophy and Public Affairs* 18 (Spring 1989): 101–132. Forthcoming in Korsgaard, *Creating the Kingdom of Ends*, chapter 13. New York: Cambridge University Press, 1995.

'Skepticism about Practical Reason'. *The Journal of Philosophy* 83 (January 1986): 5–25. Forthcoming in Korsgaard, *Creating the Kingdom of Ends*, chapter 11. New York: Cambridge University Press, 1995.

'The Normativity of Instrumental Reason'. Unpublished.

'The Reasons We Can Share: an Attack on the Distinction between Agent-Relative and Agent-Neutral Values'. *Social Philosophy & Policy* 10 (January 1993): 24–51. Forthcoming in Korsgaard, *Creating the Kingdom of Ends*, chapter 10. New York: Cambridge University Press, 1995.

'Two Arguments Against Lying'. *Argumentation* 2 (February 1988): 27–49. Forthcoming in Korsgaard, *Creating the Kingdom of Ends*, chapter 12. New York: Cambridge University Press, 1995.

'Two Distinctions in Goodness'. *The Philosophical Review* 92 (April 1983): 169–195. Forthcoming in Korsgaard, *Creating the Kingdom of Ends*, chapter 9. New York: Cambridge University Press, 1995.

Mackie, J. L. *Ethics: Inventing Right and Wrong*. New York: Penguin Books, 1977.

Mandeville, Bernard. *An Enquiry into the Origin of Honor* (1732). I have quoted from J. B. Schneewind, *Moral Philosophy from Montaigne to Kant*.

The Fable of the Bees: or, Private Vices, Public Benefits (1714). Edited by F. B. Kaye. Indianapolis: Liberty Classics, 1988. This edition is a reprint of a 1924 edition published by Oxford University Press.

Mill, John Stuart. *The Subjection of Women* (1869). Edited by Susan Moller Okin. Indianapolis: Hackett Publishing Company, 1988.

Utilitarianism (1861). Edited by George Sher. Indianapolis: Hackett Publishing Company, 1979.

Miller, Richard. *Analyzing Marx*. Princeton: Princeton University Press, 1984.

Moore, G. E. 'The Conception of Intrinsic Value'. Moore, *Philosophical Studies*. London: Kegan Paul, 1922.

Principia Ethica (1903). Cambridge: Cambridge University Press, 1971.

Nagel, Thomas. *The Possibility of Altruism*. Princeton: Princeton University Press, 1970.

The View From Nowhere. Oxford: Oxford University Press, 1986.

Nietzsche, Friedrich. *The Genealogy of Morals* (1887). Translated by Walter Kaufman and R. J. Hollingdale in Walter Kaufman, editor, *On the Genealogy of Morals and Ecce Homo*. New York: Random House Vintage Books, 1967.

Oldenquist, Andrew. 'Loyalties'. *Journal of Philosophy* (1982).

O'Neill, Onora. 'Reason and Politics in the Kantian Enterprise', in *Constructions of Reason: Explorations of Kant's Practical Philosophy*. Cambridge: Cambridge University Press, 1989.

Parfit, Derek. *Reasons and Persons*. Oxford: Clarendon Press, 1984.

Pennock, J. R. and Chapman, J. W., editors. *Marxism*, Nomos XXVI. New York: New York University Press, 1983.

Plato. *The Collected Dialogues*. Edited by Edith Hamilton and Huntington Cairns. Princeton: Princeton University Press, 1961.

Potts, Timothy C. *Conscience in Medieval Philosophy*. Cambridge: Cambridge University Press, 1980.

Price, Richard. *A Review of the Principal Questions in Morals* (1758). Edited by D. D. Raphael. Oxford: Clarendon Press, 1948. I have also cited the selections in Schneewind, *Moral Philosophy from Montaigne to Kant*, and Raphael, *British Moralists 1650–1800*.

Prichard, H. A. 'Does Moral Philosophy Rest on a Mistake?' (*Mind* 21 (1912)) and 'Duty and Interest' (Oxford: Clarendon Press, 1929). Reprinted in *Moral Obligation and Duty and Interest. Essays and Lectures by H. A. Prichard*. Edited by W. D. Ross and J. O. Urmson. Oxford: Oxford University Press, 1968.

Pufendorf, Samuel. *On The Law of Nature and of Nations* (1672). Translated by C. H. Oldfather and W. A. Oldfather. Oxford: Oxford University Press, 1934. I have quoted from J. B. Schneewind, *Moral Philosophy from Montaigne to Kant*.

On the Duty of Man and Citizen According to Natural Law (1673). Edited by James Tully and translated by Michael Silverthorne. Cambridge: Cambridge University Press, 1991.

Railton, Peter. 'Moral Realism'. *The Philosophical Review* 95 (April 1986): 163–207.

Raphael, D. D., editor *British Moralists 1650–1800*. Two volumes. Indianapolis: Hackett Publishing Company, 1991. Reprint of an edition published in Oxford: Oxford University Press, 1969. Where I have quoted from this anthology rather than original sources I have cited it as Raphael I and Raphael II.

Rawls, John. *A Theory of Justice*. Cambridge, Massachusetts: Harvard University Press, 1971.

'Kantian Constructivism in Moral Theory: The Dewey Lectures 1980'. *The Journal of Philosophy* 77 (September 1980): 515–572.

Ross, W. D. *The Right and the Good*. Oxford: Clarendon Press, 1930.

Sandel, Michael J. *Liberalism and the Limits of Justice*. Cambridge: Cambridge University Press, 1982.

Schiller, Friedrich. 'Über Anmut und Würde' (1793), in *Sämtliche Werke*. Munich: Hanser Verlag, 1967. (Band V.)

Schlegel, Friedrich. 'Fragmente', originally published in the magazine *Athenäum*. Edited by Friedrich and August Wilhelm Schlegel, 1798.

Lucinde (1799), in *Kritische Friedrich Schlegel – Ausgabe*. Edited by Ernst Behler. Munich: Paderborn–Wien, 1958–.

Schneewind, J. B., editor. *Moral Philososphy from Montaigne to Kant*. Two volumes. Cambridge: Cambridge University Press, 1990. Where I have quoted from this anthology rather than original sources I have cited it as Schneewind I and Schneewind II.

Shaftesbury (Anthony Ashley Cooper, Third Earl of Shaftesbury). *An Inquiry Concerning Virtue or Merit*. Essay IV of *Characteristics of Men, Manners, Opinions, Times* (1711). Edited by John Robertson. New York: Macmillan Library of Liberal Arts, 1964. The *Inquiry* was first published in an edition unauthorized by Shaftesbury in 1699.

Sidgwick, Henry. *The Methods of Ethics* (1874). Indianapolis: Hackett Publishing Company, 1981.

Whelan, Frederick. 'Marx and Revolutionary Virtue', in J. R. Pennock and J. W. Chapman, editors, *Marxism*, Nomos XXVI. New York: New York University Press, 1983: pp. 64–65.

Wiggins, David. 'Moral Cognitivism, Moral Relativism and Motivating Beliefs'. *Proceedings of the Aristotelian Society* 91 (1990/91).

Williams, Bernard. *Ethics and the Limits of Philosophy*. Cambridge, Massachusetts: Harvard University Press, 1985.

Moral Luck. Cambridge: Cambridge University Press, 1981.

Morality: An Introduction To Ethics. New York: Harper Torchbooks, 1972.

'Practical Necessity', in *Moral Luck*. Cambridge: Cambridge University Press, 1981.

'Präsuppositionen der Moralität', in Schaper and Vossenkuhl, editors. *Bedingungen der Möglichkeit*. Stuttgart: Klett-Cotta Verlag, 1983.

Wittgenstein, Ludwig. *Notebooks, 1914–1916*. Edited by G. H. von Wright and G. E. M. Anscombe, with an English translation by G. E. M. Anscombe. Oxford: Basil Blackwell, 1961.

Philosophical Investigations. Translated by G. E. M. Anscombe. New York: Macmillan, 1953.

Index

agent-neutral vs. agent-relative reasons, *see* reasons, publicity of
aliens: and perspective-dependent concepts, 69, 69–70, 72; will have thin ethical concepts, 115–116; bases for different ethical conceptions, 116 n. 30
Ancient Greek World View, 1–5, 18, 50, 51 n. 4, 66 *see also* Medieval Christian World View, Modern Scientific World View
animals: conscious but not self-conscious, 92–93; Aristotelian account of, 149–150; moral standing of, 130,131–132, 152–153; and pain, 145, 149–150, 150; obligations of, 157; and instinctual dominance, 157–158; value depends on attitude to our animal nature, 159; as intrinsically normative entities, 166
Aristotle: on form and matter as related to value, 2–4, 107–108; ideal of excellence vs. obligation, 3–4; role of law in ethics, 3–4; action vs. production, 44 n. 74; bases morality on human nature, 50; derives normativity from reflective endorsement and teleology, 51 n. 4; derives normativity from reflexivity, 77; whether egoistic, 77–78, 247 n. 44; theory of animals, 149–150; Williams's Aristotelianism, 50–51, 77–78, 213
Augustine, St, 4
authority, source of normativity, 18, 30; Pufendorf and Hobbes on legislative authority, 28–30; autonomy as authority over oneself, 20, 104; authority of legislator depends on sanctions, 25–26; relation of sanctions to authority over oneself, 150–151; authority of law in Hobbes, Kant, and Korsgaard, contrasted by Cohen, 167–174; reply by Korsgaard, 234–236

autonomy: imposition of form on matter, 4–5, 107–108; as source of normativity, 19–20, 91, 165; in Clarke's theory, 31–32; related to reflective endorsement, 89, 91; related to voluntarism, 104–105; of the will, leads to categorical imperative, 98, 219–220; in the deliberative standpoint, 100, 128–129; and practical identity, 101, 103, 112; and integrity, 101–102; and motivation to conform to requirements, 105–107; creates intrinsically normative entities, 112; relation to authority, in arguments of Hobbes, Kant, and Korsgaard, according to Cohen, 167–174; reply by Korsgaard, 234–236

Baldwin, Tom, 191–192 n. 4
Balguy, John, 152
beauty, normativity of, 8 n. 8, 20–21, 210
belief, normativity of, *see* theoretical reasons, normativity of
Bentham, Jeremy: transition from Hume to Utilitarianism, 86, 86 n. 69, 87 n. 70, 214–215, 217
biological origins of value, 8, 14, 149–160; *see also* evolutionary theory of ethics; human nature
Brink, David, 40
Brown, Charlotte, 52 n. 7; 60 n. 27; 258 n. 60
Butler, Joseph: distinction between authority and power, 30, 104, 226 n. 10; consistency between morality and self-interest, 56–57, 60; compared to Greek philosophers, 66 n. 37

categorical imperative, as a test of reflective endorsement, 89; employs Aristotelian notion of a maxim's form, 107–108; Kant's argument for, 97–98, 219–220,

266